MOUNTAIN BIKING
Orange County
CALIFORNIA

Randy Vogel • Larry Kuechlin

FALCON®

Guilford, Connecticut
An imprint of The Globe Pequot Press

ISBN 1-57540-011-1

Front cover: Hans Rey riding Telonics, Laguna Beach Greenbelt. Photo by Bill Freeman.
Back cover: Ira Vick riding Telonics, Laguna Beach Greenbelt. Photo by Bill Freeman.

Manufactured in the United States of America
First Edition/Fourth Printing

WARNING

IMPORTANT INFORMATION: READ BEFORE YOU USE THIS GUIDE

WARNING: MOUNTAIN BIKING IS A DANGEROUS SPORT IN WHICH SERIOUS INJURY OR DEATH OR NASTY RASHES OF ALL SORTS MAY OCCUR.

This guidebook is a compilation of information gathered from a variety of sources, which may not have been independently verified. The authors cannot guarantee the correctness of any of the information in this guidebook. The maps, the trail descriptions and the difficulty ratings may be incorrect or misleading. Trail conditions can change drastically from season to season. Natural and man-made hazards will be encountered anytime you leave the pavement. These hazards are part and parcel of the mountain biking experience. Legal access may also change. The user of any information from this guide must exercise his or her own judgment in choosing or riding a trail or ride described in this guidebook.

This is not an instructional book. You should not depend on any information derived from this guidebook for your or your party's personal safety. Mountain biking is a dangerous activity and many of the rides and trails described require expert riding techniques. Proper experience, training and/or instruction may be necessary to learn these skills.

The responsibility for safety in mountain biking rests entirely with each individual rider. If you have any doubt as to your ability to safely ride any trail or ride in this guide, do not try it.

THERE ARE NO WARRANTIES, WHETHER EXPRESS OR IMPLIED, THAT THIS GUIDEBOOK IS ACCURATE OR THAT THE INFORMATION CONTAINED IN IT IS RELIABLE. THERE ARE NO WARRANTIES OF FITNESS FOR A PARTICULAR PURPOSE OR THAT THIS GUIDE IS MERCHANTABLE. YOUR USE OF THIS BOOK INDICATES YOUR ASSUMPTION OF THE RISK THAT IT MAY CONTAIN ERRORS AND IS AN ACKNOWLEDGMENT OF YOUR SOLE RESPONSIBILITY FOR YOUR RIDING SAFETY.

FOREWORD

This guide started one night when we (Larry and Randy) started carping about the other mountain biking guidebooks we had seen or used. One of us proclaimed, "Even we could do a better job!" Such hubris. The spew became more specific. We outlined our approach and all the cool things we would include that other authors had omitted. Next thing we knew, we had actually agreed to undertake to write this guide. Think of all the expensive lightweight s—t we could buy with the royalties!

The reality of this project was quite sobering. Believe us, this guide was ten times more work than we had anticipated, and the royalties will barely pay for all the tacoed rims, worn-out and broken parts, cracked frames and such (including one stolen bike). But, hell, we rode hundreds (actually thousands) of miles of killer trails and explored places we'd never seen before. We actually became much better riders and more appreciative of access and other not-so-subtle issues facing all riders.

We strongly urge ALL mountain bikers to join the International Mountain Biking Association (IMBA). IMBA and their many volunteers work extremely hard to help preserve our access to trails. Without IMBA's work, we would be probably relegated to paved bike paths and the occasional fireroad. We have even reproduced a membership application in the back of the book, so you can't use that excuse. No, don't rip it out, use a copier. It will be the best $20 bucks you ever spent on mountain biking. You can even be a little smug about it.

Of course, we could not have completed this guide (incomplete as it is) without a lot of help from plenty of other people. Other riders shared information (knowingly and unwittingly), tolerated our frequent scribbling of mileage notes and such, and accompanied us on many uninspiring trails and rides.

Randy would like to thank: Daniel Castillo, a great riding companion who helped keep my motivation high and lent his considerable photographic talents. My wife, Sarah Tringali, helped edit my ramblings, rode trails, and endured the havoc this project wrought. My daughter Claire was a good sport and actually rode along on her mountain bike to help dad check out some mileage. Bill Freeman, for his excellent photographs. My partner in crime, Larry, who helped get me psyched for this project. David Evans, for taking me on one of my first real dirt experiences.

Larry wishes to thank: My brother, Keith, who carried me when I could go no further. My sister, Shelly, whose loyalty I can never repay. My friend, Cory, who never gave up on me. My friend, Randy Vogel, who puts up with me and manages to smile. My mom and dad, who believed in me. And, my friend, John, who's always ready for a new adventure. For Brandee, whose quiet beauty always calms my soul, and for my precious Courtney whose fire and joy renew my spirit.

Larry also wants to thank: Randy Simpson, the King of Cheese (have you got those FX Judy's working yet?). Sandy McLain, Sergio Velasquez and the gang at Performance Brea who helped me replace what I thought was irreplaceable. Ted, Bob and Bill at the Bike Beat for answering countless questions. John and Tracy at Grafton. Caroline and Madaline at Ventana for their generosity and for listening. Richard Garrett, Greg Garcia, Allen James, Dave Stelter and Louie Anderson, for not hiding when I asked them to go on documentation rides. Lastly, the guys at the Corona Fire Department's Magnolia Avenue Station for not laughing.

We would also like to express our appreciation to the Orange County Department of Harbors, Beaches and Parks. Despite shrinking budgets, the County Bankruptcy, and a nearly criminal diversion of money to balance the County's budget, this is one agency that does a tremendous job. Now, if we could only get rid of the endless series of developer-appointed/anointed Board of Supervisors...Hmm?

We would particularly like to thank Harbors, Beaches and Parks employees Tim Miller and Jeff Dickman. They care deeply about our wilderness parks, have been strong advocates of multiple use of trails, and together with many others have worked to expand our trail systems for all to enjoy. They even took the time to answer our many questions and to provide us with the most up-to-date information available. Other Harbors, Beaches and Parks rangers and employees also were of great assistance. We thank them all.

We also wish to acknowledge the excellent work of the State Park System, which has also worked hard to preserve Orange County's natural heritage. Chino Hills and Crystal Cove State Parks are tremendous resources and, as a result of the hard work of many individuals, they remain open to the mountain biking community. Similarly, the United States Forest Service has managed one of Orange County's most valuable natural and recreational resources, the Cleveland National Forest. When you ride, hike or run along the many trails and see for yourself the extraordinary beauty and diversity of the landscape and wildlife, you will appreciate how lucky we are to have this area in our backyard.

Ride Smart.

Randy Vogel and Larry Kuechlin

March 1996

TABLE OF CONTENTS

PART I

The Parks

PART II

Santa Ana Mountains/Cleveland National Forest

INTRODUCTION

We'll admit it right up front. This book is not complete. There are several reasons for this fact. First and foremost, many mountain biking trails that are commonly used may be illegal or closed to public access. We have tried our best to not include any of these trails. Riding illegal or closed trails can create access problems and then everyone suffers. Secondly, we realize that we have missed or neglected some trails. Lastly, new trails and parklands are being opened to public use. To address the last two issues, we intend to regularly update this guide with the latest information to ensure that it remains current.

Orange County is blessed with a tremendous amount of quality mountain biking. We sincerely hope that this guide will provide you the means to enjoy this sport, no matter what your level of experience. We recommend that you read the introductory material. It will explain the use of this book and give you some valuable pointers on safety and access issues.

How to Use This Guide

This guide is fairly self-explanatory. Nevertheless, there are a number of items unique to this book which need a bit of explanation.

ORGANIZATION

This guide is divided into two sections. The first part of the book covers the County, State or other Parks with mountain biking. We start in north county (Chino Hills State Park) and work our way south and then down the coast (to Aliso-Wood). The next section covers the rides in the Santa Ana Mountain Range and Cleveland National Forest. Again, we start in the north (Black Star Canyon) and work our way south (Ortega Highway Corridor).

RIDE DESCRIPTIONS

For each ride, we give certain technical information (see "Ratings" below), a short synopsis of the ride ("About This Ride"), and a point-to-point description of your route of travel ("The Ride"). Mileage markers are used for key points along the ride. Other useful or interesting information may also be provided.

BIKE COMPUTERS

We strongly recommend you purchase and use a bike (mileage) computer. Although not absolutely necessary to follow the ride descriptions, we assume you have one on your (or your partner's) bike. The mileage points and distances given for the rides are as reliable as we could make them and will help keep you on route. We used bike computers to document each ride (rather than guessing as some writers seem to have done). Bike computers are cheap ($15 on up), easy to use and reliable. We also feel the more expensive, wireless computers are probably worth the investment.

CAR DIRECTIONS

For each park or area covered, we provide you with driving directions. In the case of some parks (e.g.; Chino Hills, Santiago-Weir, Aliso-Wood and O'Neill) several entrances or parking areas are mentioned. In these cases, look at the ride you wish to do, and it will let you know to what entrance you need to drive. In the case of the Santa Ana Mountains, each canyon or area covered has its own set of driving instructions. These are generally set forth in the first ride described.

PARKING

Parking can be a sensitive access issue at many of the riding areas described. Take note of any special considerations described for a ride or area. In the past, the failure of a small minority of mountain bikers to exercise common sense and courtesy has caused closures or restrictions. This is particularly a problem when parking occurs in residential areas.

We feel silly giving you a bunch of "Do Nots," but if people stopped doing this stuff and ruining access for everyone, we wouldn't have to. Here we go:

- Do not play loud music.
- Do not pee along the road.
- Do not block parking, roadways or access to others.
- Do not leave trash—energy bar wrappers, old inner tubes, etc.
- Do not change clothes in open view.
- Avoid obnoxious and rude behavior.

MAPS

We have gone overboard in trying to prepare detailed and accurate maps for every ride and area described in this book. There is an overview map of Orange County showing the location of all the parks and forest lands. There are also overview maps of the Santa Ana Mountains and each state or county park. With rare exception, we have also made separate maps for each ride described in this book. Use the area and/or ride maps in conjunction with the verbal descriptions to ensure you find your starting point and stay on track.

The area and ride maps distinguish the type of trail you are riding (singletrack, fireroad, paved service road, etc.), and provide other details to aid in finding your way around. The individual ride maps also show your starting point, route and direction of travel, and on the longer rides, key mileage markers. All these maps use various symbols which are shown in the Sample Map Key (above).

Sample ride

Distance • 12.3 mile loop

Time Required • 1.5 to 2 hours

Route Rating • 7

Grunt Factor • 5

Technical Rating • 2

Downhill Rating • 6

Elevation • Start 500 ft.

High point 1090 ft.

Finish 500 ft.

Topos • *Topographical map;* ride map, page 150

How we rate the rides

This is always the touchy part, isn't it? We think it's a Sunday-walk-in-the park, you consider it a suicide attempt. Randy glides to the top and Larry is wheezing like a OCTD bus on a bad fuel day. Who is right? We all are. For this reason, we attempted to provide some a semblance of objectiveness to how we rate and describe the rides. We also tried to present this information in a manner that all of us can use. The following describes the type of information provided for most of the rides described in this guide.

Warning

In most cases, the ratings have not been confirmed by anyone else, or even both of us. The ratings may be misleading or just plain wrong. Always use your own judgment in sizing up a ride and your abilities.

Distance

This will include the total miles we traveled on our bike. This information was derived from our trusty bike computer (see above). Distances may be rounded to the nearest tenth of a mile. Remember that tenths of a mile represent 528 feet, or roughly the length of two football fields. This may not sound like a long way to you, but out on a remote trail a tenth of a mile can be a long, confusing length. When measuring the distances we dropped our bike where we stopped so as not to add extra feet to the length of the ride. If you are ahead of your partner and ride back to him/her, you have now added whatever the distance is back to them, multiplied by two. It is also easy to add a tenth of a mile or two over longer rides by just swerving back and forth across a fireroad. Remember this, take the measurements as approximates, and make allowances for this on your ride.

Time Required

We have given a range for most rides. On longer rides, this will include likely food, liquid and potty breaks. These times should only be used as a guide. They are not gospel. Ultimately, you must judge whether you have allotted enough time to complete a ride. On the longer or more advanced rides, we have given estimates based upon the assumption you are fit enough to complete them with some aplomb.

Route Rating

This is the overall feeling we have about the ride. This is highly subjective and we'll admit it. It's based on the other ratings and how we feel about the rest of the factors involved, like scenery, seclusion, availability of cool places to go for a cold one afterwards, or maybe the vibe we get when we balance a crystal on our forehead and spin counter-clockwise on our back wheel. For whatever reasons we use in our convoluted logic, as a general rule, the higher the rating, the better the ride. Beware, they ratings may be somewhat inconsistent from area to area. Feel free to scratch out the number and insert your own if you think it sucks.

Grunt Factor

This is a rough measure of the overall strenuousness of the ride. The factors we take into account are length and relative steepness of the uphill. If the climb is not that steep but goes on for untold miles, or if it gains elevation rapidly over a shorter distance, it might get a high grunt factor. Like all the ratings, it is our opinion.

Technical Rating

We expect to get lots of flak for trying to quantify technical difficulty of biking trails. Nevertheless, we felt most other guides either overlook this critical factor or do a poor job at letting you know what you are getting into. Use this rating to give you a rough idea of how technically difficult any given trail or ride may be. This is an open ended system. A technical rating of "0" is a paved road or very smooth dirt road. No particular dirt riding technique is required. Most fireroads would rate a "1" or so. As the trail steepens, narrows, involves rocks, obstacles or drop-offs, the handling skills required increase dramatically. So does the technical rating. The technical challenges are what make mountain biking so much fun (and hazardous).

The following guideline can be helpful in understanding the rating system. Ride some sample trails to get an idea of your abilities compared to these ratings.

0 to 2	Novice Riders
3 to 5	Intermediate Riders
6 to 8	Advanced Riders
9 and up	Expert Riders

Downhill Rating

Most of the other books that we have seen are biased in one way or another toward cross-country riding. In some cases, this tendency is a bit extreme, such as listing a ride that has a really great downhill section that the author has decided to send you up instead of down. Well, Larry has said he would climb a 2000-foot pile of unprocessed fertilizer for an awesome downhill. Randy, the sick puppy he is, actually likes the uphill and downhill of long cross-country rides. To try to balance matters a bit, in some cases we have included a "downhill rating." It is based on potential speed, uninterrupted motion and overall length. For safety reasons, we will also give crowded areas a somewhat lesser mark. Remember, respect all posted speed limits and *always* yield to (and slow to pass) hikers and, yes, horses too. *Never* go fast where vision is restricted or where you can't make an emergency stop.

Elevation

We have generally only included the starting points and the high points on the rides. Where not relevant, we have not included this information.

Topos

Egyptian for topographical maps, or more accurately, US Geological Survey Quadrangle Maps. They are not required, but are highly suggested for the rides in the Santa Ana Mountains. They can be obtained at Allied Supplies, REI, Sport Chalet, etc. They are fun to pour over and plan your own unique rides.

ON BEING PREPARED

Part of being a responsible rider is being prepared. This includes wearing a helmet, protective eyewear, and carrying a proper tool kit.

WEAR A GOOD HELMET

Riding without a helmet is irresponsible. It is far too easy to fall when riding on dirt. Even expert riders take spills. Several of our friends have been spared serious comas by wearing helmets, including one friend that fell at Snow Summit doing nearly fifty. He got one heck of a road rash over most areas of his body, but his helmet took the first shot. He mailed it in for the free replacement and kept on riding.

PROTECTIVE EYEWEAR

Protective eyewear is strongly recommended when riding off-road. Avoid glasses that can shatter upon impact. Good glasses will keep dust, dirt, rocks and brush out of your eyes. They should be considered obligatory when riding many of the narrow and brush-lined singletracks described in this guide.

TOOL KITS

Being prepared for your ride means far more than donning a stylish riding jersey or ensuring that your helmet matches the paint job on your bike. Being self-sufficient is part of responsible off-road riding. Yet too many riders give little or no thought to preparedness before setting out on the dirt. You know who we're talking about! Those people you see on the side of the road with the long, sad faces begging for anything from a spare tube to a new frame. Trail leeches are out there and they all have their own techniques to get the prepared, responsible rider to surrender his\her spare tube. "Oh, and can I use your pump?"

When contemplating putting your kit together, ask yourself these questions:

1. How long is the trip supposed to take?
2. How far away from humanity is it?
3. How far do I care to walk if I don't bring the proper item?

We regularly add and subtract items to our kits based on these questions. A ride at Chino Hills is not going to necessitate the same list of items brought on a ride in the Santa Anas.

Packs

First off, you need a way to carry your kit. This can vary from the pocket on your jersey (kind of a bummer if you fall on them), a seat bag, cases that fit in water bottle holders (where does the water go?), to various fanny packs or backpacks. We prefer to use a pack that works with our Camelback since we carry the water there anyway. It also allows you to carry enough tools, water and energy bars for a complete day of riding, or strap on a windbreaker or other extra clothing items that you may want to carry. When outfitting for a short ride we trim down the items.

Tools

This brings us to the tools themselves, which are as varied as types of mountain bike frames. They basically fall into two categories: folding type and one-piece. The tools that have impressed us the most are made by Ritchey and Avenir. Ritchey's CPR line is a one-piece type of tool. Our main gripe with these types of tools is they can be like carrying an open Swiss Army knife in your pack. If you carry one of these anywhere on your body, please don't fall on it! The Avenir Bike Knife is another favorite. It has 12 functions, including a 2mm hex for brake adjustments. It also folds up neatly so you can't accidentally impale yourself.

To round out a complete kit, include a chain breaker (e.g., Park CT-5 Chain Brute), an extra bit of chain (remember that piece you cut off when fitting a new chain?), a 3mm hex wrench for SPD adjustments (as well as tightening chain pulleys), a replacement tube (we prefer standard black tubes because they survive better), and a patch kit (or speed patches) in a case with one tire lever. Include emergency information on the inside lid of the case for those special occasions when death occurs.

If you are concerned about weight for short rides, have your partner carry some of the items. Most repairs you'll need to make in the field are minor adjustments and can be easily handled with the kit described.

Pump

A pump is also essential. On this one, your guess is as good as ours. We have a crate full of them, some of which never performed on their first try. Price, model and style don't seem to matter much: they either work great or fail miserably. It seems to be a matter of Zen, predestined luck or black magic voodoo. Whatever the secret is, Larry found a Vetta in the weeds at Carbon Canyon which has worked perfectly for over two years now and Randy has a Blackburn which he guards with his life. Go figure.

Tool Kit Additions

Some other items you might want add to your standard tool kit are: a few pain killers, three dimes (phone calls) and a five dollar bill (emergency rations). All of these can fit neatly into the patch kit if you purchase one with a large enough case.

FLUID REPLACEMENT

It should go without saying that on a ride of any length you are going to need to bring fluids. Water is cheap and readily available. Items like Gatorade, Gookenade and Powerade are good for longer rides as they replace minerals and salts you loose when you sweat. Make sure you bring enough fluids with you. Consider the length and strenuousness of the ride, the temperature, your fitness and the availability for replenishing your supplies along the route.

ENERGY BARS

We are strong believers in the use of energy bars for longer rides. They pack and travel well and provide all sorts of essential nutrients for your body. On long rides, take several along and be sure to take the time to eat and drink before you suddenly run out of power.

EXTRA CLOTHING

It can be an excellent idea to take some extra clothing, such as a windbreaker on long rides, even if the weather is not particularly cool.

MAINTENANCE

The one item which can significantly increase the enjoyment of your rides, reduce the time you spend fiddling with your bike and the amount of tools you will need to carry is a good regimen of maintenance. Whether you do this yourself, or whether you take it to the professionals, putting your bike in good working order before you hit the trail will always pay big dividends. A good mechanic is not hard to find at most reputable bike shops, but the one's that are part mechanic and part shaman are the most valuable and will see problems in the future through whatever mystical divination they seem to possess. Find a good shop close to you and develop a relationship with them. You'll never regret it.

YOUR BEHAVIOR AND ACCESS

So you went out and purchased that shining, full-suspension rocket ship and now want to know what to do with it. Well, here's a short list of things you shouldn't do with it. As stated above, many access problems start right at the parking area (see "Parking" above). If you see others engaging in irresponsible behavior, get all over them (in a nice way, of course).

But let's not be pretentious here. Everyone breaks the rules. There's not a single pair of hands holding this book that hasn't been used to steer a bike down a path marked out of bounds, or hasn't exceeded the 15 mph speed limit by at least another 15 mph. Just be ready to accept the responsibility for your actions and remember that every time someone permanently tattoos some twelve-year-old hiker with the imprint of his or her rear tire, another trail closes or another 10 mph sign goes up.

RIDE WITHIN YOUR VISION

We've been down Telegraph Canyon at least a thousand times at well over 30 miles per hour, but not once have we been close to an accident because we follow this simple rule. Every time you fly around a blind corner you spin the revolver and hope the bullet doesn't show up. Nobody's going for the World Cup down Mathis. Nobody really cares if you beat your partner by 30 seconds. We all care if you screw it up for the rest of us.

RIDE WITHIN YOUR ABILITIES

It's one thing for pro downhillers to ride at 50 miles per hour or a trials champions to float through a boulder choked trail. It's quite another for you and I. Remember, our parks are not racing venues. If you know a trail well or have been riding for years, technical sections are going to seem easier, but always be aware of other users. Less experienced riders should take enough time to learn proper skills and their personal limits.

SUPPORT AND BE A VOLUNTEER

Join your local mountain bike club and IMBA. If you see volunteers working on the trails, find out how you can help. Attend organized maintenance efforts or fund raising events whenever they occur. The more community support we give to the areas we ride the more goodwill we develop. The more goodwill we develop, the more tolerant people will be of mountain biking.

BE RESPONSIBLE (or "Don't Look for Someone Else to Blame")

If you decide to ride too fast or too hard and you crunch hard, that's your fault, not some government organization, landowner or manufacturer. The fastest way for biking to get restricted or banned is by suing someone else for your own stupidity. When you participate in an extreme sport in the wilderness, bad things can happen regardless if a sign warned you. We hear lots of talk about responsibility, but we see few examples to follow. On the contrary, we see people attempt to shirk responsibility every day. Even former Orange County Treasurer Robert Citron, who campaigned as an investment wizard, sought leniency by denigrating his intelligence and financial acumen. Break out of this mold. Accept responsibility for your actions.

HORSES

As with mountain bikers, horse riders come in all stripes; only a small percentage of equestrians are outlaw types. Even when the rider is rude, keep in mind that the horse is an innocent victim. Be courteous to the horse and tolerate its master. Most horse riders are pleasant people and would prefer not to end up being rudely tossed into the weeds because some biker scared the apples out of Trigger, Silver or Mr. Ed.

SHOW COURTESY TO OTHERS

Use your brains for something other than helmet filler. Treat others like you would like to be treated (seems like someone else may have already coined that phrase). Be friendly and greet other people on the trail. Cheerfully give each other the right of way. Nobody appreciates a rider who hogs all the room on a singletrack as they pass and never even looks up. Unwarranted acts of kindness always seem to be rewarded. It all starts with you.

OTHER RULES OF THE TRAIL

In addition to showing common sense and courtesy, observe the following IMBA Rules of the Trail:

1. RIDE ON OPEN TRAILS ONLY. Respect trail and road closures (ask if not sure), avoid possible trespass on private land, obtain permits and authorization as may be required. Federal and State wilderness areas are closed to cycling.
2. LEAVE NO TRACE. Be sensitive to the dirt beneath you. Practice low-impact cycling. This also means staying on the trail and not creating new ones. We have seen old tubes discarded along the trail in the middle of the Santa Anas. Are you that lazy? Be sure to pack out at least as much as you pack in.
3. CONTROL YOUR BICYCLE. Inattention for even a second can cause disaster. Excessive speed threatens you and others.
4. ALWAYS YIELD THE TRAIL. Make known your approach well in advance. A friendly greeting (or bell) works well; startling someone may cause loss of trail access. Show your respect when passing others by slowing to a walk or even stopping. Anticipate that other trail users may be around blind corners or in blind spots.
5. NEVER SPOOK ANIMALS. All animals are startled by an unannounced approach, a sudden movement or a loud noise. This can be dangerous to you, others and the animals. Give animals extra room and time to adjust to you. In passing, use special care.
6. PLAN AHEAD. Know your equipment, your ability and the area in which you are riding—and prepare accordingly. Be self-sufficient at all times, wear a helmet, keep your machine in good repair, and carry necessary supplies for a change in weather or other conditions. A well-executed trip is satisfying to you and not a burden to others.

NEW INFORMATION-CORRECTIONS

We are happy to get feedback from you on this book. Comments, new trails or rides and corrections are all welcome. They should be sent to:

Randy Vogel,
P.O. Box 4554
Laguna Beach, CA 92652

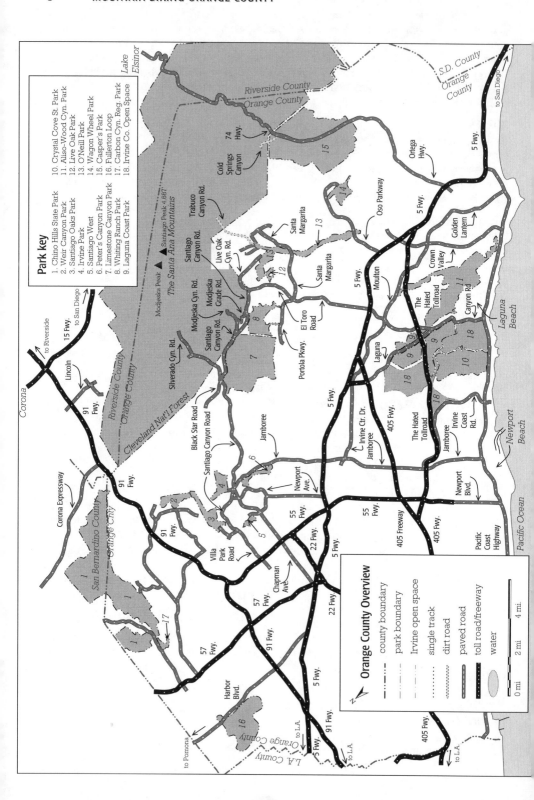

Park key

1. Chino Hills State Park
2. Weir Canyon Park
3. Santiago Oaks Park
4. Irvine Park
5. Santiago West
6. Peter's Canyon Park
7. Limestone Canyon Park
8. Whiting Ranch Park
9. Laguna Coast Park
10. Crystal Cove St. Park
11. Aliso-Wood Cyn. Park
12. Live Oak Park
13. O'Neill Park
14. Wagon Wheel Park
15. Casper's Park
16. Fullerton Loop
17. Carbon Cyn. Reg. Park
18. Irvine Co. Open Space

▲ Modjeska Peak   ▲ Santiago Peak 4,687'

The Santa Ana Mountains

Orange County Overview

- — · · — county boundary
- — · · · — park boundary
- — · · · · Irvine open space
- · · · · · · single track
- ∿∿∿∿ dirt road
- ━━━ paved road
- ━•━•━ toll road/freeway
- ⬭ water

0 mi   2 mi   4 mi

Chino Hills State Park (aka Carbon Canyon)

Chino Hills State Park
4195 Chino Hills Parkway, #E165
Chino Hills, CA 91709

WITH OVER 12,000 ACRES OF LAND, CHINO Hills State Park is an expansive and diverse park which offers riders the rare opportunity to get so deep into a riding area that you can't see any evidence of the surrounding communities. The Park is enjoyed equally by mountain bikers, hikers, nature watchers, horse owners, model glider enthusiasts and photographers.

The wildlife is plentiful and often quite visible. It is not beyond expectation to see countless rabbits, bobcats, deer and all types of raptors on the same ride. In the spring and summer, the wildlife list also includes a plentiful supply of rattlesnakes, so be careful.

Tarantulas are also found in great numbers and are frequent visitors on all the trails and fireroads. We take great lengths, and sometimes dumb chances, to avoid hitting these guys on their stroll around the park. In the spring, between the tarantulas, caterpillars and lizards, it may be hard to find a clear spot on the trail!

MOUNTAIN BIKING IN THE PARK

Chino Hills State Park, or Carbon Canyon as it is affectionately known, is a gold mine of opportunity for the fledgling mountain biker desiring to break into this terrific sport. For advanced riders it has opportunities for fast downhills and long loop rides. Chino Hills doesn't offer much in the way of technical difficulty, but it is the perfect place to "get your legs" and take those first few timid forays onto some outstanding singletracks like Gilman's, Raptor Ridge or Water Canyon.

Aside from the well-known singletracks, some long, remote and potentially outstanding singletracks are waiting to be ridden out on East and North Boundary. These trails, which seem to wax and wane with the seasons, desperately need a lot of bike traffic to both negate equestrian damage and permanently establish these trails. Razorback, Sapphire and the isolated East Boundary trail are a few of these excellent trails which see such little traffic.

HOW TO GET THERE

Chino Hills has so many entrances it would be confusing to list them all, so we will focus on those entrances that have the best parking and the easiest access to the park.

ORANGE COUNTY ENTRANCES

On the Orange county side you have two main entrances: the Rimcrest entrance and the Carbon Canyon Regional Park entrance.

CARBON CANYON ENTRANCE

Carbon Canyon Regional Park provides parking and access to the western portion of Chino Hills. From the 57 (Orange) Freeway, exit Lambert Road and proceed east for about 5.6 miles to the entrance of Carbon Canyon Regional Park. Turn right into the parking area. Note: As you pass Valencia Avenue, Lambert Road becomes Carbon Canyon Road. Be extremely careful while you are turning into this lot. Carbon Canyon is a route used by commuters who sometimes seem asleep.

As of January 1, 1996, parking fees are $2.00 during the week and $4.00 on weekends. Make sure you bring *crisp* dollar bills or plenty of quarters—the parking lot gate rejects anything else. You can also purchase a yearly pass, which is good at all Orange County Regional Parks. The passes are $50.00 and will save regular riders money and hassle.

RIMCREST ENTRANCE (aka Cheat Street)

Parking is along Rimcrest Drive in a residential area. Due to rude and crude behavior by a few (changing clothes, urinating and loud obscene language) local residents, backed by the City of Yorba Linda, have restricted parking to one side of the street and limited the hour you can park there to after 8 a.m.. If this type of behavior persists we are sure that the City of Yorba Linda will not hesitate to ban parking altogether.

From the Orange Freeway (57): Exit at Yorba Linda Boulevard and head east, past the Nixon Library, until you reach Fairmont Boulevard. Turn left onto Fairmont and travel north for 1.8 miles until you see Rimcrest. Turn left (also north) and travel 0.2 mile until you reach the corner of Rimcrest and Blue Gum. Park on the east side of the street only.

From the Riverside Freeway (91): Exit at Imperial Highway and head north. Follow Imperial until you reach Yorba Linda Blvd and follow it until you reach Fairmont Blvd. Turn left (north) and follow Fairmont 1.8 miles until you see Rimcrest. Turn left (also north) onto Rimcrest and follow it 0.2 mile to the corner of Rimcrest and Blue Gum. Park along the east side of the street.

Rimcrest is also dubbed "Cheat Street" because advanced riders can skip the relatively easy lower section of Telegraph Canyon Road and jump right into the harder, more technical riding.

SAN BERNARDINO COUNTY ENTRANCES

From the San Bernardino County side you can access the park from two different points, Bane Canyon and Prado Dam.

PRADO DAM ENTRANCE

Take the Riverside Freeway (91) east, toward Corona. Then take the Corona Expressway (Hwy. 71) north. Immediately after crossing over the Santa Ana River, you will see a small parking area on your right. It is located at the access road to Prado Dam. Park here, or continue north about 200 yards, and park at the third pullout on the west side of the road. This pullout is fairly large.

BANE CANYON ENTRANCE

Bane Canyon is the main entrance to the park and the only road open to automobile traffic. Take the Riverside Freeway (91) east to the Corona Expressway (71). Head north on the Corona Expressway to Central Avenue. Turn right (west). Turn left (south) at Pomona Rincon Road. Take Pomona Rincon to Soquel Canyon Parkway and turn right (west). Follow Soquel to Elinvar Drive (try saying that quickly three times) and turn left. Turn left again at Sapphire. The entrance should be in front of you. The gate may be closed which will add some mileage to your ride. This entrance is primarily used by equestrians.

OTHER ENTRANCES

There are at least six more entrances of which we are aware. These have been excluded for various reasons. Several, like Brush Canyon, have been closed by housing development.

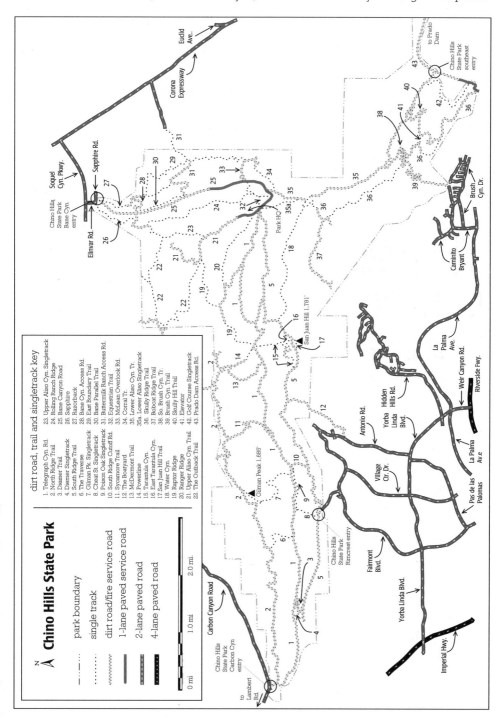

Some entrances that may have been quasi-legal, have been closed. If we demonstrate responsibility, perhaps more of these entrances could be re-opened.

FEES AND FACILITIES

The Bane Canyon Entrance is open to cars at certain times of the year. This allows you to drive all the way to the Visitor Center. Parking is $2.00 per vehicle per day. The Carbon Canyon Entrance requires parking at Carbon Canyon Regional Park, which also charges $2.00 per vehicle. Chino Hills State Park also offers plentiful camping. These are used primarily by equestrian visitors, but are quite nice and suitable for mountain bikers. Toilets are provided as well as potable water. Call the Park for camping reservations.

CHINO HILLS LOOP RIDES

The following eight rides are little more than a sampling of the tremendous riding potential in this large park. Nevertheless, these rides are some of our favorites and we think you will enjoy them too. Once you get to know the park better, you can put your own rides together using the overview map and the individual trail descriptions at the end of this chapter.

Telegraph Canyon Loop

CHINO HILLS RIDE 1

Distance • 12.0 mile loop

Time Required • 1 to 2+ hours

Route Rating • 5

Grunt Factor • 3

Technical Rating • 1

Downhill Rating • 4

Elevation • Start 580

High point 1318 ft.

Finish 480 ft.

Map • Telegraph Canyon Loop, page 13

THIS IS THE PERFECT PLACE FOR beginning riders to start their riding careers. Telegraph Canyon is also very scenic. Why ride a boring bike path to gain conditioning when you can ride one of the best trails in the area? As an in-and-out ride, you can turn around at any point. If you can ride up to Four Corners and back, you are ready for tougher rides, such as Ride #3 - The Standard Loop. The nicest feature of this ride is that the return leg is always downhill.

SAFETY HINT

Watch for traffic. Safety and courtesy go hand in hand. *Always slow down* and if required, *always yield* when passing hikers or equestrians. When passing anyone (bikers too), advise them of how many more members are in your group. This helps avoid accidents and user conflicts. Remember, user conflicts can lead to trail closures.

PARKING

Park at Carbon Canyon Regional Park. From the 57 (Orange) Freeway, take Lambert Road east for about 5.6 miles to Carbon Canyon Regional Park. Turn right into the parking area. Make sure you bring two *crisp* dollar bills or plenty of quarters – the parking lot gate rejects anything else.

THE RIDE

From the parking lot, ride east on Carbon Canyon Road to the Lemon Grove gate. Reset your mileage computer here. Beware of lemon tree branches that have huge, tire-puncturing thorns. Ride 0.2 mile to a second gate. Stay to the right, around the ridge,

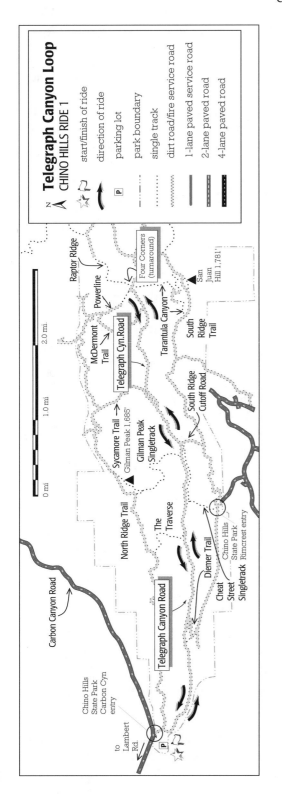

Telegraph Canyon Loop
CHINO HILLS RIDE 1

N

start/finish of ride
direction of ride
P   parking lot
park boundary
single track
dirt road/fire service road
1-lane paved service road
2-lane paved road
4-lane paved road

0 mi   1.0 mi   2.0 mi.

Carbon Canyon Road

Chino Hills State Park Carbon Cyn entry

to Lambert Rd.

P

Telegraph Canyon Road

North Ridge Trail

The Traverse

Diemer Trail

Cheat Street Singletrack

Chino Hills State Park Rimcrest entry

South Ridge Cutoff Road

South Ridge Trail

Tarantula Canyon

San Juan Hill 1,781'

Telegraph Cyn.Road

Sycamore Trail
Gilman Peak 1,685'
Gilman Peak Singletrack

McDermont Trail

Powerline

Raptor Ridge

Four Corners (turnaround)

into the mouth of Telegraph Canyon. From here, stay in the canyon bottom, avoiding any turn-offs.

After riding nearly 3.9 miles, the trail starts to feature some steeper grades. At the **5.1 mile mark**, is a beautiful clearing with a picnic table amid oak trees; a great spot for a picnic. This spot is a good goal for new riders.

The Telegraph Canyon Trail continues through riparian woods, featuring a few steep but short sections. At the **6.0 mile mark**, you reach Four Corners (where several trails converge). There is a picnic bench here and usually a gathering of riders. Grab your water and jump right into the discussion.

From wherever you decide to stop your ride, simply turn your bike around and head back to your car. Watch your downhill speed. Telegraph Canyon appears a gentle descent, but you can quickly gain speed that can exceed the abilities of beginners. This is one of the better beginner rides in Orange County. It will remain a favorite long after it ceases to be a challenge.

Gilman Peak Singletrack Loop

CHINO HILLS RIDE 2

Distance • 9.9 mile loop

Time Required • 1 to 2 hours

Route Rating • 8

Grunt Factor • 6

Technical Rating • 4/5

Downhill Rating • 4

Elevation • Start 480
High point 1680 ft.
Finish 480 ft.

Map • Gilman Peak Singletrack Loop, page 15

THE GILMAN PEAK SINGLETRACK LOOP IS one of the outstanding singletrack rides of Chino Hills. It is somewhat shorter than Water Canyon and Raptor Ridge, but it is consistently steeper and can be more technical. Because of its central location it is often the first singletrack done by visitors to the park and is a favorite of hikers and horse riders.

This singletrack starts at the second highest location of the park and offers terrific vistas of both Orange and San Bernardino Counties.

HOW TO GET THERE

You start at the Carbon Canyon Entrance. From the 57 (Orange) Freeway, exit Lambert Road and proceed east for about 5.6 miles to the entrance of Carbon Canyon Regional Park. Turn right into the parking area.

Make sure you bring two *crisp* dollar bills or plenty of quarters—the parking lot gate rejects anything else.

THE RIDE

From the Carbon Canyon Entrance follow the paved road down and through a water crossing to a gate at the 0.2 mark. This is the beginning of both Telegraph Canyon and North Ridge. Head left (east) sharply up North Ridge. (North Ridge is also known as 4 Mile Hill—the distance to the summit of Gilman Peak.)

Continue on North Ridge toward Gilman Peak. At the **3.4 mile mark** you'll see a singletrack that cuts uphill and right around the base of Gilman Peak. Stay left. Make a right-hand turn

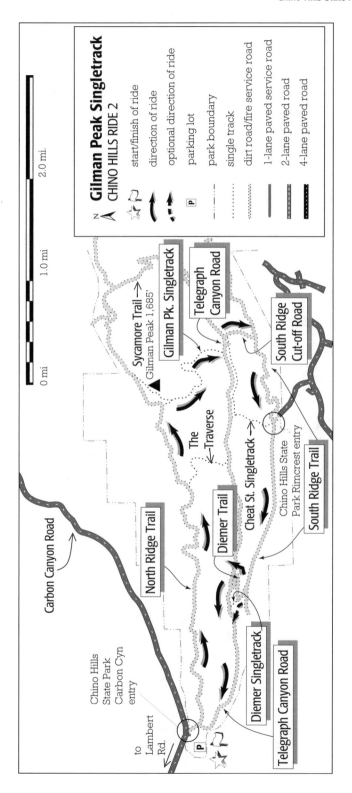

uphill toward the summit at a point just before passing downhill through a fence (3.8 mile mark). Head up to the summit of Gilman Peak (**4.1 mile mark**). Take a little time to enjoy the view. During the winter this can be a really beautiful spot with clear views of San Clemente and Catalina Islands.

From the summit, head down a singletrack on the right (west). This is the Gilman Peak Singletrack. Initially the trail is loose and rocky. Think "monster truck" and stay back over your rear wheel. This excellent, fast and somewhat technical downhill heads south and switchbacks until you reach the bottom at a junction with Telegraph Canyon Road (**5.2 mile mark**).

Head left up Telegraph Canyon where you soon will see the South Ridge Cutoff fireroad on your right. Turn right here and proceed uphill until you reach South Ridge Trail. Turn right here. Rollercoaster up and down South Ridge Trail until you descend down to the Cheat Street (Rimcrest) entrance. Continue south on South Ridge Trail.

Climb up to the top of South Ridge to Glider Hill. There are often scores of people flying all sorts of colorful radio-controlled gliders here. This activity can be really fun to watch. From Glider Hill continue west along South Ridge Trail. South Ridge is usually smooth and fast until you reach the Diemer Trail). Turn right onto Diemer Trail. The corners on Diemer can be loose so be prepared! Diemer terminates at Telegraph Canyon at the 8.2 mark. Note: At Diemer's first S-turn a short singletrack heads directly down to Telegraph Canyon. It is worth doing, if for no other reason than to ride more singletrack.

Turn left at Telegraph and ride back to the entrance.

The Standard Loop

CHINO HILLS RIDE 3

Distance • 10.3-mile loop

Time Required • 0.75 or 1.5 hours

Route Rating • 7

Grunt Factor • 4 (5 on Backwards Loop)

Technical Rating • 4

Downhill Rating • 6 (7 on Backwards Loop)

Map • The Standard Loop, page 17

THE STANDARD LOOP IS A SHORT conditioning loop designed to get your legs burning even when you don't have all day to ride. This is a great ride for beginners to start to explore singletrack and to lengthen the mileage and amount of uphill they do. This should be the next ride a beginner does after making it to Four Corners without collapsing from exhaustion.

It is also fun backwards (but then you have to call it the Standard Loop Backwards).

HOW TO GET THERE

Park at the Cheat Street (Rimcrest) entrance. From the 57 (Orange) Freeway: Take Yorba Linda Blvd. east, past the Nixon Library, to Fairmont Blvd. Turn left (north) onto Fairmont and travel 1.8 miles until you see the Rimcrest. Turn left (also north) and travel 0.2 mile to the corner of Blue Gum and Rimcrest. Park on the east side of the street.

THE RIDE

From the Cheat Street entrance take South Ridge left (west) uphill. After an initially steep uphill enjoy the roller coaster downhill 2.0 miles to the Diemer Trail. Turn right and follow the Diemer Trail downhill to Telegraph Canyon at the 2.6 mile mark. Follow

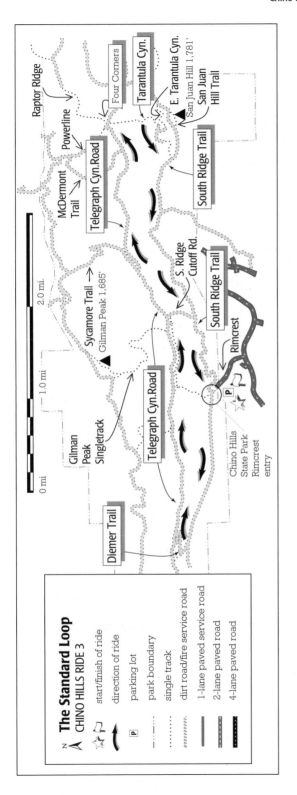

The Standard Loop
CHINO HILLS RIDE 3

≥ start/finish of ride

direction of ride

P parking lot

park boundary

single track

dirt road/fire service road

1-lane paved service road

2-lane paved road

4-lane paved road

Diemer Trail

Gilman Peak Singletrack

Telegraph Cyn.Road

Sycamore Trail →
Gilman Peak 1,685'

Telegraph Cyn.Road

McDermont Trail

Powerline

Raptor Ridge

Four Corners

Tarantula Cyn.

E. Tarantula Cyn.
San Juan Hill 1,781'

San Juan Hill Trail

South Ridge Trail

S. Ridge Cutoff Rd.

South Ridge Trail

Rimcrest

Chino Hills State Park Rimcrest entry

0 mi   1.0 mi   2.0 mi.

right and follow the Diemer Trail downhill to Telegraph Canyon at the 2.6 mile mark. Follow Telegraph Canyon to Four Corners at the **6.9 mile mark**.

From Four Corners, head right (south) up the Tarantula Canyon singletrack. Continue up Tarantula Canyon, staying right at the fork, and continue 25 feet farther to the gas pipe access road. Turn left (southwest) uphill until you reach the singletrack turn-off at the **7.6 mark**. Turn right (southwest) here and continue gently uphill on this singletrack until you reach the intersection with South Ridge fireroad at the 8.0 mile mark.

Follow South Ridge, resisting the temptaion to take any of the turn-offs, until you reach the **10.3 mile mark** and arrive back at the Cheat Street entrance. Not tired yet? Turn around and do it backwards.

Raptor Ridge Loop

CHINO HILLS RIDE 4

Distance • 12.5 mile loop

Time Required • 1.5 to 3 hours

Route Rating • 9

Grunt Factor • 5

Technical Rating • 3

Downhill Rating • 8

Map • Raptor Ridge Loop, page 19

FLYING DOWN RAPTOR RIDGE IS ONE OF the best experiences you can have at Chino Hills or all of Orange County for that matter. There are many ways to include this outstanding singletrack in a loop, but this is the version we most often choose.

HOW TO GET THERE

The loop begins at the Rimcrest entrance (see pages 10 and 16).

THE RIDE

From the Cheat Street entrance, turn right and head uphill at the South Ridge Trail fireroad. At the **2.5 mile mark** you'll find the top of the Tarantula Canyon singletrack on your left. It will be the only singletrack leading off the ridge to the north on the complete eastern length of South Ridge. Turn left (northeast). For three miles you'll be mainly singletrack all the way to the Visitors Center. Yahoo!

Continue roughly northeast on Tarantula Canyon. At the **3.0 mile mark** you intersect a short length of fireroad; continue downhill (north). After 100 yards on the fireroad, just as you make a sharp, right-hand turn, you will see the singletrack on the right as it continues downhill. (If you miss this turn you'll just dead end at the pipe and have to either rejoin the trail across a dry creek or doubleback to the singletrack). The singletrack soon forks: bear left. Continue downhill until you reach a fireroad at Four Corners (**3.6 mile mark**) marked by a picnic table.

Head across the fireroad, slightly right, and enter the singletrack running up a short ridge. This is Raptor Ridge. After some really fun banked turns and ramps, and a few uphill sections, you'll be dumped onto an access road right under a power line tower at the **4.2 mark**. This next section goes very fast as you blaze down the fireroad.

Head downhill to the sharp, left (north) turn at the **4.5 mark** to put you back on the singletrack is easy to miss. As you approach the turn, the bluff on your left drops down to about three feet. Evidence of missed turns and near death experiences are abundant here.

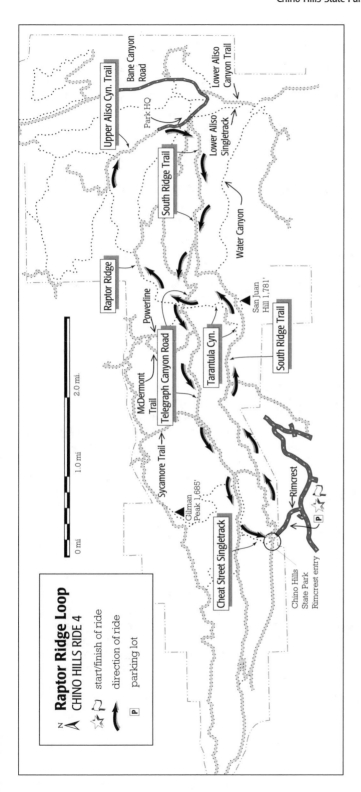

Raptor Ridge Loop
CHINO HILLS RIDE 4

★ start/finish of ride
➤ direction of ride
P parking lot

0 mi   1.0 mi   2.0 mi

Upper Aliso Cyn. Trail

Bane Canyon Road

Lower Aliso Canyon Trail

Park HQ

Lower Aliso Singletrack

South Ridge Trail

Water Canyon

Raptor Ridge

San Juan Hill 1,781'

Powerline

South Ridge Trail

McDemont Trail

Tarantula Cyn.

Telegraph Canyon Road

Sycamore Trail

Gilman Peak 1,685'

Rimcrest

Cheat Street Singletrack

Chino Hills State Park Rimcrest entry

Traditionally, Raptor Ridge concludes straight ahead, but no one I know does it that way anymore. We have renamed it to try and clear some of the confusion.

The singletrack continues down some really fast sections featuring a few hairy off-camber turns to the **5.4 mark** where the trail merges with the Aliso Canyon trail. There is an abrupt right (southeast) turn heare that crosses a dry creek as the trail continues towards the visitor center. Follow this until you dead end onto the paved access road. Turn left (east) and follow this road 50 yards to the entrance of the South Ridge road at the **6.9 mark** and turn right (west). The South Ridge entrance will be marked with a sign.

Follow South Ridge as it grinds you back up towards Four Corners. At the **8.3 mile mark**, south Ridge continues sharply uphill to the left but stay to the right to make the connection with Telegraph Canyon at the **8.7 mark**. Continue straight (northwest) at this junction as it takes you farther uphill toward the crest of Telegraph Canyon Road at the **8.8 mark**. Glide down into Four Corners at the **10.1 mark** and join in the slander if you neeed a rest.

From Four Corners continue down Telegraph Canyon (west). Put it in the big chain ring, keep peddling and continue the burn while gaining a little extra speed. Don't be distracted by the South and North Ridge cutoff roads and follow Telegraph Canyon downhill to the **12.1 mark** where a sharp left (south) turn puts you on the Cheat Street singletrack. Follow Cheat Street uphill to the Rimcrest entrance at the **12.5 mark**. Don't let tired legs deter you from trying to make it up Cheat Street clean!

Water Canyon Loop

CHINO HILLS RIDE 5

Distance • 13.5 mile loop

Time Required • 1.5 to 2.5 hours

Route Rating • 8

Grunt Factor •5

Technical Rating • 4

Downhill Rating • 7

Map • Water Canyon Loop, page 21

WATER CANYON IS PROBABLY THE crown jewel of the Chino Hills singletracks and this loop is definitely the finest ride you can do from the Bane Canyon entrance. It has sections that can be pushed to the riders limit and also features just enough obstacles to make you pay attention. Whether experienced beginner or serious hammerhead, Water Canyon has to be done. Repeatedly.

HOW TO GET THERE

The ride starts at the Bane Canyon entrance (see page 10). Park on the outside of the park and ride up Bane Canyon Road.

THE RIDE

Start up Bane Canyon Road until you reach the horse gates at the **0.5 mile mark**. At the horse gate turn right (west) continue to head uphill. You will pass around an old gate along the way and then reach a fork in the road at **0.9 mile mark** that is underneath a power tower. Turn right (west) onto the spur road that heads down to another power tower. On your right, you will see the top of the Aliso Canyon singletrack at the 1.0 mile mark just to the northwest side of the power tower.

As you head down the Upper Aliso Canyon singletrack be careful of the narrow sections that offer a really quick trip down into the canyon if you mess up. Blast down the singletrack until you reach the **2.0 mile mark** where you will intersect the Upper Aliso Canyon Trail fireroad. Turn left (southwest) and ride down Aliso Canyon past the "Barn" until you reach the three-way intersection of Bane Canyon, Telegraph Canyon and Aliso Canyon roads at the **3.0 mile mark**. This is the beginning of the real work.

Turn right (west) onto Telegraph Canyon and follow this fireroad uphill to the **3.9 mile mark**. Turn right and head up the access road that will connect you with Raptor Ridge. This is a very steep section but can be done if you have the will. Avoid entering the restricted, and Poison Oak infested, "Hills for Everybody" trail that also connects with Telegraph Canyon at this intersection.

You reach the top of the ridge at the **4.5 mile mark**. Stay left, on the fireroad which turns to singletrack. Follow the singletrack down to Four Corners at the **5.8 mile mark**. Proceed directly across the fireroad and start the Tarantula Canyon singletrack up toward South Ridge. You will take the East Tarantula Canyon trail at the **6.3 mile mark** which is a 180 degree left turn.

You reach South Ridge at the **6.7 mile mark**. Turn left (northeast) onto South Ridge. Head downhill on South Ridge until you reach the entrance to Water Canyon at the **7.0 mile mark**.

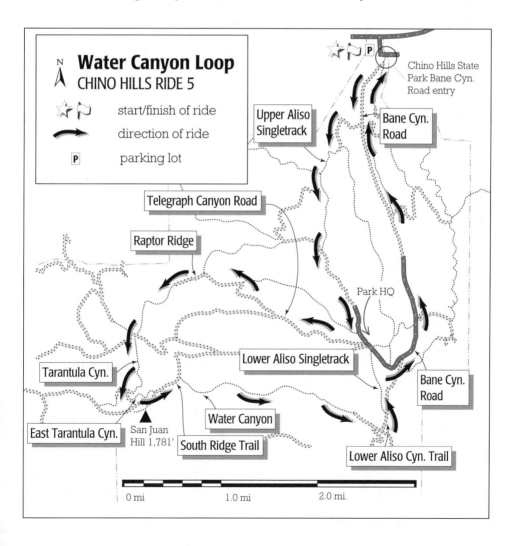

The entrance is located on the right just past a power tower and just on the downhill side of an old fence. It is easy to miss.

Water Canyon is absolutely wonderful most times of the year. Be careful at the **7.8 mile mark** where you will reach a technical section after you make a short climb up and over a shale outcropping. The lower section is not as steep, but still a lot of fun. You reach the end of Water Canyon at the **8.9 mile mark** at the Lower Aliso Canyon Trail just as it turns into Skully Ridge. Turn left and proceed a short distance and make another left turn at the 9.0 mile mark. Follow this trail as it takes you past a gate and some campsites to Bane Canyon road at the **9.7 mile mark**.

Turn right onto the paved section of Bane Canyon as it heads uphill to the southeast. Follow Bane Canyon past the fee kiosk back to your car at the **12.4 mile mark**.

Skully Ridge Loop

CHINO HILLS RIDE 6

Distance • 12.3 mile loop

Time Required • 1.5 to 2 hours

Route Rating • 7

Grunt Factor • 5

Technical Rating • 2

Downhill Rating • 6

Elevation • Start 500 ft.
High point 1090 ft.
Finish 500 ft.

Map • Skully Ridge Loop, page 23

THIS LOOP TAKES YOU THROUGH THE southeastern portion of Chino Hills, an area that offers isolated riding and good scenery. Despite the blocking of easy access points by the City of Yorba Linda and Green River Golf Course, this region still offers a few good loop possibilities. The uncrowded conditions are yet another positive attribute.

DIRECTIONS

Take the Riverside Freeway (91) east, toward Corona. Then take the Corona Expressway (Hwy. 71) north. Immediately after crossing the Santa Ana River, you will see a small parking area on your right. It is located at the access road to Prado Dam. Park here, or continue north about 200 yards, and park at the third pullout on the west side of the road. This pullout is fairly large.

THE RIDE

Take the Prado Dam access road down, then under the Corona Expressway, parallel with the Santa Ana River. Continue west between the hills and the golf course until you reach the entrance to the park on your right (**1.6 mile mark**).

Turn right and ride 3.1 miles up the Lower Aliso Canyon Trail. There are several stream crossings which can be full of water during winter and spring. At the **4.7 mile mark**, you reach a three-way intersection. Take the road on the left, which switchbacks up the hill. This is the Skully Ridge Trail.

After 0.6 mile, a fireroad heads off to the right (the Bobcat Trail), head to the left (**5.3 mile mark**). Continue southeast along Skully, passing several utility access roads on your right. Soon, the Skully Ridge Trail narrows down to singletrack. Continue straight along the ridge at the intersections with the East and West Brush Canyon Trails (**7.2 mile mark**).

After several roller coaster hills you'll reach the top of Skully Hill (**8.3 mile mark**). Begin the final and steep descent down Skully Ridge which ends at a paved access road (**9.5 mile mark**). Head left and connect with a fun singletrack that runs around an enclosed pasture. Cross the stream and rejoin the Lower Aliso Canyon Trail just above the gate (**10.6 mile mark**). Turn right, ride through the gate, then turn left back up the Prado Dam trail to your car (**12.3 miles**).

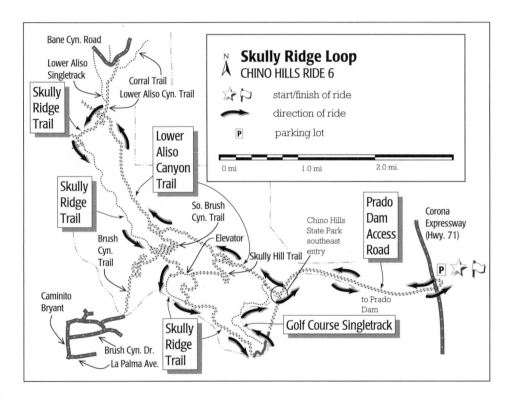

Upper Aliso Canyon Loop

CHINO HILLS RIDE 7

Distance • 6.3 mile loop

Time Required • 1 to 2 hours

Route Rating • 6

Grunt Factor • 3

Technical Rating • 2

Downhill Rating • 5

Map • Upper Aliso Canyon Loop, below

THIS IS A GREAT BEGINNER RIDE THAT takes you through some of the more isolated areas of Chino Hills. It features a very moderate singletrack that is perfect for honing your skills without incurring some nasty rashes in the process.

DIRECTIONS

You start this ride at the Bane Canyon Entrance gate. Take the Riverside Freeway (91) east to the Corona Expressway (71). Head north on the Corona Expressway to Central Avenue. Turn right (west). Turn left (south) at Pomona Rincon Road. Take Pomona Rincon to Soquel Canyon Parkway and turn right (west). Follow Soquel to Elinvar Drive; turn left. Turn left again at Sapphire. The entrance should be in front of you. Don't cheat by driving up Bane Canyon and parking near the fee kiosk!

THE RIDE
Start up Bane Canyon until you reach the **0.5 mile mark**. Head right, through a nifty horse gate and up a fireroad, around an old gate. Continue until you reach the powerline tower (**0.9 mile mark**). Turn right (west) and head down the ridge on a short access road to a point just before a second powerline tower.

You are going to turn right onto the Upper Aliso Canyon singletrack just as you reach the power tower (**1.0 mile mark**). The trail skirts around the outside of the ridge and eventually runs south-southwest in direction. Be careful on the first one hundred yards which has a steep drop-in and a couple of narrow spots with fairly steep drop-offs. Watch the trail and not the drop off!

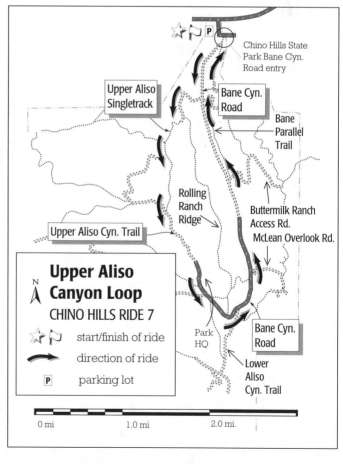

Chino Hills State Park Bane Cyn. Road entry

Upper Aliso Singletrack

Bane Cyn. Road

Bane Parallel Trail

Upper Aliso Cyn. Trail

Rolling Ranch Ridge

Buttermilk Ranch Access Rd.

McLean Overlook Rd.

Upper Aliso Canyon Loop
CHINO HILLS RIDE 7

N

⭐🚩   start/finish of ride

➤   direction of ride

P   parking lot

Park HQ

Bane Cyn. Road

Lower Aliso Cyn. Trail

0 mi   1.0 mi   2.0 mi.

Follow the singletrack as it meanders down into a pretty canyon. The singletrack eventually terminates at the Upper Aliso Canyon Trail fireroad. Turn left. Follow Upper Aliso Canyon downhill until you reach the now abandoned Visitors Center (**3.1 mile mark**). Take this opportunity to refill your water or use the only real restroom in the entire park.

Continue down Upper Aliso Canyon until it dead ends into Bane Canyon Road (**3.2 mile mark**). Turn left (east), following the short paved section of the road up to an overlook and back down the hill. Continue along Bane Canyon as it winds its way northeast. Be careful as you travel this road. There is a lot of traffic on this section of road when the Bane gate is open to car traffic. (Variation: There is a fun singletrack that parallels the east side of Bane Canyon Road that can be accessed at several spots.)

You finally reach the fee kiosk just as you begin the downhill leg of Bane Canyon (**5.7 mile mark**). Caution is strongly urged as you descend. There is often lots of foot, equestrian and automobile traffic. Additionally, gravel has been placed on this road to help with erosion, but this creates a situation where you can gain lots of speed quickly without having any real control for steering or stopping.

You'll arrive back at the Bane Canyon gate at the **6.3 mile mark**.

The Grand Tour

CHINO HILLS RIDE 8

Distance • 26.7 mile loop

Time Required • 3 to 6 hours

Route Rating • 8

Grunt Factor • 7

Technical Rating • 6

Downhill Rating • 8

Map • The Grand Tour, page 27

SO, YOU THINK YOU GOT CHINO HILLS wired? None of the loops challenge you enough to make you sweat? The Grand Tour will get your heart rate up and take you through all the best parts of the park to boot.

CAR DIRECTIONS

Park at the Carbon Canyon parking lot. From the 57 Freeway take Lambert east 5.6 miles until you reach the entrance to Carbon Canyon Regional Park. Parking is $2.00 during the week, $4.00 on weekends. Make sure to bring crisp dollar bills or lots of quarters, the gate rejects anything else.

 ### THE RIDE

From the Lemon Grove gate, follow the paved road, through a water crossing, to a horse gate (**0.2 mile mark**). The road forks past this point, take the left fork. This is the start of the North Ridge Trail, also affectionately known as 4 Mile Hill.

Keep following the North Ridge Trail upward, past several turnoffs. At the **3.8 mile mark**, immediately before a gate, make a sharp, right-hand turn. This takes you uphill to the summit of Gilman Peak (**4.1 mile mark**). Off the west side of the peak, you begin to descend the Gilman Singletrack, one of the best singletracks in Orange County. Watch those off-camber turns in the meadow! Unfortunately, the descent lasts only 1.1 miles when you reach Telegraph Canyon (**5.2 mile mark**).

Turn left, uphill on Telegraph Canyon and head east to Four Corners (**7.4 mile mark**). From Four Corners, take the Raptor Ridge Trail, a singletrack on your left (northeast of the picnic benches) which starts out slightly uphill. Raptor Ridge begins by winding through hills which feature some way-cool banked turns. Eventually, you get dumped out onto a fireroad under power line towers (**8.0 mile mark**).

Follow the fireroad downhill for a short and fast 0.3 mile, and make a sharp left turn, up a short hill and back onto singletrack (**8.3 mile mark**). Now sit back and rip down the rest of this excellent singletrack trail. Eventually, you merge with the Aliso Canyon fireroad (**9.2 mile mark**). Head right, downhill on Aliso Canyon for 0.6 mile, where you will turn left onto the Upper Aliso Canyon Singletrack (**9.8 mile mark**). Be careful of the narrow spots on this trail.

After 1.0 mile, you will reach the top of the Upper Aliso Singletrack (**10.8 mile mark**). From the top of the trail, follow the fireroad uphill (left) where you will reach another fireroad (**10.9 mile mark**). Turn left and follow the fireroad downhill to where it hits Bane Canyon Road (**11.4 mile mark**). Pass through the horse gate, cross Bane Canyon Road, then proceed through a gate on the opposite side of the road. Continue uphill on another fireroad (East Ridge Access Road) for 0.2+ mile. Turn left onto a singletrack (East Boundary Trail) and head sharply downhill. This is one of the more technical areas in the Park.

Don't be discouraged if the East Boundary Trail seems a bit unkempt. It is one of the best trails in the Park and needs to be ridden to keep it in good repair. The trail goes over several short ridges, then makes a long climb up to Buttermilk Ranch Road (**12.7 mile mark**). You'll know you have arrived when you see the old windmill. Continue across the fireroad and continue on occasionally technical singletrack and past the abandoned Slaughter Canyon Road (**13.6 mile mark**).

The East Boundary Trail now heads over to the Bane Canyon side of the ridge and will intersect two different abandoned roads. The trail terminates at the McLean Overlook fireroad (**14.1 mile mark**). Turn left here. Head 0.1 mile where you will reach the top of the Corral Trail. Make a right turn down the steep and technical Corral Trail. It ends at a campsite fitted with corrals (surprise) and a real toilet.

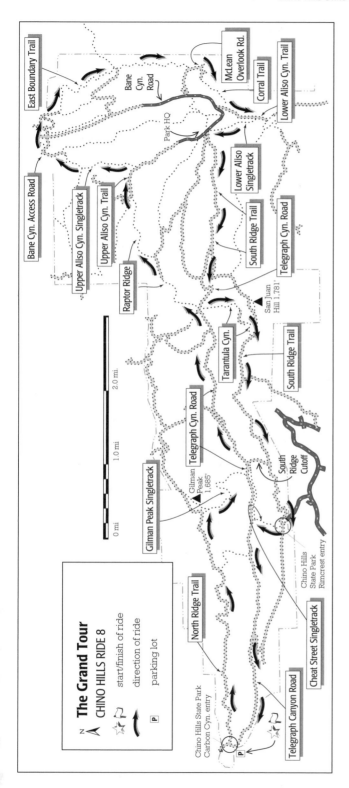

The Grand Tour
CHINO HILLS RIDE 8

⛺ start/finish of ride

➤ direction of ride

P parking lot

East Boundary Trail

Bane Cyn. Road

McLean Overlook Rd.

Corral Trail

Lower Aliso Cyn. Trail

Park HQ

Bane Cyn. Access Road

Upper Aliso Cyn. Singletrack

Upper Aliso Cyn. Trail

Lower Aliso Singletrack

Raptor Ridge

South Ridge Trail

Telegraph Cyn. Road

San Juan Hill 1,781'

Tarantula Cyn.

South Ridge Trail

Gilman Peak Singletrack

Telegraph Cyn. Road

Gilman Peak 1,685'

South Ridge Cutoff

Chino Hills State Park Rimcrest entry

North Ridge Trail

Cheat Street Singletrack

Telegraph Canyon Road

Chino Hills State Park Carbon Cyn. entry

0 mi   1.0 mi   2.0 mi

From the campsite, go left, over the gate, down Lower Aliso Canyon Road to the 14.7+ mile mark. At this point, you turn right and pick up the Lower Aliso Singletrack. This fun singletrack does not receive much traffic and takes you back north to the beginning of the South Ride Trail, at Bane Canyon Road (**15.6 mile mark**). Tired yet? Better not be, you have a long way to go pilgrim!

Turn left, and head up the South Ridge fireroad. After 1.4 miles, you reach a fork in the road (**17.0 mile mark**). Take the right-hand fork. At the 17.4 mile mark turn left, uphill. After a fun downhill section, you reach Four Corners again (**18.7 mile mark**). At Four Corners, make a left onto the Tarantula Canyon Singletrack. Ride uphill to where Tarantula Canyon joins a fireroad. Make sure to turn right off the fireroad onto the second section of Tarantula Canyon (**19.4+ mile mark**). This singletrack ends at South Ridge Trail (**19.9 mile mark**).

You can cruise down the South Ridge fireroad (be sure to fight your way up the few uphills) all the way to the Cheat Street Entrance (**22.6 mile mark**). From the Cheat Street gate, turn right onto the Cheat Street Singletrack which heads downhill, then across a stream to meet the Telegraph Canyon fireroad (**23.1 mile mark**). Turn left on Telegraph Canyon and start the last leg of your journey. Keep on those cranks as you blast back to the horse gate and then the Lemon Grove gate (26.7 miles total). Remember, the last one to finish buys the beer!

Trail Segments

The following is a partial list and description of the innumerable trails, roads and singletracks at Chino Hills. As you gain experience riding at Chino Hills, you can use the following information and the overview map of the park to create your own custom rides. Many great trails described below are not included in the suggested loop rides.

The trails are described from west to east, starting at the Carbon Canyon entrance. The numbers assigned to the trails correspond to the numbers used on the overview trail map of the park on page 29.

Some of the trails at Chino Hills are up to eight miles long. As a result, conditions and ratings may be dependent upon which side of the park you start. Telegraph Canyon Road, is a good example. It is very easy starting from the Orange County side, but has quite the uphill grind if you start from the San Bernardino side. For riders wanting additional information about the park topography, we recommend the USGS 7.5 minute topographical maps "Yorba Linda" and "Prado Dam."

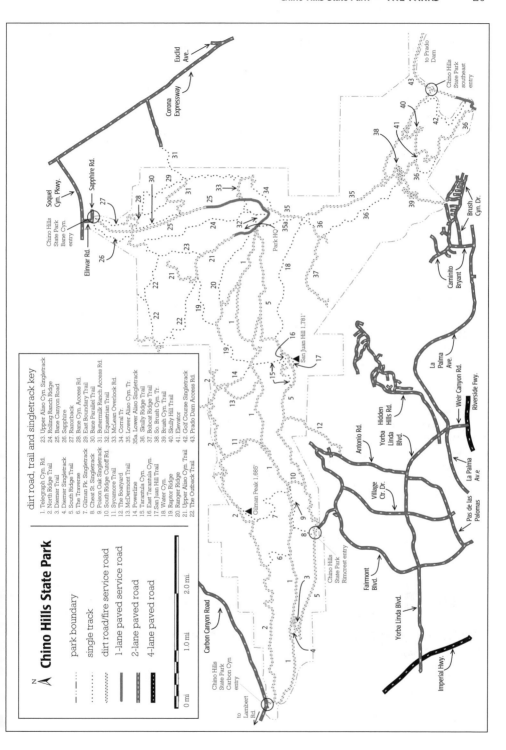

N

Chino Hills State Park

- – · – · – park boundary
- · · · · · · single track
- ◇◇◇◇◇◇ dirt road/fire service road
- ▬▬▬▬ 1-lane paved service road
- ▬▬▬▬ 2-lane paved road
- ▭▭▭▭ 4-lane paved road

0 mi   1.0 mi   2.0 mi.

dirt road, trail and singletrack key

1. Telegraph Cyn. Rd
2. North Ridge Trail
3. Diemer Trail
4. Diemer Singletrack
5. South Ridge Trail
6. The Traverse
7. Gilman Pk. Singletrack
8. Cheat St. Singletrack
9. Poison Oak Singletrack
10. South Ridge Cutoff Rd
11. Sycamore Trail
12. The Boatyard
13. McDermont Trail
14. Powerline
15. Tarantula Cyn.
16. East Tarantula Cyn.
17. San Juan Hill Trail
18. Water Cyn.
19. Raptor Ridge
20. Ranger Ridge
21. Upper Aliso Cyn. Trail
22. The Outback Trail
23. Upper Aliso Cyn. Singletrack
24. Rolling Ranch Ridge
25. Bane Canyon Road
26. Sapphire
27. Razorback
28. Bane Cyn. Access Rd.
29. East Boundary Trail
30. Bane Parallel Trail
31. Buttermilk Ranch Access Rd.
32. Equestrian Trail
33. McLean Overlook Rd.
34. Corral Tr.
35. Lower Aliso Cyn. Tr.
35a. Lower Aliso Singletrack
36. Skully Ridge Trail
37. Bobcat Ridge Trail
38. So. Brush Cyn. Tr.
39. Brush Cyn. Trail
40. Skully Hill Trail
41. Elevator
42. Golf Course Singletrack
43. Prado Dam Access Rd.

Telegraph Canyon Road

CHINO HILLS SEGMENT 1

Distance • 12.3 miles
Time Required • ? hours
Route Rating • 6
Grunt Factor • 5
Technical Rating • 1
Downhill Rating • 8
Elevation • 500 ft. at Carbon Canyon.
High point 1090 ft.
500 ft. at Aliso Canyon

THIS TRAIL IS THE PERFECT PLACE TO begin both our descriptions and your biking career. Telegraph can be accessed from either the Carbon Canyon entrance on the west, or at the Visitor's Center off Bane Canyon Road on the east. This road runs nearly the length of the park, but is usually ridden only on the Orange County side.

One of the beginning goals for new riders is to reach the picnic bench in the beautiful clearing at the **5.1 mark** from the Lemon Grove entrance. Build up your stamina and push onto Four Corners at the **6.0 mark** for the next step. Telegraph is a fun descent when done from Four Corners back to the Lemon Grove.

North Ridge Trail

CHINO HILLS SEGMENT 2

Distance • 6.4 miles
Route Rating • 5
Grunt Factor • 5
Technical Rating • 1
Downhill Rating • 6
Elevation • 490 ft. at Carbon Canyon.
High point 1686 ft.

NORTH RIDGE SERVES AS AN ACCESS point for several fun downhill trails. It is a challenging uphill ride in its own right. North Ridge is accessed from the Carbon Canyon on the west and terminates just beyond the junction with the McDermont Trail on the east. Although North Ridge continues all the way to Four Corners, it crosses private property. North Ridge is ridden in Ride 2, the Gilman Peak Loop, but can be included in as part of numerous other loop rides. One of our favorites is the return leg from Gilman Peak back down 4 Mile Hill to the Carbon Canyon entrance. What a blast!

Diemer Trail

CHINO HILLS SEGMENT 3

Distance • 0.6 mile
Route Rating • 3
Grunt Factor • 4
Technical Rating • 1+
Downhill Rating • 7
Elevation • 620 ft. at bottom
870 ft. at top

A SHORT CONNECTION BETWEEN Telegraph and South Ridge Trail. Diemer Trail is the western access for South Ridge.

It features two very sharp and usually loose switchbacks that can be scary on fast descents. The trail is usually rutted at the connection with Telegraph Canyon.

Diemer Singletrack

CHINO HILLS SEGMENT 4

Distance • 0.1 mile
Route Rating • 5
Grunt Factor • 5
Technical Rating • 3
Downhill Rating • 5
Elevation • 700 ft. at top
                590 ft. at bottom

THIS IS A SHORT SINGLETRACK THAT begins at about the middle of the top switchback on the Diemer Trail.

From Diemer Trail it returns west as you go downhill and terminates back at Telegraph. Can be fairly technical sometimes because of ruts, with two sharp dips to navigate for good measure.

South Ridge Trail

CHINO HILLS SEGMENT 5

Distance • 7.3 miles
Route Rating • 4
Grunt Factor • 6
Technical Rating • 1+
Downhill Rating • 8
Elevation • High point 1710 ft.

SOUTH RIDGE SERVES AS THE MAIN access point to many excellent downhill trails in Chino Hills. Part of the Water Canyon, Gilman Peak and Raptor Ridge Loops described above, South Ridge is fun to ride for its own sake. This trail is an absolute scream when ridden downhill (east) from the top of San Juan toward the Visitor's Center. It is reached by riding up the Diemer Trail in the west, Rimcrest in the middle, or at the gate near the Visitor's Center in the east.

The Traverse

CHINO HILLS SEGMENT 6

Distance • 0.6 mile
Route Rating • 7
Technical Rating • 5
Downhill Rating • 6
Elevation • 1270 ft. at top
                760 ft. at bottom

THIS TRAIL IS A LITTLE-KNOWN SINGLE-track that contains some of the hardest technical areas in the park, and is recommended as a downhill. To find the upper trailhead, start from the Carbon Canyon entrance and head east up North Ridge to the 2.0 mark. The Traverse is on the right side and can be clearly seen going up a short, steep section to the top of a saddle. Turn right off of North Ridge and ride up to the saddle. From here you'll head downhill as you traverse east along North Ridge and up and over several smaller ridges that wander down to the canyon floor. Near the end you negotiate two loose sections that are really steep (not Chino Hills steep, but rear-tire-rashes-on-your-butt steep). You exit at Telegraph Canyon Road just above (east of) the third water crossing as you are going up canyon.

Gilman Peak Singletrack

CHINO HILLS SEGMENT 7

Distance • 1.1 miles
Route Rating • 8
Grunt Factor • 7
Technical Rating • 4
Downhill Rating • 7
Elevation • 500 ft. at top
             970 ft. at bottom

THIS OUTSTANDING RIDE IS DESCRIBED in the Gilman Peak Singletrack Loop. One of the jewels of the Chino Hills experience with all the classic traits that make the singletracks here so fun: smooth and fast (unless, of course, thoughtless people on horses have destroyed it again!) There is a fledgling singletrack heading southeast off the peak that is not finished.

Cheat Street Singletrack

CHINO HILLS SEGMENT 8

Distance • 0.4 mile
Route Rating • 6
Grunt Factor • 5
Technical Rating • 3
Downhill Rating • 6

CHEAT STREET IS A SHORT SINGLETRACK that runs from the Rimcrest entrance downhill (north) to Telegraph Canyon Road. There was some question to the legality of riding this trail, but it seems there is some unspoken approval. The trail is no longer marked and most people that ride it are blissfully unaware of any controversy. Evidence of constant traffic is well established as this is a main access to Telegraph Canyon. Help keep the peace and tread lightly here, always giving foot traffic the right of way!

Poison Oaks Singletrack

CHINO HILLS SEGMENT 9

Distance • 0.6 mile
Route Rating • 1
Grunt Factor • 0
Technical Rating • 2

POISON OAK IS A SHORT SINGLETRACK that runs parallel to the stream in Telegraph Canyon on its south bank. You enter at the fork at the bottom of Cheat Street and exit onto Telegraph Canyon just west of the lower entrance to Gilman. I have never been on this trail when I didn't get a patch of the dripping crud on one part of my body or another. A big tree laying across the middle of the path doesn't help matters. Not worth the tread wear.

Little Canyon (aka South Ridge Cut-off Road)

CHINO HILLS SEGMENT 10

Distance • 0.3 miles
Route Rating • 3
Grunt Factor • 5
Technical Rating • 1
Downhill Rating • 6
Elevation • 1500 ft. at top
600 ft. at bottom

LITTLE CANYON IS A SHORT ROAD THAT connects Telegraph Canyon at the **3.8+ mile mark** upstream from the Carbon Canyon entrance. In an awkward location to include in loops, it is sometimes used to reach Telegraph Canyon from the Rimcrest entrance. Fun on the descent!

Sycamore Trail (aka North Ridge Cut-off Road)

CHINO HILLS SEGMENT 11

Distance • 1.1 miles
Route Rating • 4
Grunt Factor • 6
Technical Rating • 3
Downhill Rating • 8
Elevation • 1495 ft. at top
960 ft. at bottom

THIS ROAD CONNECTS NORTH RIDGE east of Gilman Peak with Telegraph Canyon Road at the **4.4 mark** upstream from the Carbon Canyon Entrance. There is a sign that marks this trail near a water crossing. It is a good way to reach Gilman Peak. A fun downhill that has challenging corners and terrain.

The Boatyard

CHINO HILLS SEGMENT 12

Distance • 1.3 miles
Route Rating • 4
Grunt Factor • 5
Technical Rating • 1
Downhill Rating • 6
Elevation • 1500 ft. at top
600 ft. at bottom

THE IS ONE OF THE SEVERAL ACCESS roads that lead off South Ridge. It is located 0.5 mile west of the access to Tarantula Canyon. It heads southeast and quickly downhill, ending at San Antonio and Casino Ridge roads, just east of Rimcrest. Technically not in the park, it is openly used by a variety of users. Access does not seem to be a problem as long as you're not adding to the collection of rusted hulks and landfill product that seems to be collecting here. The boat adds a surreal aspect to your descent down this trail.

McDermont Trail

CHINO HILLS SEGMENT 13

Distance • 1.0 mile
Route Rating • 3
Grunt Factor • 7
Technical Rating • 2
Downhill Rating • 8
Elevation • 1545 ft. at top
1220 ft. at bottom

AN EXCRUCIATINGLY STEEP WAY TO GET to the North Ridge. Starts just west of McDermont Spring at the **5.8 mark** on Telegraph Canyon Road as you leave from the Carbon Canyon entrance. Fast, but pointless downhill. Did I say that this trail is steep? Larry found a piece of shale with fossils in it on this trail. That is about the only redeeming thing we have to say about it.

Powerline

CHINO HILLS SEGMENT 14

Distance • 0.4 mile
Route Rating • 4
Technical Rating • 3
Downhill Rating • 7
Elevation • 1545 ft. at top
1295 ft. at bottom

AN ACCESS ROAD THAT BRANCHES downhill (south) from the top of McDermont Trail to a power line tower. Someone has cleverly added a singletrack to this road so that it finishes just above McDermont Spring on Telegraph Canyon Road. Short, but not bad when run south from the intersection of North Ridge and McDermont Trail.

Tarantula Canyon (aka Bovine Delight)

CHINO HILLS SEGMENT 15

Distance • 1.1 miles
Route Rating • 7
Grunt Factor • 4
Technical Rating • 3
Downhill Rating • 8
Elevation • 1590 ft. at top
1318 ft. at bottom

A FUN SINGLETRACK THAT RUNS FROM Four Corners to South Ridge. It is described in detail in the Raptor Ridge Loop and included in several others. It's definitely the best way to the summit of San Juan.

East Tarantula Canyon

CHINO HILLS SEGMENT 16

Distance • 0.5 miles
Route Rating • 6
Grunt Factor • 4
Technical Rating • 3
Downhill Rating • 5
Elevation • 1620 ft. at top
             1540 ft. at bottom

A SHORT SINGLETRACK THAT STARTS AT the **0.5 mark** up Tarantula Canyon from Four Corners and heads up to South Ridge just above Water Canyon. A short technical climb—always a challenge—makes it clean. This trail is sometimes overgrown but should always be visible enough to ride.

San Juan Hill Trail

CHINO HILLS SEGMENT 17

Distance • 0.1 mile
Route Rating • 4
Grunt Factor • 3
Technical Rating • 1+
Downhill Rating • 3
Elevation • 1781 ft. at top
             1700 ft. at bottom

A SHORT TRAIL THAT RUNS UP TO THE summit of San Juan from either side of the hill as you approach on South Ridge. The northeast access is a fireroad, while the western access is a singletrack that adds just that little extra fun to a Raptor Ridge run if you want to continue up to San Juan and head straight back again. Do it once to see the summit monument and the view!

[Note: There is also an access road that heads off from the summit in a southern direction. This road then splits into three sections. The first of these three roads is very short, the second dead-ends after about a mile, and the third goes all the way down into unfriendly Yorba Linda across land marked "No Trespassing." Avoid creating access problems and stay off this trail.]

Water Canyon

CHINO HILLS SEGMENT 18

Distance • 2.0 miles
Route Rating • 9
Technical Rating • 4
Downhill Rating • 9
Elevation • 1590 ft. at top
             680 ft. at bottom

OUR FAVORITE SINGLETRACK AT CHINO Hills. An absolute must do! Easy enough for beginners to crawl down if they are careful, and wild enough for the most experienced riders. This is it! You haven't ridden Chino Hills until you've ridden Water Canyon. (It's even pretty.) Described in detail in the Water Canyon Loop. Connects South Ridge with Lower Aliso Canyon Trail.

Raptor Ridge

CHINO HILLS SEGMENT 19

Distance • 1.8 miles
Route Rating • 8
Grunt Factor • 7
Technical Rating • 3
Downhill Rating • 8
Elevation • 1318 ft. at top

DESCRIBED IN DETAIL IN THE LOOP THAT bears it's name (see page 18), this is one of the premier singletracks in Chino Hills. Not as steep as Water Canyon, but it has a lot of interesting banked turns and air opportunities that the others don't have. Connects Four Corners with Aliso Canyon Trail as you ride east.

Ranger Ridge Access Road and Singletrack

CHINO HILLS SEGMENT 20

Distance • 1.2 miles
Route Rating • 4
Grunt Factor • 6
Technical Rating • 3
Downhill Rating • 3
Elevation • 1195 ft. at top
         750 ft. at bottom

ANOTHER CLEVER PERSON HAS ADDED this singletrack finish to an access road that is part of the Raptor Ridge Trail. Ranger Ridge continues downhill and southeast past the left turn that connects the two singletrack sections of Raptor Ridge. The trail roller coasters enough to force you to pedal the uphill sections.

This trail is a death crawl to nowhere. It dumps you out behind the ranger's work facility directly across (west) from the Visitor's Center. Take our advice and do Raptor Ridge, or even South Ridge, instead!

There is a short spur road that starts at the **1.1 mile mark** on Telegraph Canyon as you leave from the San Bernardino side and connects with Ranger Ridge. It has no endearing qualities at all.

Upper Aliso Canyon Trail

CHINO HILLS SEGMENT 21

Distance • 1.4 miles
Route Rating • 3
Grunt Factor • 4
Technical Rating • 1
Downhill Rating • 4
Elevation • 1010 ft. at top
           740 ft. at bottom

AN ACCESS ROAD THAT STRETCHES BACK up Aliso Canyon from the Visitor's Center. It's part of the Raptor Ridge and Outback loops. It can be used to make a continuous loop that starts at the Visitor's Center, heads uphill north and winds to the east eventually joining the Upper Aliso Singletrack allowing one to end up at Bane Canyon Road just north of the kiosk.

The Outback Trail

CHINO HILLS SEGMENT 22

Distance • 2.9 miles
Route Rating • 7
Grunt Factor • 7
Technical Rating • 4
Downhill Rating • 5

A POTENTIALLY EXCELLENT SINGLE-track. Begins at Aliso Canyon Road just north of the junction with Raptor Ridge. Proceed up Aliso Canyon, past the Raptor junction. Within 100 feet you'll see a singletrack heading uphill just behind the pond and windmill, across a small gully. This trail ends at the Upper Aliso Canyon Trail.

This singletrack takes you through some of the most remote and least disturbed sections of the park. An outstanding trip for cross-country riders. When done from the Bane Canyon entrance, this could well become the best all around singletrack in the park. However, a few selfish horse riders habitually destroy this trail. On our documentation ride we suffered gravely in our efforts to complete this ride. This trail desperately needs bike traffic to smooth out the trail.

Upper Aliso Canyon Singletrack

CHINO HILLS SEGMENT 23

Distance • 1.1 miles
Route Rating • 7
Grunt Factor • 3
Technical Rating • 3
Downhill Rating • 5

THIS SHORT TRAIL STARTS AT ALISO Canyon Road, below the junction with Raptor Ridge. It terminates at the top of the ridge at Rolling Ranch Ridge.

Rolling Ranch Ridge

CHINO HILLS SEGMENT 24
Distance • 2.1 miles
Route Rating • 6
Grunt Factor • 6
Technical Rating • 4
Downhill Rating • 4
Elevation • 1150 ft. at top
          740 ft. at bottom

THIS TRAIL SKIRTS ALONG THE WEST ridge of Bane Canyon. The trail starts on the Canyon's northern end at a right (west) turn on Upper Aliso Canyon Trail at the **0.4 mark** from the Bane Canyon Road entrance underneath an electrical tower. As you go south from this entrance, you'll intersect a singletrack that heads back down to Bane Canyon (east) at the **0.1 mark**. The trail roller coasters along the top of the ridge offering good uphill challenges as well as steep downhill. You will reach a fork in the road at the **0.8 mark** under three towers. This is an access road that also heads left (east) back down into Bane Canyon. At the **1.9 mark** you'll reach the equestrian camp and an intersection with another singletrack that runs east to Bane Canyon. Follow the trail to the **2.1 mark** and the intersection with Bane Canyon at the paved section, just downhill from the overlook.

Bane Canyon Road

CHINO HILLS SEGMENT 25
Distance • 3.2 miles
Route Rating • 4
Grunt Factor • 3
Technical Rating • 1
Downhill Rating • 6

THIS ROAD, WHICH IS PARTIALLY paved, runs from the Sapphire Road gate to the Visitors Center. It is used mostly as an avenue for easy entrance to the heart of the park. It is very heavily traveled by both horses and hikers so keep a sharp eye out and keep the speed down, especially on the weekend.

Sapphire

CHINO HILLS SEGMENT 26
Distance • 0.5miles
Route Rating • 6
Technical Rating • 6
Downhill Rating • 6
Elevation • 1080 ft. at top
          790 ft. at bottom

THIS TRAIL RUNS FROM AN ENTRANCE off Upper Aliso Canyon Trail and heads north along the ridge on the west side of Bane Canyon. In Its final 50 the trail drops sharply down to Sapphire Road, just west of the gate.

Razorback

CHINO HILLS SEGMENT 10

Distance • 0.3 mile
Route Rating • 6
Technical Rating • 5/6
Downhill Rating • 7
Elevation • 1200 ft. at top
          820 ft. at bottom

SCARY! THIS TRAIL STARTS AT THE SUMMIT of the Bane Canyon Access Trail on the left side of the upper tower. (Look close, the trail is there!) The first half of the trail is along a narrow (six- to eight-foot wide) ridge line giving you an eerie feeling of exposure as you descend. This is a fairly serious descent because any fall could cause you to slide down the steep sides of the ridge. Forget trying to climb it. It has a short technical section about midway as you head down over a short bump on the ridge. Finishes just above the Bane Canyon gate.

Bane Canyon Access Road

CHINO HILLS SEGMENT 28

Distance • 0.4 mile
Route Rating • 3
Grunt Factor • 3
Technical Rating • 1
Downhill Rating • 5

THIS TRAIL RUNS UP THE EAST SIDE OF Bane Canyon and terminates at two towers that overlook the Bane Canyon gate. The entrance is at the 0.5 mark as you head south up Bane Canyon. Although sometimes the entrance is barb wired, this is the best access to Razorback, East Boundary and The Spine.

Photo: Larry Kuechlin

East Boundary Trail

CHINO HILLS SEGMENT 29
Distance • 3.3 miles
Route Rating • 10
Grunt Factor • 7
Technical Rating • 6
Downhill Rating • 3

THIS IS THE CREAM OF THE CROP IF YOU are interested in cross-country experiences. Downhill speed is not the point of this trail which takes you to the absolute quietest and most beautiful spots in the park. Rarely done, it can sometimes be a challenge to find the trail, let alone stay on it. The hardest technical sections in the park are also along this trail. These sections are short enough that even beginners will not be too intimidated. The only drawback is lack of traffic. This trail needs regular riding to keep the trail clear and smooth. Even if you walk half of it because of its difficulty, you have to do this one! There is some poison oak and stinging nettles so be careful.

Start on it's northern end at the right (south) turn-off at the trail sign posted at the **0.3 mark** on the Bane Access Road. From the sign you'll travel 0.3 mile to a sharp left (east) turn downhill as you reach the entrance to The Spine that continues uphill and south along the ridge line. This is the longest downhill section of the trail and features several technical sections. Continue up and over several ridges as the trail follows a canyon. At the **1.3 mark**, as you approach the power lines, you will begin a steep technical climb that is tough but can be done with persistence.

At the 1.8 mark you'll intersect the Buttermilk Ranch Access Road as you reach an old windmill. If you are tired, you can follow this road west uphill until you reach the summit and then follow the road downhill to Bane Canyon. If you continue east you reach a tricky technical downhill section at the **2.5 mark**. As you continue, you'll cross the barely visible Slaughter Canyon at the **2.7 mark**. The trail ends at an access road at the **3.3 mark**. You can continue south along access roads and singletrack to link enough trails to ride almost the entire East Boundary.

Bane Parallel Trail

CHINO HILLS SEGMENT 30
Distance • 0.5 mile
Route Rating • 4
Grunt Factor • 2
Technical Rating • 2
Downhill Rating • 1

A SHORT SINGLETRACK THAT RUNS PARallel to Bane Canyon from just south of the fee kiosk until it ends at the intersection of Buttermilk Ranch and Bane Canyon. Might be worth doing instead of heading down Bane constantly, otherwise just so-so.

Equestrian Trail

CHINO HILLS SEGMENT 31

Distance • 0.1mile
Route Rating • 3
Grunt Factor • 2
Technical Rating • 2
Downhill Rating • 3

THIS TRAIL RUNS UP AND OVER THE ridge that is between Bane Canyon and Aliso Canyon at the Park Headquarters. Intersects Rolling Ranch Ridge at the summit of the ridge near a small campground. It is supposed to continue down to the Visitor's Center. If you find this portion of the trail, mark it please.

Buttermilk Ranch Access Road

CHINO HILLS SEGMENT 32

Distance • 2.6 miles
Route Rating • 4
Grunt Factor • 5
Technical Rating • 3
Downhill Rating • 6
Elevation • 900 ft. at Bane Canyon
1200 ft. high point

AN ACCESS ROAD THAT BISECTS THE East Boundary. It runs from the sign on Bane Canyon at about the **1.1 mark** from the Bane gate, east up and over the ridge and down until it ends at Buttermilk Ranch Road. The last half of this road, past the windmill, is of dubious legality and might require some sketchy tactics to finish.

McLean Overlook Road

CHINO HILLS SEGMENT 33

Distance • 1.2 miles
Route Rating • 2
Grunt Factor • 5
Technical Rating • 2
Downhill Rating • 3
Elevation • 1050 ft. at top
765 ft. at bottom

A SHORT ROAD THAT DEAD-ENDS JUST past the Corral Trail—the length depends on how motivated the road crew is. This road is not ridden very frequently.

Corral Trail

CHINO HILLS SEGMENT 34
Distance • 0.5 mile
Route Rating • 5
Technical Rating • 4
Downhill Rating • 4

A STEEP AND LOOSE WAY TO DESCEND down from the East Boundary area. Can be accessed at the top from McLean Overlook Road at the sign, or at the equestrian camp and corral at the gate just south of Bane Canyon Road. Usually very rutted and cut up making it quite a challenge. Crosses the streambed at the bottom entrance.

Lower Aliso Canyon Trail

CHINO HILLS SEGMENT 35
Distance • 3.9 miles
Route Rating • 5
Grunt Factor • 2
Technical Rating • 0
Downhill Rating • 3
Elevation • 440 ft. at Bane Canyon
440 ft. at South East entrance

LOWER ALISO CANYON TRAIL IS A ROAD that runs from the Chino Hills State Park South East entrance, which has a golf course blocking easy access, and terminates at the Bane Canyon Road. It is an easy ride and is isolated from traffic and very beautiful. This canyon can have a lot of water running through it during rainy periods, and should have water running through it most times of the year. Lots of little singletracks parallel this road here and there and are too short to report.

Photo: Keith Young

Skully Ridge Trail

CHINO HILLS SEGMENT 36

Distance • 4.8 miles
Route Rating • 7
Grunt Factor • 6
Technical Rating • 3
Downhill Rating • 7
Elevation • 1090 ft. high point
790 ft. at Water Canyon

A GREAT RIDE THROUGH SOME OF THE outmost regions of the park. It offers great views with enough good downhill to keep your eyes off the scenery and on the trail. Wavers between fireroad and singletrack without any rhyme or reason. Skully's northern entrance is located at the exit to Water Canyon and the turn-off from Lower Aliso Canyon past the campgrounds toward the ranger compound. In the south, the entrance is located directly north of the golf course's club house and shoots straight up the ridge toward the summit.

Bobcat Ridge Trail

CHINO HILLS SEGMENT 37

Distance • Dead end
Route Rating • 0
Grunt Factor • 4
Technical Rating • 2
Downhill Rating • 2

FORGET IT. SINCE ACCESS TO THIS END of the park has been severely restricted, this trail has fallen into serious disrepair. It may be passable at certain times of the year, but not enough to report. Some people do use this in conjunction with illegal access to the park.

South Brush Canyon Trail

CHINO HILLS SEGMENT 38

Distance • 1.0 mile
Route Rating • 5
Grunt Factor • 2
Technical Rating • 1
Downhill Rating • 6
Elevation • 890 ft. at top
580 ft. at bottom

THIS PROVIDES THE BEST, OR AT LEAST easiest, way to reach Skully Ridge. Don't be fooled by the sign denoting the turn-off of Lower Aliso Canyon which has Brush Canyon in tiny letters and Skully Canyon in huge letters. Well-thought-out switchbacks take all the grunt out of the climb. At the top, when you intersect Skully Ridge, if you continue right (north) maybe fifty yards you can see the top of Brush Canyon Trail as it descends another 1.1 miles and ends at intolerant Yorba Linda.

Brush Canyon

CHINO HILLS SEGMENT 39

Off limits

THE ENTRANCE TO BRUSH CANYON HAS been effectively blocked with signs warning of imminent arrest and financial penalty. Letters to Yorba Linda Policy Wonks would be a good way to perhaps convince these idiots that mountain bikers are not an unwashed horde of pillaging vermin. Blocking access to this entrance makes absolutely no sense and really creates a situation where access to this end of the park is tricky. Tell those uptight suburbanites to chill out and let us use the gate!

Skully Hill Trail

CHINO HILLS SEGMENT 40

Distance • 1.5 miles
Route Rating • 3
Grunt Factor • 5
Technical Rating • 2
Downhill Rating • 6
Elevation • 1030 ft. at top
          480 ft. at bottom

AN ACCESS ROAD THAT CONNECTS Skully Ridge with Lower Aliso Canyon. It starts at three entrances on Lower Aliso Canyon at the **0.6**, **0.7** and **0.8 mark** as you leave from the Lower Aliso Canyon gate and intersects Skully Ridge 1.2 miles from the southern entrance.

Elevator

CHINO HILLS SEGMENT 41

Distance • 0.1 mile
Route Rating • 6
Technical Rating • 4
Downhill Rating • 3

A FUN BUT EXTREMELY SHORT SINGLE-track that connects Skully Ridge with Skully Hill. Starts downhill 0.4 mile south of the South Brush Canyon connection. Very cool.

Golf Course Singletrack

A FUN SINGLETRACK THAT RUNS AROUND an enclosed pasture between Skully Ridge at its west end and the Lower Aliso Canyon entrance in the east. A fun way to connect the two segments. Some air opportunities and good speed through some sections.

CHINO HILLS SEGMENT 42

Distance • 0.9 mile
Route Rating • 5
Grunt Factor • 3
Technical Rating • 2
Downhill Rating • 6

Prado Dam Access Road

THIS IS THE ROAD THAT RUNS ALONG THE north side of the Santa Ana River from Prado Dam, past the golf course and then merges with Lower Aliso Canyon at the signed gate. This trail can be really scenic in the winter and spring.

CHINO HILLS SEGMENT 43

Distance • 1.6 miles
Route Rating • 7
Grunt Factor • 1
Technical Rating • 0
Downhill Rating • 0

Photo: Larry Kuechlin

Fullerton Bike Loop

Fullerton Bike Loop

Distance • 11.5 mile loop

Time Required • 1 to 2 hours

Route Rating • 7

Grunt Factor • 4

Technical Rating • 3

Map • Fullerton Bike Loop, page 47

YES, IT'S TRUE. THE VAGUE RUMORS OF cool riding in the heart of metropolis are correct. You can stop laughing at all those full-suspension bikes riding into the hills in the heart of Fullerton. The Fullerton Bike Loop has exciting singletracks, fast fireroads and great conditioning characteristics. All this and plenty of spoke-breaking, rim-twisting air. In fact, jumps are the dominant feature that really separate these trails from other more traditional riding areas.

This is also an outstanding area for beginners because the uphill sections are not lengthy or overly steep and you are never far from civilization. The Fullerton Loop does not offer "true" mountain trail riding, nor is it the most inspiring spot. It is, however, fun.

ACCESS ISSUES

This trail is shared by local residents who also own horses. So far, mountain bikes and equestrians have coexisted without major incident. However, failure to exercise caution and common courtesy could result in access problems. These paths have a tendency to be narrow with lots of blind turns or obstructed views. Avoiding conflicts with other trail users requires that you watch your speed in these sections. Remember, this is their backyard. Ride smart.

HOW TO GET THERE

There are about a million entrances and exits to this ride as well as a million ways to make a ride out of these trails. We will describe only one loop and only one parking area. As you ride the loop you will be able to find other areas to park and other ways to start the loop.

We park in the North Orange County Municipal Court lot. From the 91 Freeway, take Harbor Blvd. north to Berkeley. Turn left (west) onto Berkeley and enter the parking lot for the Court at the first entrance. Park next to the trees at the furthest point south from the courthouse, as close to Berkeley as you can get. This is were you start.

LOCAL BETA

Every Thursday night of the year at 6:00 P.M. the guys at Bike Beat lead a ride through the loop. They break it into three groups based on riding ability. Lights are required some of the year. It is a fun way to learn the ropes as well as hook up with other riders to train with.

PRELIMINARY CONSIDERATIONS

The following trail description is somewhat complicated, but once you get out on the trail it is pretty easy to see which way the trail goes. For the most part, the trail continues straight across, over and through things until you come to the obvious turns. When in doubt, go straight. Remember, you are never more than 5 minutes from a major street where you can get help in finding your way.

THE RIDE

To get an accurate reading, start at the sidewalk on Berkeley where the dirt path starts. Follow the path in a west-northwest direction. At **0.3 mile mark**, head straight across Valley View. The path forks here and either path is okay to follow. Notice the signs here. You will see them consistently throughout the ride, so if you get lost you can look for this type of sign. At **0.6 mile mark** you cross Richman and continue straight.

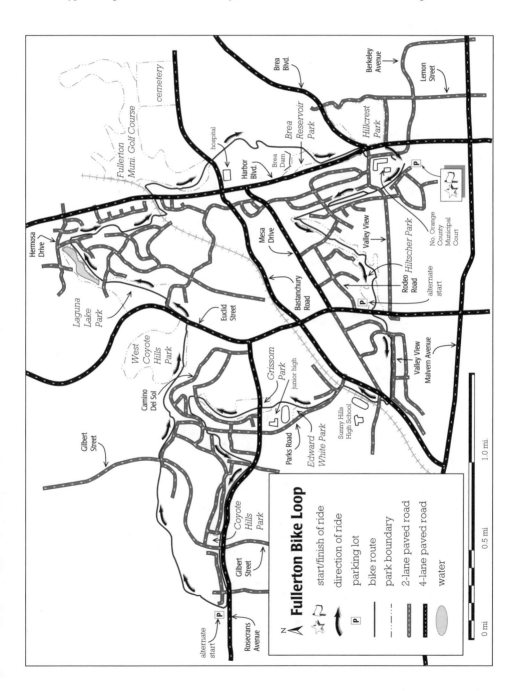

At the **0.8 mile mark** you make a sharp left (southwest) turn downhill into a beautiful valley. This is the upper end of Hiltscher Park. This entire singletrack is really fun. At the **1.0 mark** head straight across Richman Knoll Dr. and continue down the Hiltscher singletrack. Cut across the dry creekbed just after you cross the street so that you can ride the singletrack on the east side of the creek. Continue to follow the singletrack on the east side of the creekbed. Watch for sand at the apex of turns. You will pass an area with some jumps made by BMX riders that are fun to play around on if you have the guts.

At the **1.7 mark** you reach the bottom of Hiltscher Park as the trail intersects Euclid Avenue. When it is *safe*, cross Euclid and pick up the trail again just past the telephone pole that is about 20 feet south (left) of where you exited Hiltscher Park. It is the only path and almost directly across the street. Drop down into a short valley before heading up a short, technical trail that ends at a dirt lot at the intersection of Valley View and Fern Drive (**1.9 mark**). Go straight (west) on Valley View until it bends slightly right and terminates into Bastanchury.

Turn right on Bastanchury and head northeast until you reach the first traffic light which is Warburton Way. Cross Bastanchury and head west on Warburton until you reach the railroad tracks at the **2.4 mark**. Turn right (north) onto a path that follows the east side of the train tracks. At the **2.6 mark** turn left onto Parks Road (the first left) and head to the corral-type entrance to the bridle path that is just past Peacock Lane at the **2.7 mark**. As you continue up the bridle path, resist the temptation to turn right onto the various exits onto the neighborhood streets.

At the **3.2 mark** you reach Rosecrans. When it is *safe*, head straight across and pick up the trail again at the asphalt path that is just east of the big sign which proudly exclaims this to be "Virgil 'Gus' Grissom Park." Follow this path north to the **3.6 mark** where you veer right just before you come to Camino Rey at the **3.7 mark**. Head straight across the street into a small, and I mean *small*, park. The trail continues at the left rear corner of this small parcel of land and heads up a narrow path. Watch out for the big sand trap!

At the **3.9 mark** you reach Parks Road. When it is safe, cross and you pick up the loop by following the left trail located on the top of the bluff along the fence line. *Don't take the right-hand trail.* The left-hand trail follows a roller coaster ride along the top of the bluff, then heads down an extremely steep hill, crosses a concrete culvert and dead-ends onto a sidewalk at the **4.3 mark**. Turn left (south) and ride a short distance to Rosecrans and turn right (west) onto the path that follows the sidewalk along Rosecrans.

As you continue along Rosecrans, you will cross traffic lights at Gilbert and then Sunny Ridge. Just past Sunny Ridge, at the **5.1 mark**, turn right (north) at the marked trailhead. You'll see a sign here. The trail skirts along the Chevron oil fields—they are definitely O.B. (out-of-bounds). At the **5.8 mark** you will take the left-hand uphill fork. *Do not take downhill right-hand fork.* Other paths that head left are encountered beyond this point. When in doubt, follow the well-worn path.

At the **6.4 mark** the trail exits at the intersection of Chantilly and Castlewood. About 30 feet farther you cross Gilbert, when it is safe, and continue straight onto the path that is on the left (west) side of Castlewood. Follow this fenced-in section of the path to the **6.7 mark** where you exit to the left, up a steep, technical singletrack featuring several boards laid across the trail to divert water. After negotiating this section and continuing uphill for a short while, you reach the best launch ramps on the ride. Big, big air! Be very careful.

At the **7.4 mark** you cross Euclid, when it is safe, and turn left (north) as you follow Euclid up the lower entrance to Laguna Lake Park. The trail starts just 40 feet east of Euclid at the intersection of Euclid and Laguna. Follow the path uphill on the east side of the corral until you reach, then cross, Clarion Drive (**8.0 mark**). Stay on the east side of the park, riding along the beautiful lake, being careful to avoid getting snared in the head by the fly fishermen.

At the **8.3 mark** you will cross Hermosa and pick up the trail just on the other side of the street. Turn right (east). As you follow the path, note the fun parallel singletracks on the left side. Follow either a short distance over a fun jump, then re-cross the main path diagonally and head up the singletrack that heads up the right side of the trail. A big tree blocks the path about halfway down the right trail but it's easy to walk over.

At the **9.0 mark**, just after you cross a bridge, make a sharp left turn down a steep singletrack to the railroad tracks and head right (northeast). Follow the railroad tracks under Harbor Boulevard until you reach a palm tree (**9.3 mark**). Make a 180 degree turn here. Head a short uphill and cross the street at the crosswalk. This puts you on the top of a rock levee above the Fullerton Golf Course. Turn right (south). The trail follows the west side of the golf course through heavy brush. At the **9.8 mark** leave the trail (at the first tall pole) and head across to twin tunnels. Take the left tunnel and turn left just after you exit.

Follow a trail through heavy brush in the dry Brea Dam Reservoir. Around the **10.1 mark** you will see three other trails joining into the trail you are riding. The first is from the right, the next two are from the left. Bear right at the third junction. You will begin to ascend to the top of the dam on a fireroad then descend, next to a driving range. Notice the numerous balls placed upon the path by both the unskilled golfer and the expert marksman. Keep an eye out in either case.

At the **10.9 mark**, just opposite the driving line, turn left at the culvert, heading downhill. Continue left, around the fence and you'll end up in the National Sports Bar parking lot. (Remember that emergency money in your kit?) Head down the east side of Harbor and cross at the intersection with Brea Boulevard. Brea turns into Valley View as you ride across Harbor. Make the first left off Valley View just behind the shopping center. This is Berkeley which leads you back to the courthouse lot. You are back to your car at the **11.6 mark**. Way cool!

Santiago Oaks – Weir Canyon – Irvine Regional Parks

c/o Santiago Oaks Regional Park
2145 North Windes Drive
Orange, CA 92669
(714)538-4400

SANTIAGO OAKS RESTS ON A PORTION OF the old Rancho Santiago de Santa Ana which was granted to José Yorba by the Spanish Governor Arillaga in 1810. Weir Canyon and Irvine Parks are part of the former Irvine Ranch lands purchased by James Irvine in 1897.

In the late 1800s this area was prowled by several notorious bandits such as Joaquin Murietta and Three-Finger Jack. The outlaws would often sweep down from the hills and terrorize local communities or rob the Butterfield Stage which once passed through the lower Santiago Canyon area. Robber's Roost was often used as a lookout by these desperados to spot and flee from sheriffs' posses into the surrounding canyons.

Irvine Park is one of the oldest county regional parks and was donated by the Irvine family for public enjoyment, long before the foundation of the present-day development-oriented Irvine Company. As additional lands surrounding Irvine Park are acquired by the County, a larger contiguous area of open space has and will become available to public use.

Santiago Oaks was originally acquired in the mid-1970s, and through additions, has grown to more than 350 acres. Santiago Oaks preserves the early agricultural history of Orange County as well as surrounding native habitat.

Weir Canyon is the newest of these three regional parks, the present acreage being donated to the County in exchange for the right to overdevelop the surrounding Anaheim Hills. Plans are in the works for considerable additional acreage in Weir Canyon to come into a public domain in the near future. Once these additions are completed, a vast area of natural beauty will not only be preserved, but will be legally open to public recreation.

MOUNTAIN BIKING IN THESE PARKS

So you're standing around like the Mountain Dew Crew complaining, "Been there, done that." Well. Here is an area that will throw everything at you that mountain biking has to offer: gorgeous scenery, great beginner loops, hills that will make your legs burn, incredibly technical side-trips and the kind of long, twisting, uninterrupted singletracks that we all dream.

However, our experience riding here has not been all positive. On our first ride at Santiago Oaks, we had a park ranger drive up to us and hand us a brochure to Peters Canyon and then give us a sales pitch on leaving the park and heading over there. On the same ride we met another park ranger

THE RIDES

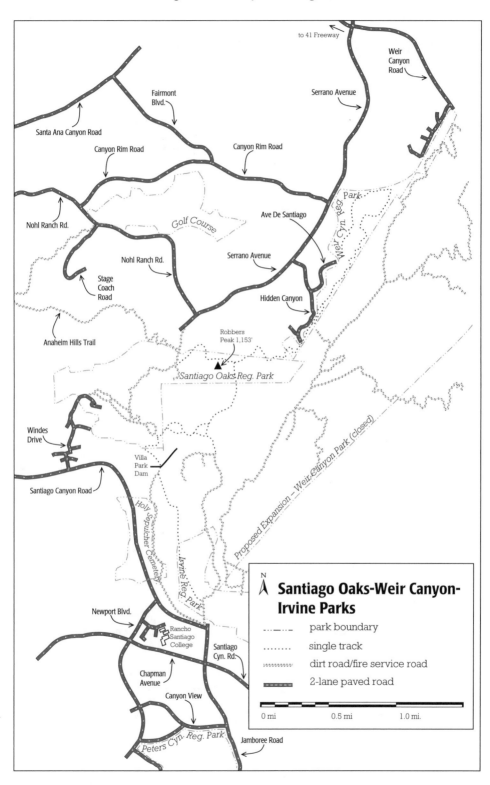

to 41 Freeway

Weir Canyon Road

Serrano Avenue

Fairmont Blvd.

Santa Ana Canyon Road

Canyon Rim Road

Canyon Rim Road

Weir Cyn. Reg. Park

Nohl Ranch Rd.

Golf Course

Ave De Santiago

Serrano Avenue

Nohl Ranch Rd.

Stage Coach Road

Hidden Canyon

Anaheim Hills Trail

Robbers Peak 1,153'

Santiago Oaks Reg. Park

Windes Drive

Villa Park Dam

Proposed Expansion – Weir Canyon Park (closed)

Santiago Canyon Road

Holy Sepulcher Cemetery

Irvine Reg. Park

Newport Blvd.

Rancho Santiago College

Santiago Cyn. Rd.

Chapman Avenue

Canyon View

Peters Cyn. Reg. Park

Jamboree Road

N

Santiago Oaks-Weir Canyon-Irvine Parks

— ·· — ··   park boundary

· · · · · · ·   single track

dirt road/fire service road

2-lane paved road

0 mi   0.5 mi   1.0 mi.

who gave us a ten-minute lecture on how this area was just infested with mountain lions and that we may want to head over to Peters Canyon. Later in that same ride we had two different horse riders give us precisely the same warning and the same solution—Peters Canyon. Also, a disturbing number of trails are marked O.B. for bikes. The vibe has been definitely negative.

We understand that these problems are being addressed by the County and that a more consistent, Countywide policy on trail closures and users is in the works. We support these efforts, and encourage you to show the County, and those who would limit access, that mountain bikers are good users. Be *extra* courteous and watch your speed whenever other users are present or visibility is restricted.

HOW TO GET THERE

There are many places to park to access these areas. You can park at Santiago Oaks Regional Park or Irvine Regional Park. There is no official parking at this time for Weir Canyon Regional Park.

Irvine Regional Park

From the Newport Freeway (55): Exit at Chapman and head east to Jamboree Road. Turn left and briefly follow Jamboree straight through the signal into the entrance of Irvine Regional Park. The trail begins on the northwest corner of this second signal before you turn down into Irvine Regional Park.

From the Santa Ana Freeway (5): Exit at Jamboree and head north for about 6.1 miles. Stay right as the road heads downhill into the park. Jamboree heads straight into Irvine Park if you make no turns whatsoever!

Santiago Oaks

From the 55 Freeway: Take the Katella Avenue exit and head east. Turn left at Windes Street. The sign can be easy to miss. Follow Windes to the park gate.

From the 5 Freeway: Take the Jamboree exit and proceed north. Follow Jamboree north for 6.1 miles (just past the Chapman-Santiago Road crossing). At the next signal (Santiago-Katella) turn left and continue northwest until you reach Windes Street (keep a sharp eye out for the Santiago Oaks Sign). Turn right and follow Windes to the park gate.

Weir Canyon Regional Park

From the 91 Freeway: Exit at Weir Canyon and head south. Turn right (west) at Serrano Avenue. Follow Serrano until you reach Hidden Canyon Road. Turn left (south) onto Hidden Canyon Road and follow it until you reach the dead end at Overlook Terrace. Park at the corner by the barrier. *Do not park in the residential areas or along Avenida de Santiago. Do not start access problems!*

FEES AND FACILITIES

Santiago Oaks has plenty of picnic tables and barbecue grills and features a nice playground for children of all ages. Irvine Park has all of this plus a small zoo and a lake. Both Santiago Oaks and Irvine parks currently charge two dollars for entrance/parking. Remember to bring either quarters or very crisp dollar bills for the finicky machine at Santiago Oaks. Irvine will have a ranger at the front gate. Weir Canyon has no facilities and currently there are no fees. All parks close at 7:00 P.M. or sunset, whichever comes first.

Santiago-Irvine Tour

SANTIAGO-WEIR RIDE 1

Distance • 4.3 miles

Time Required • 0.5 to 1.0 hour

Route Rating • 6

Grunt Factor • 2/3

Technical Rating • 2

Map • Santiago-Irvine Tour, below

THIS RIDE TAKES YOU ALONG THE   stream and through the arroyo that makes up Irvine and Santiago Oaks Regional Parks. It features some really scenic terrain, especially as you ride along the river at Santiago Oaks. This is a great ride for beginners and features enough distance and technical challenges to keep you on your toes while not being hard enough to threaten your life!

PARKING

For this loop you'll want to park at Santiago Oaks Regional Park. See page 52.

THE RIDE

Start the loop at the horse gate just below the parking area. Follow the main path across the stream. Just on the other side of the stream is a large sign. You will see a trail heading straight uphill and the Riverside Trail heading off to your right. Head straight up. At the **0.1 mile mark** turn right on a singletrack marked O.B. for horses. This singletrack roughly parallels the Riverside Trail.

You will reach a fork in the trail at the **0.2 mile mark**, bear left. Where this singletrack ends, turn right onto a fireroad (**0.3 mile mark**). Just 25 yards farther, make a right turn, head downhill and then make an immediate left (**0.4 mile mark**). Avoid heading up the steep hill with the railroad ties. Continue until the trail you are on dead-ends onto the Riverside Trail. Turn right here. Follow the Riverside Trail until you reach a singletrack which is marked by an "Irvine Park - 3 miles" sign (**0.5 mile mark**).

Turn left and follow this trail across Santiago Creek, up the gully, until you see another sign telling you that you're leaving Santiago Oaks (**0.6 mile mark**). You are now at a parking lot. Head across the lot and pick up the steep trail on the other side.

Take the steep trail up to the top of the hill. You are now on the south side of the Villa Park Dam spillway on a paved road. Abide the trespassing signs and continue to

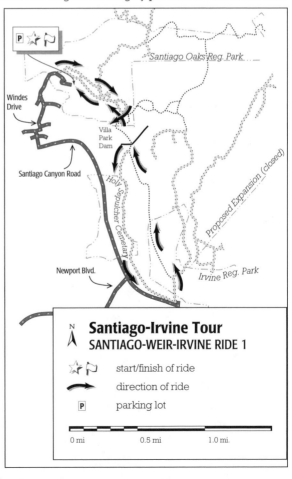

Santiago-Irvine Tour
SANTIAGO-WEIR-IRVINE RIDE 1

☆🏳 start/finish of ride

➤ direction of ride

P parking lot

N

0 mi   0.5 mi   1.0 mi.

the **0.8 mile mark** where the road forks. As you start downhill, take the first right turn, down a short steep singletrack. Be careful here. You will pass directly under and along a dam on the south side of the canyon.

This is the Santiago Creek Trail and you will see signs marking this trail clearly all the way to Windy Ridge Road at Irvine Park. Ignore the various trails leading off toward the bottom of the flood plain and continue southeast until you reach Windy Ridge Road (**2.3 mile mark**) Turn left, and follow Windy Ridge Road to the second trail and turn left (**2.5 mile mark**). This takes you along a tree-lined path that runs along the top of a levee.

At the **3.2 mile mark** the path turns into a singletrack. At the **3.4 mile mark** the trail veers left (west) off the top of the levee and connects with a series of trails that will lead back to the base of the spillway. Bear right through two branches in the trail.

You reach the paved road again at the **3.8 mile mark**. Follow it back the parking area (**3.9 mile mark**). Cross the lot and pick up the trail on the left side of the "Santiago Oaks Regional Park" sign. Be careful as you descend down this section, especially as you navigate the railroad ties. Cross the stream (**4.1 mile mark**) and continue along the Santiago Creek trail until it terminates into the Riverside Trail (**4.2 mile mark**). Turn left onto the Riverside Trail and follow this back across the stream and back to your starting point (**4.6 miles**).

Chutes

SANTIAGO-WEIR RIDE 2

Distance • 6.2 mile loop

Time Required • 1.0 to 1.5 hours

Route Rating • 7

Grunt Factor • 5

Technical Rating • 5/6

Map • Chutes, page 55

THIS IS A GREAT RIDE FOR THE MORE advanced riders. Although not a long ride, these trails gain altitude like a NASA rocket. Your legs will definitely tell you that they have been worked out!
This ride also provides some technical challenges to interest experienced riders.

PARKING

Park at Irvine Regional Park (see page 52). Start your ride at the apex of the turn that takes Jamboree down into Irvine Park.

You will see part of an old asphalt road heading north and downhill into the park. The ride starts at the gate. Reset your computer here.

THE RIDE

From the gate, head north past two left turns. (Note: The first left is the way you'll want to go during periods of rain.) Take the third left from the gate onto the road that runs on top of a dike in the middle of the wash area (**0.2 mile mark**). Head west along this road, past a turn-off into the trees. The road becomes singletrack, drops down left off the dike, continues through a field, finally ending at another trail (**1.1 mile mark**). There can be water on both sides of the dike, so watch your route carefully!

Turn right and head straight for the spillway. Climb uphill and reach a gravel road (**1.4 mile mark**). Bear left, meeting a paved road which is followed along the west side of the spillway until connecting with a steep downhill section that is marked with a trail sign.(Don't go across the spillway bridge!)

At the bottom of this hill pass through a horse gate into a large parking area (**1.6 mile mark**). Head straight across the lot and pick up the trail again at the large sign marking Santiago Oaks Regional Park. This will lead you down a staircase of four-by-fours into a loose gully. Cross a stream and head straight until you reach the Riverside Trail (**1.9 mile mark**). Turn left, then make an immediate right onto the Anaheim Hills Trail. There is a large sign here showing you the trail and warning you of impending death by several nasty critters.

Take the Anaheim Hills Trail uphill past two gates (ignoring two intersecting roads and two short singletracks), up a gut-wrenching steep section until the trail terminates at an unmarked fireroad (**2.6 mile mark**). Turn right and continue uphill onto a gravel road, and make a right turn just before the fence (**3.0 mile mark**). Descend a short distance, then turn right at the second trail you encounter. You begin a steep descent into a

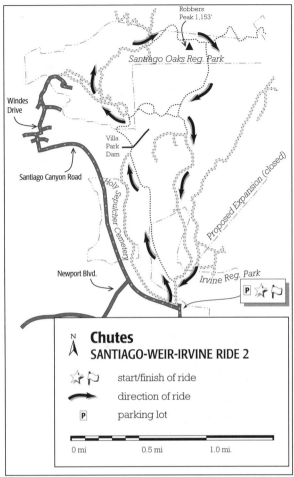

canyon then steeply back uphill to the top (**3.5 mile mark**). Don't follow the trail sign urging you to the left, be a rebel and head right onto the singletrack that follows the ridge line. This begins the real fun.

After a short climb, ride the roller coaster over rock outcroppings and short staircases until you reach a left turn-off (**4.2 mile mark**). Turn left here. This is the beginning of a section called Chutes. If you travel 15 yards farther there is another trail leading left down onto Chutes.

At the **4.4 mark** stay left and continue downhill. Very soon you'll understand why this is called Chutes as you head down the narrow slot cut into the hillside. Yahoo! At **4.8 miles** take the turn left, up a short bump in the trail (or head off a cliff). Cross a sandy arroyo, follow along a chainlink fence to a "Y" in the trail (**5.0 mile mark**). Head left, across a field and down to a fireroad. Turn right.

At the **5.6 mark**, turn right. A short distance farther you join a dirt road that leads you straight back to the start gate.

VARIATION

For Expert Riders Only. If you want more, here is a little side-trip that will add a few extra miles and a few more spills to your ride.

Take the first turn-off to the right after the **4.2 mark**. This is Waterfall. After a short drop, take the first right turn located in a small saddle. What follows are a five-foot "waterfall drop," rock staircases and other nasty surprises to make even the most daring rider have nightmares. This is a technical 11.

As you exit this little treasure, follow the fireroads back down to the Riverside Trail and head right. You'll reach the bottom of the Anaheim Hills Trail after a short distance. Finish the loop the way it was originally described or go for another tumble down the Waterfall.

Weir Canyon Loop

SANTIAGO-WEIR RIDE 3

Distance • 3.9 mile loop

Time Required • 0.66 to 1.0+ hours

Route Rating • 7

Grunt Factor • 4

Technical Rating • 3

Map • Weir Canyon Loop, page 57

WEIR CANYON IS ONE OF THE BEST KEPT secrets in Orange County mountain biking. Weir Canyon, which is suitable for both intermediates and experienced beginners, is an extremely scenic area and rarely sees traffic. This small sliver of land is slated to be expanded eastward to the Eastern Transportation Corridor, more than tripling its size. Although the following ride is a little short, it is well worth doing.

PARKING

You will need to park at the corner of Hidden Canyon Road and Overlook Terrace, see page 52. *Don't park on residential streets and ruin access for everyone else!*

THE RIDE

From your car, head north up Hidden Canyon Road 0.2 mile to Avenida de Santiago. Turn right and head uphill until you reach a cul-de-sac (**0.5 mile mark**). Pick up the trail on the left side of the cul-de-sac. This trail heads up and down, passes a water tank, and veers sharply right until you reach a green fence just before a housing tract (**1.5 mile mark**).

From here, the trail makes another sharp right and heads downhill into the canyon. As you continue, you will head up two steep climbs eventually reaching a singletrack that heads off to your right (**3.6 mile mark**). *Note: Inexperienced riders should take this singletrack. It avoids some technical sections and will lead you back to your car.*

If you continue left, make several technical descents, and reach the access road (**3.8 mile mark**). Turn right, and head back uphill to the Anaheim Hills Trail gate and your car (**3.9 miles**).

Not tired? Go for it again!

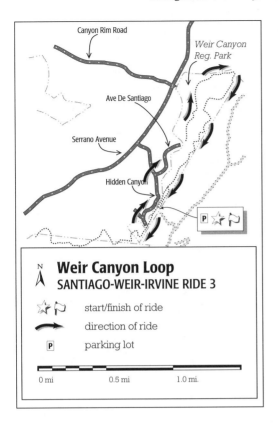

N

Weir Canyon Loop
SANTIAGO-WEIR-IRVINE RIDE 3

☆🏁   start/finish of ride

➤   direction of ride

P   parking lot

0 mi   0.5 mi   1.0 mi.

The Ironman

SANTIAGO-WEIR RIDE 4

Distance • 12.1 mile loop

Time Required • 2.0 to 4.0 hours

Route Rating • 7

Grunt Factor • 6+

Technical Rating • 5/6

Downhill Rating • 6

Map • The Ironman, page 58

THIS OUTSTANDING LOOP ENCOMPASSES all the best parts of the three adjoining regional parks. It is only 12.1 miles but it seems like a century ride. If you can do this loop without getting tired, you're ready for the podium.

PARKING

Park at the corner of Hidden Canyon Road and Overlook Terrace. Park by the barrier (See directions on page 52).

THE RIDE

Ride Hidden Canyon Road north to Avenida de Santiago and turn right. Pick up the trail on the left side of Avenida de Santiago (**0.5 mile mark**). Take the trail up and down. Just as you reach a housing project, the trail heads sharply right along a fence and drops you down into the canyon.

Continue up and over several ridges, bear left at the 3.5+ mile mark and continue to the end of the Weir Canyon Trail (**3.8 mile mark**). Head right until you reach the Anaheim Hills Trail (**3.9 mile mark**). Turn left. Stay straight on the Anaheim Hills Trail until it turns right

(**5.0 mile mark**). Take the singletrack that continues straight along the ridge line.

Follow the ridge until you reach two trails that head off to the left (**5.7 mile mark**). Turn on either trail (they join later). Stay left and descend. Soon you drop into "The Chute." Keep those elbows in! Below, the trail jogs left up a short mound (**6.3 mile mark**) to avoid dropping off a cliff.

Cross a wash, up a short hill, and follow the singletrack that heads along a fence. At a "Y" in the trail, stay left and connect with Windy Ridge Road (**6.6 mile mark**). Turn right onto Windy Ridge Road. Proceed 0.4 mile across a stream, and take the second right (**7.0 mile mark**). Take the trail that parallels the paved Irvine Regional Park road at the **7.1 mile mark** going southeast, until you reach the turn off

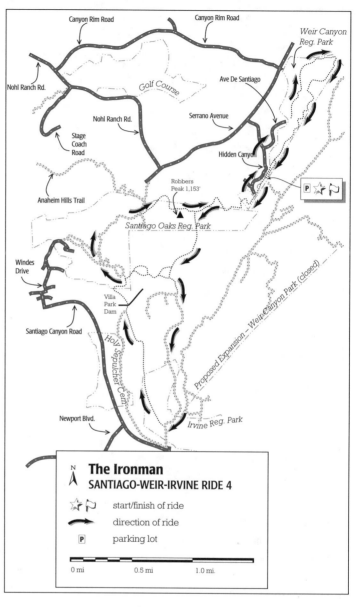

that heads right (northwest) along the road that sits atop the dike in the middle of the wash area at the **7.5 mile mark**.

This road eventually narrows to a singletrack, then heads left off the dike. (This can be flooded after rain.) At the **8.2 mile mark**, go right toward the dam. Climb uphill and reach a gravel road. Bear left, meeting a paved road which is followed along the west side of the spillway until connecting with a steep downhill section that is marked with a trail sign. *Don't go across the spillway bridge!*

At the bottom of this hill, pass through a horse gate into a large parking area (**8.7 mile mark**). Head straight across the lot and pick up the trail again. Follow it down a staircase of four-by-fours, across a stream and up to the Santiago Oaks Trail (**9.0 mile mark**). Turn left, go a short distance and make an immediate right at a sign. Proceed past two gates to reach the Anaheim Hills Trail (**9.6 mile mark**).

Turn right and continue uphill to until you a right turn just before a fence (**10.0 mile mark**). You'll be just under the summit of the ridge. Follow the trail to a second right turn which has a trail sign. Descend into the canyon then make a very hard climb to the top of the ridge (**10.5 mile mark**).

This time, head left, back toward Weir Canyon, on a mostly downhill section of the Anaheim Hills Trail until you reach an access road (**11.5 mile mark**). Turn left and head up to the gate (**11.6 mile mark**).

Santiago Oaks West

c/o Santiago Oaks Regional Park
2145 N. Windes Drive
Orange, CA 92669
(714)538-4400

THIS PARK IS NOT OFFICIALLY OPEN AS OF the date of this writing. Neither has the trail system been fully developed. Several short hiking trails on the west side seem to have been stopped in mid-progress. Nevertheless, there is some very good, but limited, riding available. With some new trail development, this place could be a small jewel. This may be your opportunity to volunteer for trail construction projects and ensure that mountain biking is not only welcome, but that we have some input on trail connections to make enjoyable loops. Call (714)834-5372 for more information about volunteering for trail projects.

Santiago Oaks West is not only geographically isolated from the main park, but is geologically and biologically unique. The park consists of an island of steep hillsides. Many of the slopes of the park's hillsides are covered in dense cactus, making a fall in the wrong place potentially disastrous. The park's hills are largely formed from volcanic basalts which protrude on the western sides (some rock climbing here) and underlay most of the soil. Housing developments surround the park, but the hilltops provide fine vistas on clear days. Horses are common users.

Vegetation varies from dense cactus patches to grassland and coastal sage scrub. There is wildlife in these hills, but the park's isolation and increasing development in the surrounding hills will preclude most large mammals. Rattlesnakes are common.

MOUNTAIN BIKING IN THE PARK

Unless you are very experienced on rocky, technical singletrack don't plan on riding here. Until more trails are developed, loop possibilities are limited and in a few places, some bike-and-hike is necessary. The good news is that many of the existing trails are steep on rocky or technical ground. Completion of singletrack trails on the western and the northeastern sides of the park could make for excellent loop connections. For now, the park offers mostly in and out riding on wild technical ridges, with limited loop potentials. The rocky terrain and frequent cactus patches demand caution. *This is not a place for inexperienced riders.* Accidents could be nasty. When in doubt, walk your bike.

THE RIDE
Santiago Oaks West Overview (p. 61) and Loop . . .60

HOW TO GET THERE

Santiago Oaks West is a separate isolated section of Santiago Oaks Regional Park and lies roughly between the main Park and Peters Canyon Regional Park. It is located north of Chapman Avenue between Rancho Santiago Boulevard and Crawford Canyon Road. From the 55 Freeway, simply take Chapman Avenue east to Crawford Canyon Road. Turn left (north) and proceed for about 0.2 mile to where the park is located on the left. Parking access will no doubt change in the future. For now, park on Stillwater, a right-hand turn off Crawford Canyon.

FEES AND FACILITIES

There are no fees and no facilities as of this writing.

Ridge Loop

SANTIAGO OAKS WEST

Distance • 2.2 miles

Time Required • 0.5 to 1.0 hour

Route Rating • 4

Grunt Factor • 3

Technical Rating • 6

Map • Ridge Loop, page 61

The Ride

FROM THE CORNER OF Crawford Canyon and Stillwater (start your computer here), head north and cross over to the west side of the Crawford Canyon. A fireroad will be seen on your right. Proceed on Crawford Canyon, past this this fireroad, until you are able to ride on a dirt service road that parallels Crawford Canyon. At the **0.1+ mile mark**, turn left on the East Connector Trail which heads uphill. This is the second and wider of two trails heading up the hill. Plan on walking your bike up some or most of this.

At the top of the East Connector, you intersect with the Ridge Trail (**0.2+ mile mark**). Turn right and continue uphill on the Ridge Trail on rocky and loose terrain, followed by a downhill ride to Four Corners (**0.5 mark**). Proceed straight ahead, then up more rocky and loose riding which soon levels. As you wind around the western side of the hill, the trail will split (**0.7 mile mark**).

Keep your momentum going (crank hard!) and turn up and right where the trail splits (technical uphill). Soon you are on the ridge and shortly reach a clearing. From the clearing, tend to the left, following a smaller singletrack which descends. Continue downhill to the **0.9 mile mark**. Although the trail keeps going (eventually it dead-ends), turn left here onto a faint singletrack which after 20 yards T's into another trail. Turn left again on this other trail (going right ends up on surface streets) and proceed south until you rejoin the Ridge Trail. (**1.1 mile mark**).

From here, retrace your ride back along the Ridge Trail and continue on the Ridge Trail past the East Connector, heading up to the top of the South Summit (**1.7 mile mark**). At the top of the South Summit, hang a right down a wide, somewhat steep and rocky trail, which soon splits.

[VARIATION 1: Take the right-hand fork in the trail (technical rating 5/6) and try not to land in a cactus until you can turn left onto a singletrack (**1.8 mile mark**). Don't go too far down the hill as you will have to walk-it back up. Head left on the singletrack until you reach some trees and then a wide clearing where teen-partying trash abounds (**1.9 mile mark**).

VARIATION 2: Take the left-hand fork (technical rating 7/8) which leads directly down to the wide clearing (**1.8+ mile mark**). Turn left.]

Pick up some trash, and ride the fireroad down to Crawford Canyon across the street from your car (2.2 miles total).

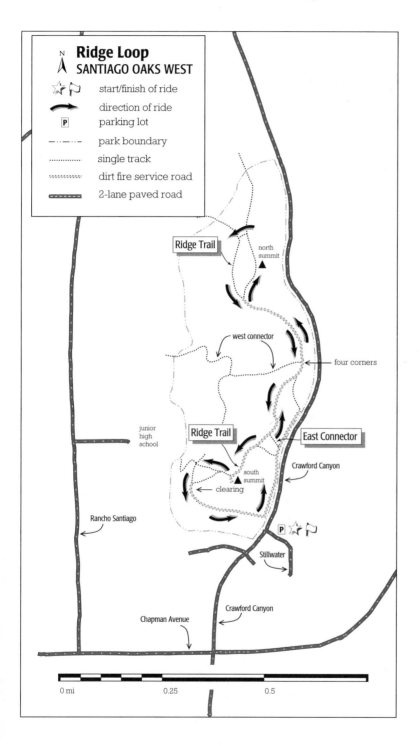

Peters Canyon Regional Park

c/o Santiago Oaks Regional Park
2145 North Windes Drive
Orange, CA 92669
(714) 538-4400
Open daily from 7:00 A.M. to sunset

PETERS CANYON CONSISTS OF 354 ACRES of coastal sage scrub, riparian habitat, freshwater marsh and grassland habitats. The large 55-acre Upper Peters Canyon Reservoir provides valuable habitat to migrating waterfowl. The area is popular with hikers, mountain bikers and equestrians. The park is located between the hills of north Tustin and Jamboree Boulevard.

The wildlife population includes mule deer, bobcats, coyotes, opossums, raccoons and occasionally mountain lion. A wide variety of amphibians, reptiles and bird life is also found here.

Peters Canyon Regional Park was originally part of the spanish Rancho Lomas de Santiago. During those days, Peters Canyon was called Cañon de las Ranas or "Canyon of the Frogs." This was attributed to the canyon's drainage into the Cienega de las Ranas or "Marsh of the Frogs," which is known today as Upper Newport Bay.

The Rancho was purchased in 1897 by James Irvine, who leased out the canyon to various farmers. One of the early farmers was James Peters, for whom the canyon is named. The Upper Peters Canyon Reservoir was completed in 1931, the Lower in 1940. Today only the Upper Reservoir has water.

In 1992, the present parklands were donated to the County of Orange by the Irvine Company, greasing the wheels of the County government for yet further development.

MOUNTAIN BIKING IN THE PARK

Peters Canyon is a great place to get a quick ride in at some place close. Although the trails are short, and the traffic sometimes crushing, good riding is definitely on the agenda. Most trails are suitable for beginners, a few require intermediate riding skills.

Peters Canyon is regularly featured as the backdrop for pictures in the various bike magazines. It is not just an easy stroll through the park. Steep but short climbs and short but challenging singletracks are the park's closely held secret. Quick circuits around this park build stamina, sprinting ability and technical capability.

HOW TO GET THERE

From 55 Freeway, take Chapman Avenue east to Jamboree Road. Turn right (southwest) on Jamboree. After about 0.6 mile turn right on Canyon View Avenue. Proceed a short distance and turn left into the park. A large parking lot will be found here.

From the 5 Freeway, take Jamboree Road north for 5.3 miles. Turn left on Canyon View Avenue, proceed a short distance and then left into the park's parking area.

THE RIDES

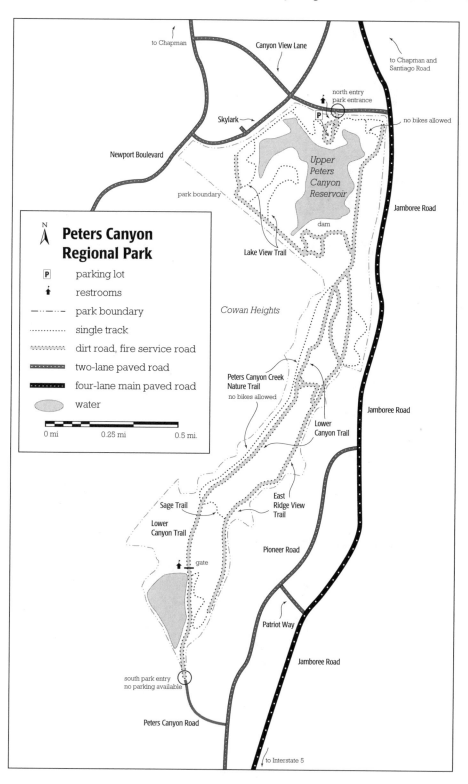

FEES, FACILITIES AND RESTRICTIONS

There is a $2.00 fee for parking. A box to collect the parking fee is located in the lot. Water and toilets will be found near the parking area. Minors must be accompanied by an adult at all times.

THE RIDES

We have given two sample loops to ride. Obviously, more possibilities can be worked out.

Lake Loop

PETERS CANYON RIDE 1

Distance • 2.5 mile loop

Time Required • 0.33 to 1.0 hour

Route Rating • 5

Grunt Factor • 2

Technical Rating • 1

Map • Lake Loop, below

PETERS CANYON IS A GREAT PLACE FOR beginners to taste real dirt and test their skills on both hill climbing and singletrack trails. This loop is suitable for most any rider and should get you familiar with the area. The views are nice for such a short ride in a suburban area.

THE RIDE

From the Parking lot, start the ride by heading east, toward the picnic tables. You will see a trail on your left just before you reach the tables. Turn left (north) onto the trail. This singletrack takes you toward Canyon View and then parallels Canyon View as it takes you to the corner of Canyon View and Jamboree.

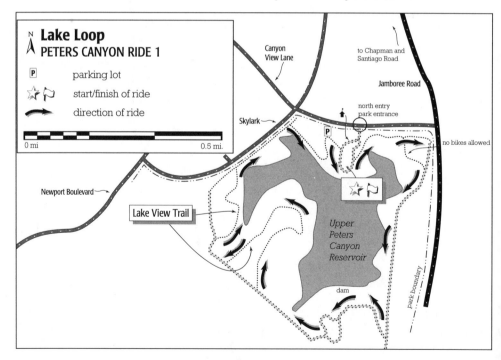

Turn right and go up and over the gate (**0.2 mile mark**) and follow the trail as it parallels Jamboree. Soon you reach a fork in the trail (**0.4 mile mark**). Take the right fork up a short hill until you intersect Peters Canyon Road (**0.5 mile mark**). Turn right and head downhill.

After 0.1 mile, turn right again on a fireroad that heads below the dam (**0.6 mile mark**). You'll reach the most strenuous part of the trip as you take the right fork up the short but steep hill that sits above the dam. The left fork takes you to the same place. There is a bench at the top of the hill (**1.1 mile mark**), if you would like to sit and enjoy the view.

Turn right and follow the road through a few roller coaster hills until you reach the Lake View Trail singletrack (**1.3 mile mark**). Turn right and follow this fun, mostly downhill, trail toward and along the lake shore.

You exit the Lake View Trail at the 1.8 mile mark, and turn right. Continue to follow the path that skirts around the lake. At the **1.9 mile mark** take the right fork. The path narrows at this point and runs in and out of some brush as you head back toward the parking area. Follow the singletrack to the **2.4 mile mark**, then take the left fork back to your car (**2.5 miles**).

Park Loop

PETERS CANYON RIDE 2

Distance • 6.3 mile loop

Time Required • 0.75 to 1.5+ hours

Route Rating • 5

Grunt Factor • 4

Technical Rating • 3

Map • Park Loop, page 66

THIS RIDE CONNECTS SEVERAL SEGMENTS of the park's fun and moderately technical singletrack while making a wide loop of the entire park. This is a fun, but short, ride that will appeal to riders with better bike handling skills.

THE RIDE

From the parking lot, head east toward the picnic tables, then turn left onto a singletrack that takes you toward, then parallels, Canyon View. Proceed to the corner of Canyon View and Jamboree. Turn right and go over the barrier. Follow the singletrack to the upper end of Lower Canyon Road (**0.5 mile mark**). Stay right and head downhill.

At the 0.8 mark turn left (uphill) on the East Ridge View Trail. At the crest of the hill (**1.0 mile mark**) turn left onto a singletrack that continues up a bit then descends to hook back up with the East Ridge Trail at the **1.1 mark**. Turn left. Continue along East Ridge until you reach the Sage Trail singletrack (**1.8 mile mark**). Turn right and descend this shady trail under eucalyptus trees until you reach the Lower Canyon Trail fireroad (**2.0 mile mark**). Turn left here.

Proceed downhill until you reach a gate (**2.5 mile mark**). Just beyond the gate, turn left (uphill) on a singletrack that connects with the East Ridge Trail (**2.9 mile mark**). Turn left, and take the East Ridge Trail until you again reach the Sage Trail (**3.5 mile mark**). Turn left (back over the same ground). This time when you reach the bottom (**3.7 mile mark**), turn right onto Lower Canyon Trail and head uphill to where the road splits at the dry side of the dam (**4.6 mile mark**). Turn left here.

Take either fork in the road to the top of the hill, descend, and then go uphill to where the Lake View Trail singletrack will be seen on your right (**5.0 mile mark**). Turn right. At the **5.5**

mark you rejoin the fireroad. Turn right. Follow the road, then tend right onto a singletrack along the edge of the lake back to the parking area (6.3 miles).

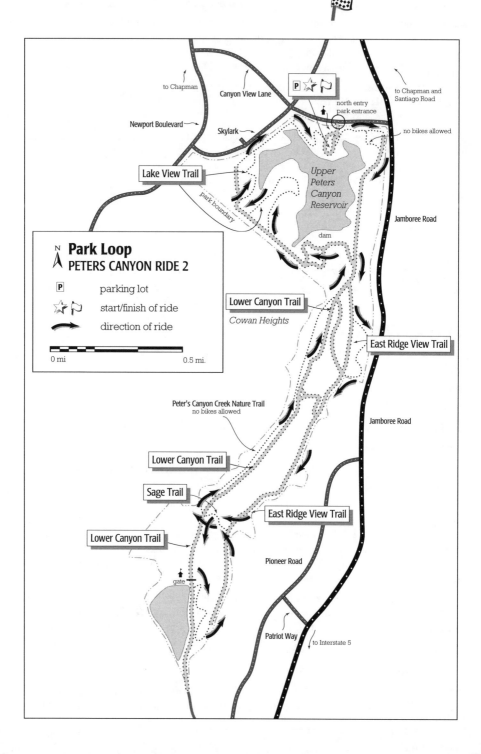

to Chapman

Canyon View Lane

P ☆ ⇃⟍

to Chapman and Santiago Road

north entry park entrance

Newport Boulevard

Skylark

no bikes allowed

Lake View Trail

Upper Peters Canyon Reservoir

park boundary

Jamboree Road

dam

N

Park Loop
PETERS CANYON RIDE 2

P   parking lot

☆ ⇃⟍   start/finish of ride

➤   direction of ride

0 mi   0.5 mi.

Lower Canyon Trail

Cowan Heights

East Ridge View Trail

Peter's Canyon Creek Nature Trail
no bikes allowed

Jamboree Road

Lower Canyon Trail

Sage Trail

East Ridge View Trail

Lower Canyon Trail

Pioneer Road

gate

Patriot Way

to Interstate 5

Limestone Canyon Park

Under the Supervision of
The Nature Conservancy
3142 Irvine Blvd.
Irvine, CA 92720
(714)832-7478

LIMESTONE CANYON PARK IS A LARGE section of undeveloped countryside and a future county regional park located north of Whiting Ranch. The hills and canyons which lie between Santiago Canyon and the plains to the west are full of geological and biological wonders of which most Orange County residents are unaware. Whiting Ranch Park lies in the southern section of this region and has seen tremendous intrusion by development. Limestone Canyon Park is the central section of these undeveloped lands.

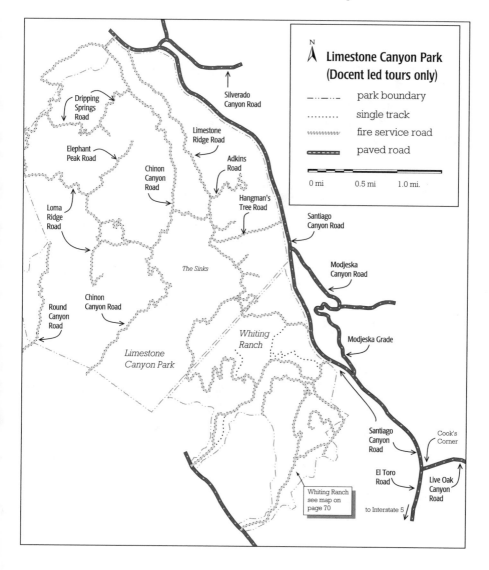

N

Limestone Canyon Park
(Docent led tours only)

_ . . _ . . _   park boundary
. . . .   single track
~~~~~~~   fire service road
▭▬▭▬▭   paved road

0 mi   0.5 mi   1.0 mi.

Dripping Springs Road
Silverado Canyon Road
Limestone Ridge Road
Elephant Peak Road
Adkins Road
Chinon Canyon Road
Hangman's Tree Road
Loma Ridge Road
Santiago Canyon Road
The Sinks
Modjeska Canyon Road
Chinon Canyon Road
Round Canyon Road
Whiting Ranch
Modjeska Grade
Limestone Canyon Park
Santiago Canyon Road
Cook's Corner
El Toro Road
Live Oak Canyon Road

Whiting Ranch see map on page 70

to Interstate 5

Within Limestone Canyon Park are many canyons, creeks and steep ridges. But perhaps the park's most inspiring bit of geography is The Sinks. The Sinks are located in the central section of the park where erosion has caused the sandstone layers under the hills to form a basin with many sheer cliffs of up to four hundred feet. In the past, some commentators referred to The Sinks as the "Grand Canyon of the Santa Anas." While this rather overstates the case, the place has a definite visual power not otherwise associated with the region.

Current open space planning calls for this area and perhaps other land north of Limestone Canyon Park to come into public ownership or at least to be preserved as open space for the immediate future. The possibilities for contiguous off-road riding would be excellent. Mountain bikers should strongly support preservation of these hills, canyons and the other unique geological and biological resources which are so quickly falling prey to the bulldozer's blade.

As with Irvine Company Open Space in Laguna (see page 112), the area is currently closed to public access except by docent lead tours under supervision of the Nature Conservancy. (714)832-7478.

Claire Vogel and Brandee Kuechlin at Whiting Ranch.   Photo: Larry Kuechlin

Whiting Ranch Wilderness Park

P.O. Box 156
Trabuco Canyon, CA 92678
(714)589-4729
Open 7 A.M. to sunset every day

WHITING RANCH IS A APPROXIMATELY 1500 acres of "wilderness" park that were opened in 1991. The community of Foothill Ranch intrudes upon and surrounds the southern and western portion of the park giving it an odd upside down "U" shape. The eastern portion of the park bounds Santiago Canyon Road. Some sections of the southern area are still privately owned, but access is generously allowed. Wildlife abounds, including snakes, bobcats and the occasional mountain lion. Eventually, private holdings to the south and southeast of the park will be acquired by the County. This should open several fine singletrack and expand riding possibilities. The future Limestone Canyon Wilderness Park bounds the northern section of Whiting Ranch, and once open may provide for greatly expanded riding possibilities.

MOUNTAIN BIKING IN THE PARK

Whiting Ranch is extremely popular with mountain bikers. It is easy to access and has a short, but fun loop ride. Although mountain bikers of all abilities ride Whiting Ranch, the park is particularly popular with novice riders. As a result, Whiting Ranch has seen a disproportionally large number of accidents and user conflict problems involving cyclists. To make matters worse, there have been threats of legal action against the County and private landowners by injured cyclists. This has led to some trail closures, speed limits and construction of a few wooden bridges.

Perhaps it bears repeating here: *If you have an accident on a mountain bike it is your fault.* Yes, you can get seriously hurt or possibly killed while riding your bike. Accept the risks or sell your bike. Trying to blame someone else for your lack of judgment in reality means that everyone suffers as a result of your mistakes. *If: (1) you can not see clearly ahead, (2) other users are present on the trail, or (3) could not make a safe panic stop, you are going too fast, and should slow down.* If you feel out of control on your bike, the trail may exceed your abilities and you should walk your bike through difficult terrain.

The northwestern entrance to the park is a one-way trail, so most loop rides start here. The Red Rock and Billy Goat Trails in the northern section of the Park are off-limits to bicycle traffic. The Vista Trail and Mustard Road in the northern section of the park are open to cycling. However, because Borrego Trail is a one-way biking trail, riding Vista Trail or Mustard Road are more properly detours from the standard loop described below. *Trails not shown on the park map in this guide are closed and cross into private property.* Although there are plans to acquire some of these private parcels in the future, riding these trails could jeopardize these plans and lead to their permanent closure. *Night riding in the park is not permitted.* Wildlife needs time to recuperate from the daily onslaught of visitors.

HOW TO GET THERE

Whiting Ranch Wilderness Park lies in the western foothills of the Santa Ana Mountains between the Foothill Tollroad and Santiago Canyon Road. From the 5

THE RIDE

Whiting Ranch Overview (p. 70) and Loop 71

Freeway, take the El Toro Road exit and drive east for 4.7 miles to Portola Parkway. Turn left (north) on Portola and follow it 1.8 miles to Market (a signal), turn right and then make an immediate left. Here you will find parking for the Whiting Ranch. The Park entrance is located in the northern end of the Foothill Ranch Marketplace shopping center. You will see the Whiting Ranch sign and trail map in the small plaza next to the parking area. The trailhead is well marked.

Another new parking area is being built along Glenn Ranch Road for entry to the southern (Serrano Canyon) area of the park. It should be open sometime in 1996. *This parking area is not used for the loop ride described.*

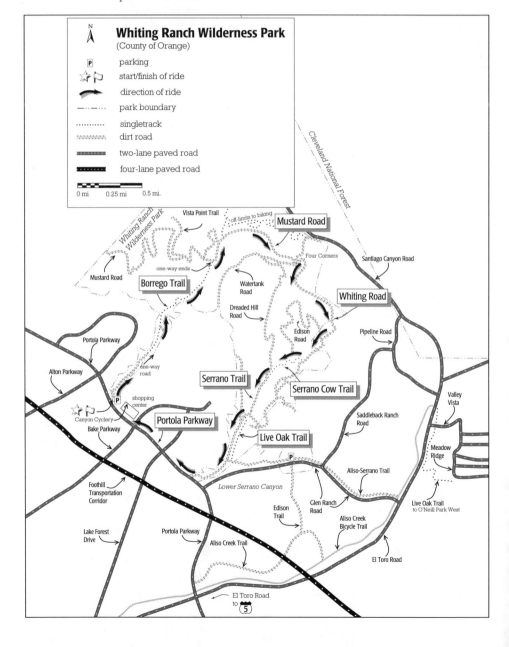

FEES AND FACILITIES

A bulletin board is the only facility available. No camping or water is to be found in the park. There is, however, a large shopping center, with food market, gas station and a fine bike shop immediately adjacent to the main parking area.

Whiting Ranch Loop

Distance • 6.0 miles

Time Required • 0.5 to 1.0 hour

Route Rating • 5+

Grunt Factor • 4

Technical Rating • 2

Elevation • Start 800 ft.

High point 1460 ft.

Finish 800 ft.

Map • Whiting Ranch Loop, page 70

THIS LOOP COMBINES THE BEST TRAILS of Whiting Ranch and takes in a complete circle around and through the park. You begin by riding up a shaded canyon, eventually climbing to a high ridge, then descend again into a oak-shaded canyon. A short section on Portola Parkway brings you back to your starting point. Singletrack, fireroad, climbs and descents are all found on this ride.

PARKING

Park at the entrance located in the northern end of the Foothill Ranch Marketplace shopping center (see "How To Get There," on page 69).

THE RIDE

From the entry gate, head downhill about 25 yards until you intersect with the Borrego Trail and bear right. It will be obvious which direction you are to take. Continue up the canyon through several dry wash crossings until you dead-end into Mustard Road at the **1.6 mile mark**. All trails are clearly marked by large posts. Turn right (east) and start up the longest climb. You will see a few trails that head off to the left, but they are marked out-of-bounds. After gaining 575 feet, you reach the summit of your climb at the Four Corners (**2.4 mile mark**). This ends the uphill section of the ride.

At Four Corners, head a few yards left (east) then make a sharp right onto Whiting Road. Follow Whiting Road downhill, in a southeasterly direction. At the first "Y" (**3.2 mile mark**), bear right onto the fireroad and continue downhill. At the next intersection (**3.4 mile mark**), again bear right on the Serrano Cow Trail singletrack that roughly parallels Serrano Road.

The Serrano Cow Trail dumps you directly onto Serrano Road fireroad (**3.9 mile mark**). Continue straight on Serrano Road for 0.3 mile, then turn left (south) onto a singletrack—the Live Oak Trail (**4.2 mile mark**). The Live Oak Trail roughly parallels Serrano Road and eventually ends at an abandoned fireroad (**4.6 mile mark**). Turn right and you soon join Serrano Road again. Turn left onto Serrano Road, and continue to the park gate (**5.0 mile mark**). Turn right onto Portola Parkway and ride 0.9 mile back to your car (6.0 miles total).

Other Mountain Biking Trails

MUSTARD ROAD

Distance: 3.0 miles

This fireroad runs from Four Corners in the south to the northern edge of the park (Limestone Canyon Park). The standard loop described above includes the southern section of Mustard Road. Although an in-and-back diversion ride, Mustard Road north is worth the side-trip to get glimpses of the scenery of the northern section of the park and The Sinks of Limestone Canyon Park. It is also the access route to the Vista Lookout Trail

VISTA LOOKOUT TRAIL
Distance: 0.5 mile

This trail begins off the northern part of Mustard Road and continues on a six-foot-wide trail to the Vista Look Out. The Look Out provides views of Redrock Canyon and Saddleback as well as the northern areas of the Park. This is well worth the side-trip to visit.

DREADED HILL ROAD
Distance: 1.0 mile

A steep fireroad that runs from Four Corners to the Serrano Road fireroad. Sections of 20% to 30% grades exist. In either direction, the uphill challenge is rewarded by 0.5 mile of downhill. A great view from the top of the hill is provided in all directions.

WATERTANK ROAD
Distance: 1.0 mile

This fireroad travels east to west from Dreaded Hill Road to an abrupt end at a water tank. The trail is not particularly steep, but it terminates (no outlet) and does not connect to any loop rides. Hence it is not very popular.

EDISON ROAD
Distance: 1.0 mile

Another dead-end ride to nowhere. This trail runs from Whiting Road in upper Serrano Canyon to an Edison Company power line. The lack of loop opportunities minimizes its use.

LINE SHACK ROAD
Distance: 1.0 mile

A fireroad that runs from Whiting Road in Upper Serrano Canyon along the ridge of Serrano Canyon then descends again to meet Serrano Road. This fireroad offers an option to and more physical challenge than the heavily used Serrano Road and Cow Trail Singletrack that run along the canyon bottom.

EDISON TRAIL
Distance: 0.7 mile

This fireroad runs south from the Glenn Ranch Road parking area to meet the Aliso Creek Riding and Hiking Trail near the over-crossing of the Foothill Toll Road. You can then connect with the Aliso Creek Bicycle Trail.

ALISO CREEK RIDING AND HIKING TRAIL
Distance: 1.3 miles

Starts near the corner of Portola and El Toro and runs east, meets the Edison Trail and then loops down to join the Aliso Creek Bicycle Trail.

ALISO SERRANO TRAIL
Distance: 1.0 mile

A dirt trail/path located adjacent to Glenn Ranch Road running from El Toro Road to the Glenn Ranch parking area. Cyclists will probably just ride the pavement. Can be used to connect the Live Oak Trail in O'Neill Park to Whiting Ranch. Hint-Loop Suggestion: This trail could be used as a link in a Santiago Trail to Joplin Truck Trail to Live Oak Trail to Serrano Road to Whiting Road to "your start" loop ride!

O'Neill Regional Park

P.O. Box 372
Trabuco Canyon, CA 92678
(714)858-9365
Open daily from 7:00 A.M. to sunset

O'NEILL REGIONAL PARK IS ONE OF THE oldest regional parks in Orange County. When the park opened in 1948, it consisted of 278 acres of land along Trabuco Canyon and Live Oak Canyon Roads. Today the park has grown to more than 2000 acres. The only positive aspect of plans for further development of south Orange County is the potential expansion of this and other "wilderness" parks. O'Neill Park's proximity to the Santa Ana Mountains and the rural Live Oak and Trabuco Canyons make it seem larger and more remote than is the case. The park supports a diverse variety of wildlife (including mountain lions) and native plant communities, including: riparian, oak and sycamore woodland, coastal sage scrub, chaparral and grassland. However, the park's primary natural resource is Trabuco Creek which descends through Arroyo Trabuco. The park has over 26 miles of trails, most of which are multiple use.

MOUNTAIN BIKING IN THE PARK
By the time you read this book, a countywide trail assessment will be implemented which will have opened several of O'Neill's singletrack trails to mountain bike use. This is a reversal of prior park policy which limited bikes to only a few short sections of singletrack. Several trails remain off-limits to bicycle traffic; please respect these closures and show that we can ride responsibly. Riding in the park is mixed with fireroad and singletrack. Recent trail openings have provided for several fun loop rides and logically link trails together. Riding is mostly concentrated in the West Group Area of the park. These trails provide the most technical and uphill challenges for riders. The Arroyo Trabuco area is largely flat riding, with multiple stream crossings. The recently opened Tijeras Creek Trail allows for a long loop ride that connects with the Arroyo Trabuco.

HOW TO GET THERE
O'Neill Regional Park lies at the western base of the Santa Ana Mountains, along the lower end of Trabuco Canyon. For directions to the park and the following rides, see specific driving directions for the rides below.

FEES AND FACILITIES
Day-use fees (as of January 1, 1996) are $2.00 per vehicle for weekdays and $4.00 per vehicle on weekends. Plenty of campsites are also available at $12.00 per night. Call the park for reservations.

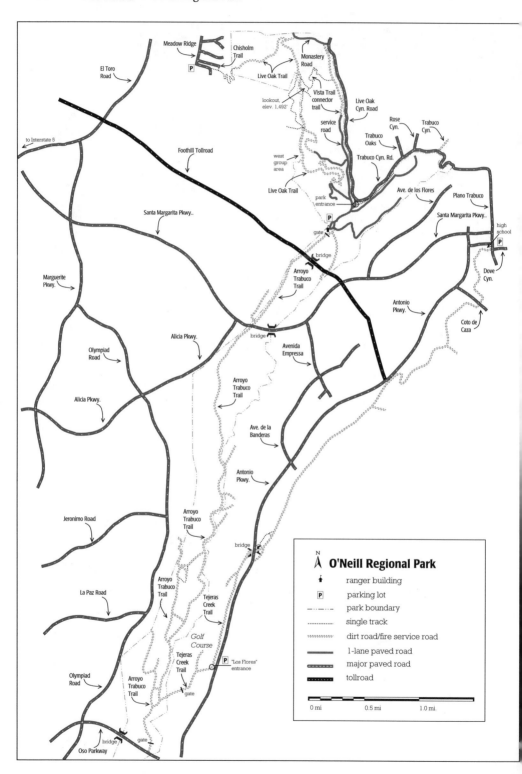

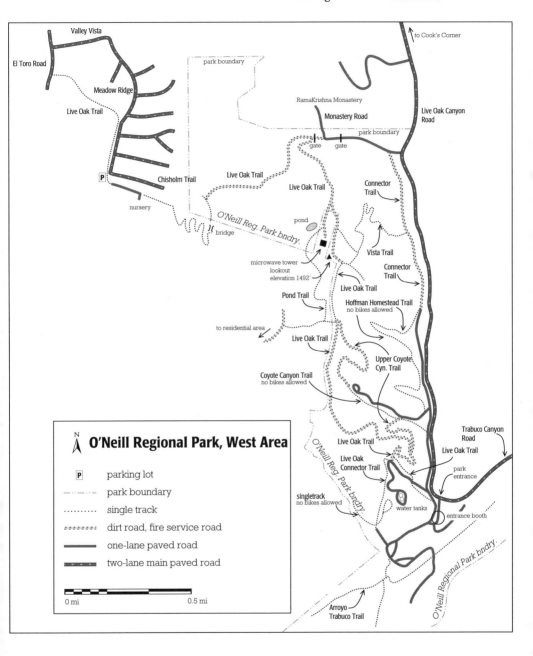

O'Neill Regional Park, West Area

P — parking lot

----- park boundary

.... single track

≈≈≈≈≈≈ dirt road, fire service road

▬▬▬▬▬ one-lane paved road

▬▬▬▬▬ two-lane main paved road

0 mi   0.5 mi

Live Oak Trail Loop

O'NEILL PARK RIDE 1

Distance • 6.4 mile loop

Time Required • 0.75 to 1.5 hours

Route Rating • 6

Grunt Factor • 4

Technical Rating • 3+

Elevation • Start 990 ft.

High point 1492 ft.

Finish 990 ft.

Map • Live Oak Trail Loop, page 77

THE LIVE OAK TRAIL PASSES ONTO private land on the west end (start and finish) of this ride. This ride climbs some 600 feet to a great observation point then drops another 600 feet into Trabuco Canyon to the east. The return trip takes other trails, then follows the last 1.4 miles back to the car.

PARKING

From the 5 Freeway: Take El Toro east for nearly 7.0 miles to Valley Vista (a signal). Turn right. From the 55 Freeway: Take Chapman Avenue east to Jamboree and continue straight (Chapman becomes Santiago Canyon Road here). Follow Santiago Canyon Road 13.4 miles to Valley Vista. Turn left. Proceed up Valley Vista a short distance to Meadow Ridge, make a right. Follow Meadow Ridge to its end. Parking is available at a small lot at the end of the street or along the west side of Meadow Ridge.

ACCESS NOTE Do not block the access road. Do not park on Chisholm Trail as has been suggested by another author. Be quiet and respectful of the residents. This means: no loud music, no urinating in the parking area, no changing clothes (yes, some bikers have done all of the above). If you see this type of behavior, it is your responsibility to educate these people. Let's not create access problems.

THE RIDE

From the car, head straight and then make a left down a paved service road (access to a nursery). Continue straight until you are on a dirt trail that proceeds behind residences then breaks out toward the hills. Put the bike in your granny gear to pedal up the short, steep and winding singletrack which then drops down the other side of a small ridge. After 0.4+ mile, you cross a small bridge and turn right onto a fireroad.

Proceed up the fireroad to where another road intersects at a sharp right-hand angle (**1.0 mile mark**). Make a severe right and proceed up the fireroad, through an unpleasant graveled section, to where another road splits off to your left (1.3+ mile). Take the left-hand road which narrows and heads up to the top of the hill. The top of the hill (**1.5 mile mark**) is the high point of the ride (1492 ft.), and has picnic tables and a plaque describing the view.

From here proceed ahead, and take the first right-hand turn-off (marked with a "Trail" sign), down a somewhat steep and mildly technical singletrack. At the 1.7 mile mark, this trail joins two fireroads and a singletrack on the right—the Four-Way Junction. Take the left-hand fireroad (Upper Coyote Canyon Trail) downhill for 0.5 mile (**2.2 mile mark**) to a paved park service road. Continue down the paved road for 0.2+ mile (**2.4+ mile mark**) where the continuation of the Upper Coyote Canyon Trail will be seen to your right. Turn right here.

After proceeding up this trail a very short distance, a trail junction is encountered. Continue straight (uphill) on the Upper Coyote Canyon Trail until you rejoin the Live Oak Trail at the 2.7 mile point. Proceed straight ahead and downhill for nearly 0.2 mile (**2.9 mile mark**) to where the Live Oak Trail makes a sharp left turn and becomes singletrack. This turn is immediately before a paved road (Watertank Road).

Head down this singletrack to a paved road, which you cross, and continue on the singletrack under large oaks until you reach a paved service road behind the park entrance (**3.1 mile mark**). Turn right on this paved road. Turn right at the stop sign, then stay right as the paved road intersects others. At the 3.3 mile mark, where the road curves sharply left, turn right on a paved connector trail. Ride a short distance on this trail to where it splits three ways at an intersection. Head straight ahead and uphill on a singletrack (the Live Oak Connector Trail). This trail goes up and over the ridge to the paved Watertank Road, and the Live Oak Trail (**3.7 mile mark**).

From here, ride up Live Oak Trail (stay left at the junction with Upper Coyote Canyon Trail) for 1.0 mile (**4.7 mile mark**). You are again at the Four-Way Junction. Now, make a quick left, through an opening in the fence-line, and then a quick right onto a singletrack (don't take the trail that heads straight west). The singletrack climbs uphill and passes a small pond. After

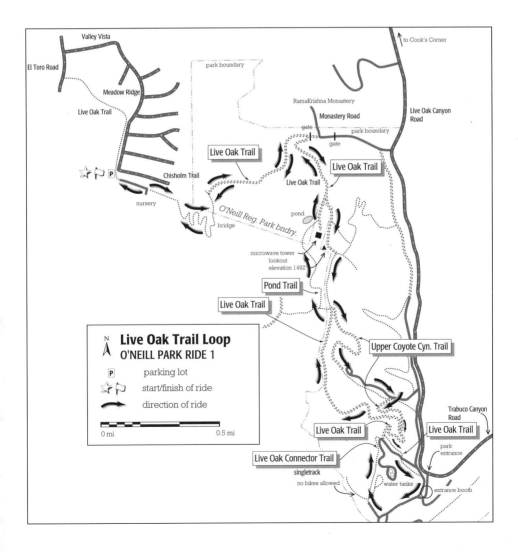

0.4 mile (**5.1 mile mark**) you join your previous route, below the 1492-foot summit. From here, retrace your ride back to your car. Total distance: 6.4 miles.

East Loop

O'NEILL PARK RIDE 2

Distance • 3.8 mile loop

Time Required • 0.5 to 1.5 hours

Route Rating • 4

Grunt Factor • 3+

Technical Rating • 2+

Elevation • Start 920 ft.

High point 1435 ft.

Finish 920 ft.

Map • East Loop, page 79

THIS SHORT RIDE WILL GIVE YOU A GOOD workout and is a good place to gain experience on singletrack riding. The ride makes a loop of the perimeter of the West Group Area of the Park. The trail surface varies from paved service road to excellent singletrack with everything in between. The initial portion of the ride is mostly uphill, with a great downhill singletrack bringing back down into Live Oak Canyon. As an option, you can take a short detour up to the 1492-foot scenic lookout.

PARKING

Park inside O'Neill Park. From the 5 Freeway, take the El Toro exit and drive east for 7.6 miles to Live Oak Canyon Road (Cook's Corner). From the 55 Freeway take Chapman Avenue east to Jamboree and continue straight (Chapman becomes Santiago Canyon Road here). Follow Santiago Canyon Road 12.8 miles to Live Oak Canyon Road (Cook's Corner). Turn east on Live Oak Canyon Road and drive about 3 miles to the Park Entrance (on your right). After paying the entry fee, go straight a short distance, make a very sharp right turn, and proceed a few hundred yards north to the first road heading left. Park near here.

THE RIDE

From where you have parked your car (see above), ride up the paved service road to a point where you are roughly behind the entrance booth. A short distance farther, you will see a singletrack trail on the left. This is the beginning of the Live Oak Trail. Reset your mileage computer here. Follow the singletrack (formerly called the Pawfoot Trail) under the old oak trees then cross a paved road, and continue uphill on singletrack (can be a bit loose here) until you reach a fireroad (**0.2 mile mark**). Turn right. After 0.2 mile, you reach the junction with the Upper Coyote Trail (on your right). Proceed on the left-hand fork, heading uphill.

Continue up Live Oak Trail for nearly another 0.8 mile to where you arrive at the Four-Way Junction (**1.2 mile mark**). Make a quick left, through an opening in the fence-line, and then a quick right onto a singletrack (don't take the trail that heads straight west). This singletrack climbs upward, then passes a small pond and joins another road.

A short distance farther, another fireroad joins in from the right (**1.6 mile mark**). Here you make a very sharp right-hand turn. After a very short distance, you will see a singletrack on your left (the Vista Trail). Turn left. Follow the Vista Trail downhill to a "T" junction; turn left and continue downhill, through switchbacks, eventually joining a wide dirt trail (**2.3 mile mark**). Turn right.

(Scenic Lookout Variation: After making the sharp right mentioned above, continue straight, past the Vista Trail, up the steep hill to the Lookout Point. Enjoy the view, then continue along the ridge, to its eastern point, where a singletrack will be seen heading down the ridge—*do not take the Live Oak turn-off on your right.* Follow this singletrack a very short distance, then turn left onto another singletrack. This joins up with the Vista Trail at the "T" intersection.)

Follow the dirt trail until it joins a paved service road (**2.5+ mile mark**). Follow the paved service road 0.3+ mile to where you can turn right, up another paved road. Follow this road 0.1+ mile where you will see the Upper Coyote Canyon trail on your left (**3.0+ mile mark**). Turn left, follow the trail uphill, crossing the Coyote Canyon singletrack (closed to bikes). Upper Coyote Canyon Trail soon becomes fireroad and eventually joins Live Oak Trail (**3.3+ mile mark**). Head left, down Live Oak Trail, retracing your ride back to the starting point (3.8 total miles).

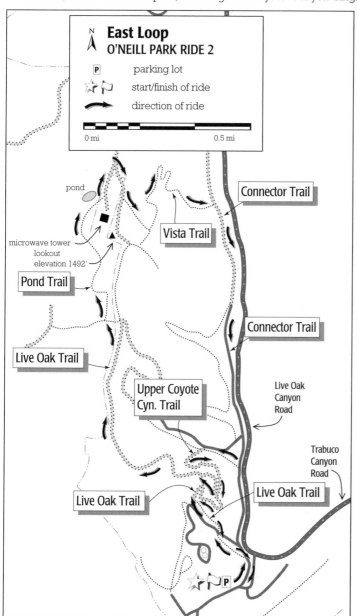

Arroyo Trabuco Trail

O'NEILL PARK RIDE 3

Distance • 10.8 miles

Time Required • 1.2 to 2+ hours

Route Rating • 4

Grunt Factor • 2

Technical Rating • 2

Downhill Rating • 6

Elevation • Start 870 ft.

High point 450 ft.

Finish 870 ft.

Map • Arroyo Trabuco Trail, page 81

ONLY RECENTLY OPENED TO THE PUBLIC, the Arroyo Trabuco Wilderness is really only a thin strip of river bottom and surrounding bluffs, sandwiched between urban development. Nevertheless, this long arm of the Arroyo Trabuco provides a valuable wildlife corridor and preserves a riparian habitat.

The riding is along fireroad. Some of the riding is behind housing developments, but most is in the depths of the arroyo where only the high bridge over-crossings disturb the illusion of being much further away from the madding crowds. The ride is often rocky or sandy and one encounters frequent stream crossings (even in summer) and an abundance of large old sycamore. Avoid this route when water is high.

PARKING
See driving directions for Ride 2, on page 78. After entering the park, proceed straight, then tend slightly right until you reach the Oak Grove day-use area. Park here.

THE RIDE
From the car, proceed to the southern apex of the Oak Grove day-use area, then down a dirt road which heads just left of a park trailer/building. A gate and warning sign (mountain lion habitat and other potentially dangerous creatures) are encountered. Start your odometer at the gate.

Generally, the ride down (and up) the arroyo stays to the right. This allows you to ride somewhat of a loop on what is otherwise an in-and-back ride. At the **2.3 mile mark**, you have climbed out of the arroyo and pass a gate on the east side of the canyon. For the next 1.1 miles you ride behind residential development (avoid any of the left-hand access roads) until the road splits (**3.4 mile mark**). Take the right-hand fireroad down into the arroyo.

After crossing the stream and heading up the other embankment, you may be tempted to take a singletrack shortcut on the left to what appears to be fireroad—don't. The trails seen were made by fire-crews and don't provide good riding. Rather, head uphill, then bear left, following the line of power towers. Continue straight (past a left-hand turn at 4.1 miles) and make several crossings of the stream. At the last crossing, the road heads left and joins another fireroad on the left bank (**4.5 mile mark**).

Continue downstream on the left side of the arroyo, past several side roads (4.8 to 5.0 miles), make a last big stream crossing and proceed to the gate just shy of the Oso Parkway bridge (**5.4 mile mark**). This is the end of the trail, and where you turn around. (Note: The recently opened Tijeras Canyon Trail climbs out of arroyo to your left (east) at the 5.0 mile mark and heads northeast to a point near Rancho Santa Margarita High School. See Rides 4 and 5 on pages 82 and 84.)

Head back upstream, bearing right at the **6.4 mile mark**, climb back out of the arroyo and join your route downstream at the **7.4 mile mark**. From here, stay left and retrace your route, through a gate on the left at the **8.5 mile mark**, then 2.3 more miles back to your car (10.8 miles).

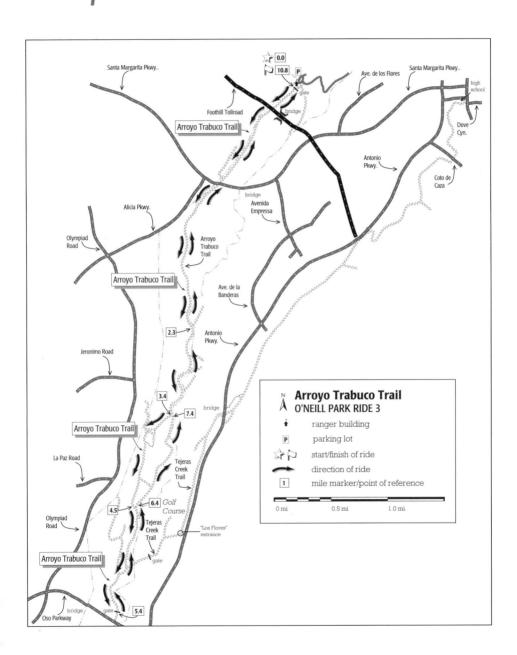

Arroyo Trabuco Trail
O'NEILL PARK RIDE 3

- 🛉   ranger building
- P   parking lot
- ☆ 🏳   start/finish of ride
- ➤   direction of ride
- 1   mile marker/point of reference

Tijeras Canyon Trail

O'NEILL PARK RIDE 4

Distance • 11.0 miles

Time Required • 1.5 to 2.5+ hours

Route Rating • 4

Grunt Factor • 4

Technical Rating • 1

Elevation • Start 1085 ft.

High point 1150 ft.

Finish 500 ft.

Map • Tijeras Canyon Trail, page 83

THIS IS ONE OF THE MOST RECENT additions to the Orange County riding and hiking trail system. It was officially dedicated and opened in November 1995. Ride it now before further over-development destroys the natural vistas which still remain. The trail extends between the confluence of Arroyo Trabuco and Tijeras Creek and Plano Trabuco Road, near Rancho Santa Margarita High School. As with the Arroyo Trabuco ride, the natural areas are (or will be) a thin strip of river bottom and surrounding bluffs, sandwiched between urban development. This trail is best utilized as part of the larger loop ride described below.

PARKING

Several approaches are possible. From the 5 Freeway, take Oso Parkway east for 2.6 miles to Antonio Parkway. Turn left. Take Antonio 5.7 miles to Dove Canyon. Turn right, then proceed to Plano Trabuco. Turn right again. Park along Plano Trabuco. A high school is on your right. The trail starts between the high school parking lot and a private parking area on the right (currently unmarked).

THE RIDE

The initial section of this ride proceeds behind the high school and residential neighborhoods. After 0.8 mile, you cross Coto de Caza Rd. and begin some hill climbing into more (currently) undeveloped terrain. At the **1.8+ mile mark**, you reach your high point on the ride at a road junction. Stay to the right and head downhill and into the Tijeras Creek drainage. Generally, you follow the drainage.

Eventually, you pass under large bridge—Antonio Parkway (**3.8 mile mark**). A short distance farther, the trail tends to the left (a golf course lies along the creek bottom) and follows some ups and downs alongside Antonio Parkway. After another mile, you come to a large "Las Flores" sign and trail entrance (**4.8 mile mark**). The trail turns right here to skirt this residential development, then soon comes to a gate and descends back into the drainage (**5.1 mile mark**). Eventually you reach a stream crossing and then the Arroyo Trabuco Trail (**5.5 mile mark**). Retrace your ride.

Santa Margarita Pkwy..

Foothill Tollroad

gate

bridge

Ave. de los Flores

Santa Margarita Pkwy..

high school

P

Dove Cyn.

Antonio Pkwy.

Coto de Caza

1.8

Tijeras Cyn. Road

bridge

Avenida Empressa

Alicia Pkwy.

Olympiad Road

Arroyo Trabuco Trail

Ave. de la Banderas

Arroyo Trabuco Trail

Antonio Pkwy.

Olympiad Road

Tijeras Creek Trail

bridge

3.8

Tijeras Cyn. Road

Golf Course

Tijeras Creek Trail

"Las Flores" entrance

turnaround point

Arroyo Trabuco Trail

gate

5.5

bridge

Oso Parkway

gate

Tijeras Canyon Trail
O'NEILL PARK RIDE 4

N

i   ranger building

P   parking lot

⭐🚩   start/finish of ride

➤   direction of ride

1   mile marker/point of reference

0 mi   0.5 mi   1.0 mi.

Arroyo Trabuco-Tijeras Creek Loop

O'NEILL PARK RIDE 5

Distance • 20.1+ mile loop

Time Required • 2.5 to 4 hours

Route Rating • 6

Grunt Factor • 5

Technical Rating • 2+

Elevation • Start 990 ft.

low point 500 ft.

High point 1440 ft.

Finish 990 ft.

Map • Arroyo Trabuco-Tijeras Creek Loop, page 85

THIS RIDE TAKES FULL ADVANTAGE OF A number of trails that have opened to public use in 1995 and 1996. This ride is long, but lacks long uphill (and downhill) stretches common to the comparable rides in the adjacent Santa Ana Mountains. Despite this ride's proximity of urban development, the scenery is still pleasant. The ride takes you along the Live Oak, Arroyo Trabuco and Tijeras Creek Trails and a bit of pavement to connect them all. Avoid this route when runoff is high.

PARKING

Park as per Ride 1 (Live Oak Loop) at the end of Meadow Ridge (see page 76).

THE RIDE

From the end of Meadow Ridge, head straight and then make a left down a paved service road which turns to a dirt trail behind residences. The trail heads up a short, steep and winding singletrack which then drops down the other side of a small ridge and crosses a small bridge. Turn right onto a fireroad (**0.4+ mile mark**).

Follow the fireroad uphill to a road intersection (**1.0 mile mark**). Make a sharp right and head up the fireroad to where another road splits off to your left

(**1.3+ mile mark**). Take the left-hand road and after a very short distance, you will see a singletrack on your left (the Vista Trail). Turn left. Follow the Vista Trail downhill to a "T" junction; turn left and continue downhill, through switchbacks, eventually joining a wide dirt trail (**2.0+ mile mark**). Turn right.

Follow the dirt trail to a paved road (**2.3 mile mark**) and continue on the paved road 0.3+ mile to where you can turn right, up another paved road. Follow this road 0.1+ mile where you will see the Upper Coyote Canyon trail on your left (**2.8 mile mark**). Turn left, follow the trail uphill, crossing a singletrack and eventually join Live Oak Trail (**3.0 mile mark**). Head left, down Live Oak Trail, for nearly 0.2 mile (**3.2 mile mark**) to where the Live Oak Trail makes a sharp left turn and becomes singletrack. This turn is immediately before a paved road (Watertank Road) is reached.

Head down this singletrack, cross a paved road and continue on the singletrack under large oaks until you reach a paved service road behind the park entrance (**3.3 mile mark**). Turn right on this paved road. Turn right at the stop sign, then stay right, until the road curves sharply left at the Oak Grove day area (**3.5 mile mark**). A very short distance farther, you will see a dirt road on your right, just left of a park trailer/building. Turn right and head to a gate and trailhead sign for the Arroyo Trabuco Trail (**3.6 mile mark**).

Stay right at the first junction then continue down the canyon until you climb out of the east side of the arroyo and pass a gate (**5.9 mile mark**). For the next 1.1 miles you ride behind

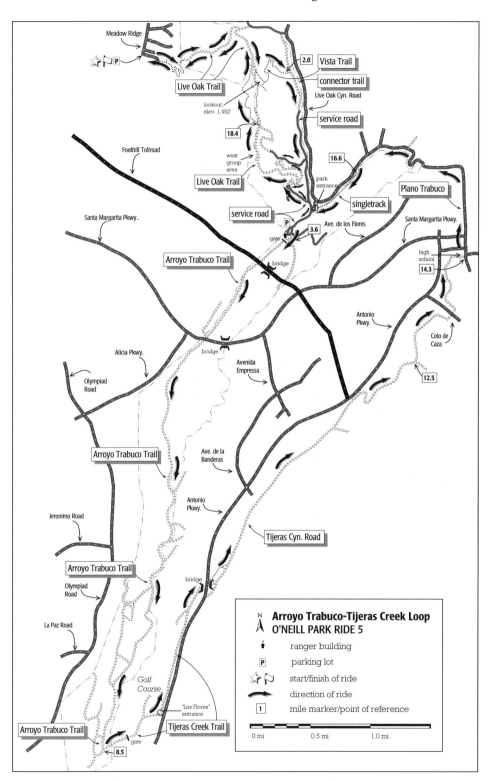

Meadow Ridge

Vista Trail
2.0

connector trail

Live Oak Trail

Live Oak Cyn. Road

lookout,
elev. 1,492'

service road

18.4

Foothill Tollroad

16.6

west
group
area

Live Oak Trail

park
entrance

Plano Trabuco

Santa Margarita Pkwy..

service road

singletrack

P

Santa Margarita Pkwy.

gate

3.6

Ave. de los Flores

high
school

14.3

Arroyo Trabuco Trail

bridge

Antonio
Pkwy.

Coto de
Caza

Alicia Pkwy.

bridge

Avenida
Empressa

12.5

Olympiad
Road

Arroyo Trabuco Trail

Ave. de la
Banderas

Jeronimo Road

Antonio
Pkwy.

Tijeras Cyn. Road

Arroyo Trabuco Trail

Olympiad
Road

bridge

La Paz Road

Golf
Course

N
Arroyo Trabuco-Tijeras Creek Loop
O'NEILL PARK RIDE 5

ranger building

P   parking lot

start/finish of ride

direction of ride

1   mile marker/point of reference

Arroyo Trabuco Trail

"Los Flores"
entrance

Tijeras Creek Trail

gate

8.5

0 mi   0.5 mi   1.0 mi.

residential development until the road splits (**7.0 mile mark**). Take the left-hand fork. This fireroad eventually heads down into the arroyo again. Stay left and eventually make a big water crossing. A short distance farther, you will see the Tijeras Creek Trail on your left (**8.5 mile mark**). Turn left, cross a stream, then head up Tijeras Canyon.

After 0.4 mile, you climb out of the canyon and arrive at a gate (**8.9 mile mark**). Head left, behind houses eventually reaching Antonio Parkway near a large "Los Flores" sign. Proceed on fireroad parallel to Antonio until the trail heads back down into Tijeras Canyon and under a bridge (**10.2 mile mark**). Continue up the Tijeras drainage for 2.1 miles to where the trail heads right and switchbacks up the steep hillside (**12.3 mile mark**). After a loose climb, you reach a junction at the crest of the hill (**12.5 mile mark**). Head straight ahead and downhill, eventually reaching Coto de Caza Road (**13.5 mile mark**). Cross the street and head up the trail on the other side. After 0.8 more mile, the trail ends on Plano Trabuco Road, next to Rancho Santa Margarita High School (**14.3 mile mark**).

Cross the street, and turn left on Plano Trabuco. Ride north on Plano Trabuco. Soon Plano Trabuco makes a 90 degree turn left and heads down into Trabuco Canyon. After passing Emory's General Store on your right (**16.4 mile mark**), cross to the left side of the road and proceed 0.2 mile to a gated entrance to O'Neill Park (**16.6 mile mark**). Head past the gate and make an immediate right onto a singletrack trail that parallels Trabuco Canyon Road. Follow this trail for 0.6 mile, eventually crossing the main park entrance road and meeting your prior route where the Live Oak Trail ended at the paved service road (**17.2 mile mark**).

Head up the Live Oak Trail singletrack 0.2 mile to the fireroad. Turn right. Head up the Live Oak fireroad for 0.2 mile, to the Upper Coyote Trail junction (on your right). Stay left, heading uphill. Continue up Live Oak Trail for nearly another 0.8 mile to where you arrive at the Four-Way Junction (**18.4 mile mark**). Make a quick left through an opening in the fence-line, and then a quick right onto a singletrack (don't take the trail that heads straight west). This singletrack climbs upward, then passes a small pond and joins another road.

A short distance farther, you rejoin your previous route again—where you headed down the Vista Trail singletrack (**18.8 mile mark**). From this point, merely retrace your route back to your car (20.1+ total miles).

Wagon Wheel Wilderness Park

Currently c/o Caspers Wilderness Park
Contact Caspers for up-to-date information at
(714)728-0235

WAGON WHEEL IS A SPARE 475-ACRE wilderness park which was dedicated to the County of Orange in 1983. The park officially opened December 10, 1994 and was renamed after a former Orange County Supervisor to commemorate (some would say celebrate) his retirement.

Wagon Wheel Canyon was once part of the original land grant of 47,432 acres by the Mexican government to John Foster in the 1820s. Foster, an English trader, married the Mexican governor's daughter and changed his name to Don Juan Forster. Due to financial problems, Forster's family sold the land to Richard O'Neill for $250,000.00. O'Neill, an Irish cattleman who had moved to California during the Gold Rush, became a prominent rancher.

Many people hope that more of the beautiful surrounding hills and valleys will be preserved and added to this small park. Barring this, Wagon Wheel may become only a curious anomaly in a otherwise barren landscape of ubiquitous development. Do you vote for preservation-minded candidates for Board of Supervisors or the hand-picked representatives of major developers?

HOW TO GET THERE

Wagon Wheel Wilderness Park (aka General Thomas F. Riley Wilderness Park) lies east of Mission Viejo and just west of Coto de Caza at the junction of Oso Parkway and Coto de Caza Drive. From the 5 Freeway, take the Oso Parkway exit and drive east for 6.0 miles. The park entrance (a right-hand turn) lies about 50 yards before the stop sign at the Oso Parkway and Coto de Caza Drive intersection. A short dirt road (0.2 mile) leads to the parking area and ranger station.

FEES AND FACILITIES

There is a $2.00 per vehicle parking fee. A toilet and bulletin board are the only facilities available. No camping or water is to be found in the park.

MOUNTAIN BIKING IN THE PARK

Although Wagon Wheel is small, there is a very positive and friendly staff and an open attitude to multiple trail use. Currently, all trails are open to all users (sorry no pets allowed). Several fun singletracks are found along with rolling terrain and fast fireroad. Trail surfaces are excellent, although hardly technical.

Thus far, there have been no user conflicts in the park. Here is your chance to keep things that way. Don't speed past other users, but slow down to pass. Be friendly. If you see someone abuse common courtesy (to other users, including other bikers) stop them, let them know how their inconsiderate attitude can ruin the fun for everyone. Let the positive experience at Wagon Wheel serve as an example at other Orange County Regional Parks. It is your responsibility.

THE RIDE
Wagon Wheel overview (p. 88) and loop 89

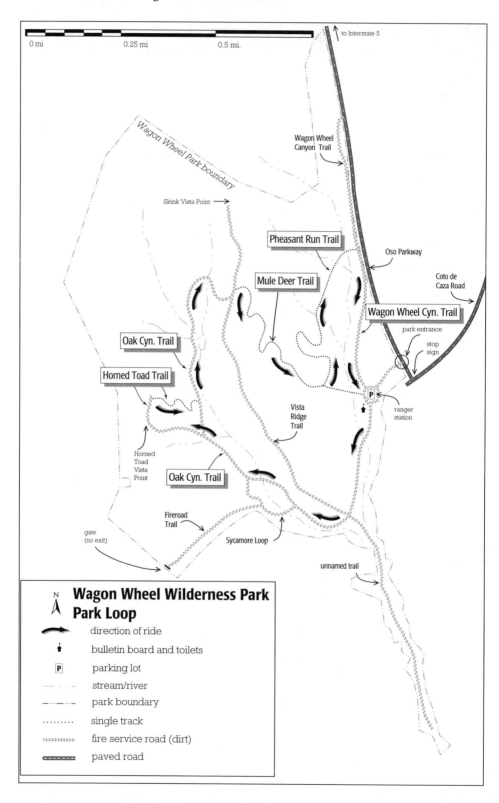

0 mi   0.25 mi   0.5 mi.

to Interstate 5

Wagon Wheel Park boundary

Wagon Wheel
Canyon Trail

Skink Vista Point

Pheasant Run Trail

Oso Parkway

Mule Deer Trail

Coto de
Caza Road

Wagon Wheel Cyn. Trail

park entrance

Oak Cyn. Trail

stop
sign

Horned Toad Trail

Vista
Ridge
Trail

P

ranger
station

Horned
Toad
Vista
Point

Oak Cyn. Trail

Fireroad
Trail

gate
(no exit)

Sycamore Loop

unnamed trail

Wagon Wheel Wilderness Park
Park Loop

N

→	direction of ride
♦	bulletin board and toilets
P	parking lot
—··—	stream/river
—··—	park boundary
········	single track
~~	fire service road (dirt)
▬▬▬	paved road

Park Loop

Distance • 2.7 mile loop

Option: 4.8 miles

Time Required • 20 to 30 minutes

Option: 35 minutes to 1.0 hour

Route Rating • 6

Grunt Factor • 3

Technical Rating • 2

Downhill Rating • 6

Elevation • Start 525ft.

High point 760 ft.

Finish 525 ft. (with lots of up and

down)

Map • Park Loop, page 88

FROM THE PARKING AREA, HEAD south past the bulletin board on the Oak Canyon Trail. At about the 0.2 mile point, the Vista Ridge Trail heads up right, an unnamed fireroad heads left. Keep going straight ahead. At **0.3 mile** (and again at **0.5 mile**), you will pass the Sycamore Loop turn-off on your left. Continue straight ahead.

At **0.7 mile**, the Oak Canyon Trail takes a right-hand turn, you should continue straight ahead on Horned Toad Trail, up the hill. At the top of the hill, the Horned Toad Trail turns to singletrack and winds back down to Oak Canyon Trail (**1.0+ mile mark**). Turn left and follow Oak Canyon Trail. At **1.5 miles** you intersect the Vista Ridge Trail fireroad. Directly across the fireroad is the top of Mule Deer Trail, a fun singletrack.

Take Mule Deer Trail down, through some tight corners, until the **1.9 mile mark**. Another singletrack, Pheasant Run Trail, heads uphill on your left. Take this enjoyable trail over a low hill then down and about for 0.4 mile where it ends at the Wagon Wheel Canyon Trail fireroad. Turn right here, and head back under old oak trees back to the parking area at its north end (2.7 miles).

CONTINUATION

For your continuation and second loop of the park, cross the parking area, and again head south on Oak Canyon Trail. At the **3.0+ mile** point, take the Sycamore Loop Trail turnoff on your left. After 0.3 mile, it again rejoins Oak Canyon Trail (**3.3 mile mark**). Another 0.2 mile brings you to the Horned Toad Trail junction, this time turn right and follow the Oak Canyon Trail for 0.5 mile until it ends at the Vista Ridge Trail (**4.0 mile mark**). Turn right and head down Vista Ridge Trail fireroad (watch your speed and for other users) 0.6 mile until it ends at the Oak Canyon Trail. Turn left and ride back to the parking area (**4.8 miles total**).

OPTIONS

Option 1: The unnamed trail heading south off Oak Canyon Trail is a pleasant 0.7-mile detour (1.4 mile roundtrip).

Option 2: A short 0.3 uphill dead-end trail off Sycamore Loop takes you to a gate (private property).

Option 3: The Skink Vista Point is a 0.2-mile side-trip off the top of the Vista Ridge Trail. Nice views.

Caspers Wilderness Park

33401 Ortega Highway
P.O. Box 395
San Juan Capistrano, CA 92675-0395
(714)728-0235

CASPERS IS A 7,600-ACRE WILDERNESS park located on the western slope of the Santa Ana Mountains and running on both sides of the Ortega Highway. Caspers' eastern boundary abuts with the Cleveland National Forest. Of Orange County's many regional and wilderness parks, Caspers is one of the largest. Caspers first and foremost is a sanctuary of pristine foothills amid South Orange County's ever-growing sea of over-development. The core of the park is the southern portion of the Starr Ranch. The northern section of the Starr Ranch is managed by the National Audubon Society as a wilderness sanctuary which is off-limits to all users.

The park has an abundance of wildlife, including mountain lions, rattlesnakes and other nasty things. Entry into the park requires completion of a Wilderness Permit, which is essentially a Disclosure/Waiver of Liability form. So if you get attacked by a mountain lion or you stub your toe, you can't sue. A number of years ago, a small child was attacked by a mountain lion in the park. Of course the parents sued the County and since everyone felt sorry for the little child, she collected a fat sum. For many years the park was closed to *all* children.

Starting in late 1995, minors are allowed limited access to the park. But since they are *not* allowed out of the camping and picnicking areas, don't plan on a family biking trip to Caspers. There are signs everywhere warning of imminent mountain lion attack. Frankly, even we were a bit paranoid. You must keep your Wilderness Permit with you when riding any trails.

MOUNTAIN BIKING IN THE PARK
Over the last few years, Caspers park officials had arbitrarily excluded biking from a growing number of trails. By 1995, no singletracks were open to multiple use, few loop possibilities existed, and the vibe was definitely not positive. Mountain bikers can thank County Harbors, Beaches and Parks officials and a trail assessment committee for turning this situation around. The County has also directed that the fireroad, which parallels Ortega Highway, be graded so that it is ridable (currently it is "disked" for fire control). This trail will become the San Juan Creek Trail. Although not the most scenic excursion, it is the only legal off-road connector between the Badger Pass, Cold Springs and Oso trails and the park entrance.

The San Juan Creek Trail may connect with the San Juan Trail and the Cleveland National Forest in the foreseeable future. Eventually, there are plans to link Caspers with Wagon Wheel and/or O'Neill Parks. If these plans come to fruition, incredible, legal off-road loop rides should be possible.

Fireroads at Caspers tend to be graded at least once a year, usually in early summer. Dry conditions after grading usually leave the steeper sections of the fireroads unpleasantly soft and loose. After a small amount of rain, the soil consolidates and provides for better riding. All trail junctions are marked with signposts. Mileage given for suggested rides is usually between these markers.

THE RIDES

HOW TO GET THERE

Caspers Wilderness Park lies in the Santa Ana Mountain foothills, east of San Juan Capistrano off Ortega Highway. From the 5 Freeway, take the Ortega Highway exit and drive east for 7.5 miles to the park entrance (a left-hand turn).

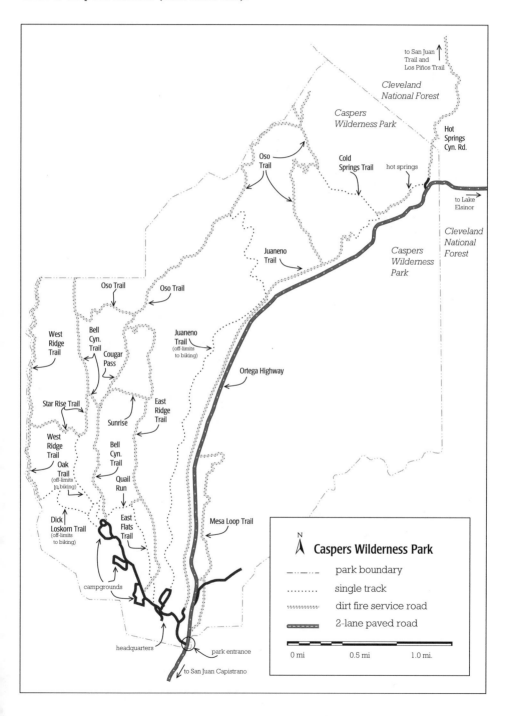

to San Juan Trail and Los Piños Trail

Cleveland National Forest

Caspers Wilderness Park

Hot Springs Cyn. Rd.

Oso Trail

Cold Springs Trail

hot springs

to Lake Elsinor

Cleveland National Forest

Juaneno Trail

Caspers Wilderness Park

Oso Trail

Oso Trail

West Ridge Trail

Bell Cyn. Trail

Cougar Pass

Juaneno Trail (off-limits to biking)

Ortega Highway

Star Rise Trail

East Ridge Trail

Sunrise

West Ridge Trail

Oak Trail (off-limits to biking)

Bell Cyn. Trail

Quail Run

Dick Loskorn Trail (off-limits to biking)

East Flats Trail

Mesa Loop Trail

campgrounds

N

Caspers Wilderness Park

- -·-·-· park boundary
- ········· single track
- wwwwww dirt fire service road
- ===== 2-lane paved road

headquarters

park entrance

to San Juan Capistrano

0 mi   0.5 mi   1.0 mi.

FEES AND FACILITIES

Day-use fees currently are $2.00 per vehicle and $10.00 per bus. Campsites are also available for $10.00 per night, and reservations are suggested (714-728-0235). Minors (less than 18) are restricted to campground and picnic areas (see page 90).

Bell Canyon-Oso-Cougar Pass Loop

CASPERS RIDE 1

Distance • 4.6+ mile loop

Time Required • 0.5 to 1+ hours

Route Rating • 4

Grunt Factor • 2+

Technical Rating • 1

Elevation • Start 420 ft.

High point 560 ft.

Finish 420 ft.

Map • Bell Canyon-Oso-Cougar Loop, page 93

THIS RIDE INVOLVES WELL-GRADED DIRT roads with very moderate elevation gain. The ride proceeds up the wide Bell Canyon. Sections of Bell Canyon Trail pass through streambeds which are full of small rocks and soft sand. After reaching the upper section of Bell Canyon, you climb onto the grassy hillsides and then head back down to join Bell Canyon. The terrain ranges from open grasslands to oak and sycamore-shaded areas and provides a good introductory ride to Caspers Park. Bell Canyon was named for a special boulder that when struck would make a loud bell noise. Many years ago the Bell Boulder was removed to Bowers Museum in Santa Ana.

PARKING

From the park entrance drive up the main paved road to its end (about 1.2+ miles). Park in the unpaved lot on your left. The Bell Canyon Trail begins on your right, where the paved road ends.

THE RIDE

Start up the Bell Canyon Trail. After about 100 yards is a gate. Continue straight ahead following the gentle ups and downs for 1.0 mile. Here, at a fork in the road, tend left. At the 1.1 mile mark, another road heads off left, stay right. Near the **1.5 mile mark**, the road follow the sandy and rocky bottom of a stream. A low gear and fast revolutions help you plow ahead. At the **1.9 mile mark**, you turn right on the Oso Trail junction on your right. Ride 0.7 mile with some uphill to the junction of the Oso Trail and Cougar Pass Trail (**2.6 mile mark**). Head right.

Now you are on Cougar Pass Trail. Stay left at junctions encountered at the **2.9** and **3.4 mile marks**. A short distance past the second junction (the Sun Rise Trail), the road splits. Stay left and you soon join Bell Canyon Trail again (**3.5+ mile mark**). Stay left and it is an easy 1.0 mile ride back to the gate and your car (4.6+ miles total).

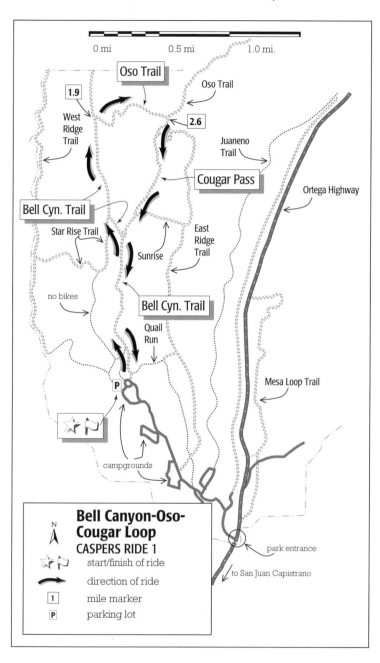

0 mi   0.5 mi   1.0 mi.

Oso Trail

1.9

West
Ridge
Trail

Oso Trail

2.6

Juaneno
Trail

Cougar Pass

Ortega Highway

Bell Cyn. Trail

Star Rise Trail

East
Ridge
Trail

Sunrise

no bikes

Bell Cyn. Trail

Quail
Run

Mesa Loop Trail

P

campgrounds

park entrance

to San Juan Capistrano

N

**Bell Canyon-Oso-
Cougar Loop**
CASPERS RIDE 1

start/finish of ride

direction of ride

1   mile marker

P   parking lot

East Ridge-Bell Canyon

CASPERS RIDE 2

Distance • 5.2 mile loop

Time Required • 0.75 to 1.3+ hours.

Route Rating • 4

Grunt Factor • 3+

Technical Rating • 1+

Elevation • Start 395 ft.

High point 920 ft.

Finish 385 ft.

Map • East Ridge-Bell Canyon, below

THIS LOOP RIDE FOLLOWS A WELL-graded dirt road (East Ridge Trail) up a long, but gradual, ridgeline climb with good views, then drops down into the wide Bell Canyon Valley. The last leg of the ride is along singletrack back to your car.

PARKING

From the Park Entrance drive up the main paved road to a stop sign. Continue straight (slightly right) on the road for about 0.1+ mile farther where a dirt road and gate will be seen on your right. This is the start of the East Ridge Trail. Park legally, off the pavement, nearby.

THE RIDE

Follow the East Ridge fireroad as it climbs over 500 feet along the ridgeline. As you ride, note the sharp drop-off to San Juan Creek (Ortega Highway) on your right and the gentle grassy valley of Bell Canyon on the left. Just shy of the end of

the East Ridge Trail (**2.5 mile mark**) turn left down a fireroad. After 0.3 mile (2.8 mile mark) you intersect the Cougar Pass Trail. Turn left here.

Follow the Cougar Pass fireroad for nearly 0.6 mile to another road junction (the Sun Rise Trail). Tend to the right. A very short distance farther, the road forks. Now take the left fork. Soon you reach the junction with the Bell Canyon Trail (**3.5 mile mark**). Turn left here. The ride is mostly downhill and after 1.0 mile, you reach a gate (**4.5 mile mark**). At the gate, a singletrack heads off left (Quail Run Trail); turn left here. This trail widens, but starts to gain elevation. After 0.3 mile, turn right onto the East Flats Trail singletrack (**4.8 mile mark**). This trail descends and after 0.7+ mile, crosses the East Ridge fireroad. Turn right on the East Ridge Trail, and return to your car (5.7 miles total).

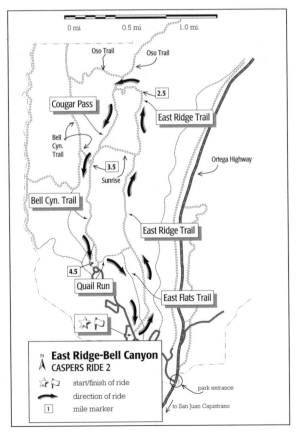

0 mi   0.5 mi   1.0 mi.

Oso Trail   Oso Trail

Cougar Pass

2.5

East Ridge Trail

Bell Cyn. Trail

Ortega Highway

3.5

Sunrise

Bell Cyn. Trail

East Ridge Trail

4.5

Quail Run

East Flats Trail

East Ridge-Bell Canyon
N CASPERS RIDE 2

☆🏳 start/finish of ride

➤ direction of ride

1 mile marker

park entrance

to San Juan Capistrano

Variation: Cross the East Ridge Trail and continue down the East Flats singletrack for another 0.3 mile to the paved park road. Turn right and ride 0.2 mile back to your car (6.1 miles total) 🏁

East Ridge-Badger Pass-San Juan Creek Trail

CASPERS RIDE 3

Distance • 9.6 mile loop

Time Required • 1.5 to 2+ hours

Route Rating • 5

Grunt Factor • 5+

Technical Rating • 2-3 (condition dependent)

Downhill Rating • 6

Elevation • Start 395 ft.

High point 1465 ft.

Finish 395 ft.

Map • East Ridge-Badger Pass-San Juan Creek Trail, page 96

THIS LOOP RIDE FOLLOWS FIREROAD UP two long and often tiring ridgeline climbs then drops steeply down singletrack and old fireroad into the San Juan Creek basin, next to Ortega Highway. You ride along the San Juan Creek Trail (or if it is unridable, along Ortega Highway) back to the park entrance and then to your car. Until the San Juan Creek Trail is properly graded, the car shuttle at Ortega Highway is recommended.

PARKING

From the Park Entrance drive up the main paved road to a stop sign. Continue straight (slightly right) on the road for almost 0.2 mile farther where a dirt road and gate will be seen on your right. This is the start of the East Ridge Trail. Park legally, off the pavement, nearby.

THE RIDE

Follow the East Ridge fireroad as it climbs over 500 feet along the ridgeline. San Juan Creek and Ortega Highway will be below on your right and Bell Canyon will be seen on the left. After 2.5 miles the East Ridge Trail ends. Take the left-hand turn downhill on fireroad for 0.3 mile to where you intersect the Cougar Pass Trail (**2.8 mile mark**). Turn right here. After 0.3 mile, you will see the Oso (meaning Bear) Trail heading steeply up the ridge. Yes, you turn right and head uphill again.

After 1.4 miles (**4.5 mile mark**) and over 700 feet in elevation gain, you will see a rest area with a shaded picnic table located on your right. This section of the Oso Trail can be torturously loose and soft after it has been graded and before it rains. Turn right at the rest area. At 1465 feet, this is the high point on the ride; a great place to re-hydrate and enjoy the view.

Now comes the fun part, the steep descent of the Badger Pass Trail. This singletrack and old fireroad heads straight down the ridge to the right of the rest area. Be careful and watch your speed and for other users as you descend over 900 feet in the next 1.5 miles to the San Juan Creek Trail below (**6.0 mile mark**). Cross the Juaneno Trail (closed to bikes) and head toward Ortega Highway. Here the San Juan Creek Trail heads west and roughly parallel to Ortega Highway for about 3.0 miles to the Ortega Flats Picnic Area near the park entrance

(**9.0 mile mark**). Ride through the picnic area to the paved road, turn right and ride back
to your car. 9.6 total miles.

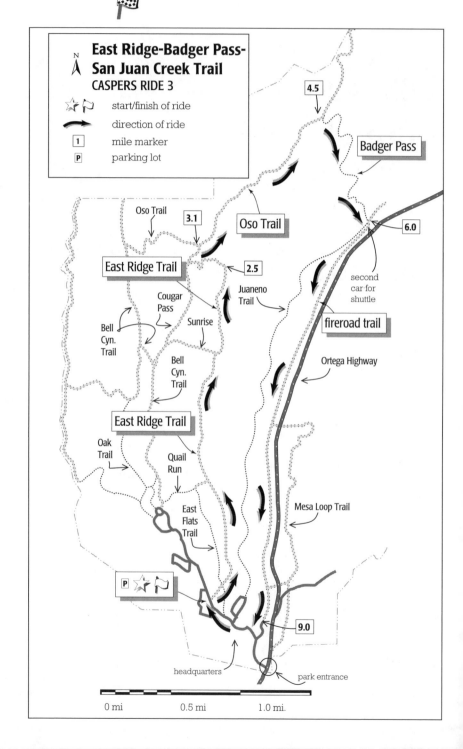

Crystal Cove State Park

8471 Pacific Coast Highway
Laguna Beach, CA 92651
(714)494-3539

CRYSTAL COVE STATE PARK CONSISTS OF approximately 2700 acres of coastal hills in the central section of the San Joaquin Hills. Nearly the entire El Moro watershed is included in the park. Surrounding land includes Laguna Coast Wilderness Park and Irvine Co. Open Space Reserve, both remain undeveloped, but public access is restricted. See pages 112 to 113 for more information. From the upper ridges of the park, the swath of destruction of the San Joaquin Hills Tollroad, which has permanently destroyed the biological integrity of the San Joaquin Hills, can be seen to the north and east.

The park includes open beautiful grasslands, riparian woodland and coastal sage scrub. Although swept by the 1993 Laguna Fire, the area is quickly recovering. Heavy rains in early 1995 did considerable damage to trails and roads, most of which have been repaired. Trail conditions are always weather dependent.

MOUNTAIN BIKING IN THE PARK
Mountain biking is a welcome and popular activity in the park, and often the trails are crowded. Nevertheless, it is a privilege that could be restricted or curtailed. Respect for other users and riders is particularly critical to keeping this area open. Also important to continued access is staying on maintained trails.

There are over 17 miles of fireroad and singletrack in the park. Most of the trails are suitable for novice to intermediate riders. All the rides in the park start near the coast and work their way inland and uphill to the crest of the San Joaquin Hills. This translates to rides with mostly uphill in the beginning and downhill to finish. It is possible to combine various Trail Segments (see page 106), providing variety and longer loop rides.

HOW TO GET THERE
Crystal Cove State Park (often referred to simply as El Moro) is situated adjacent to PCH (Pacific Coast Highway) between Corona Del Mar on the north and Laguna Beach on the south. Drive PCH to El Moro Road. There is an elementary school here and a signal light. Turn east and drive up the road to the entrance booth (a right-hand turn), either pay here or at the self-serve pay machine in the parking area a short distance ahead.

FEES AND FACILITIES
Day-use fees currently are $6.00 per vehicle (if the kiosk is open, otherwise pay only $5.00 at the self-serve machine). Primitive camping is also available (campgrounds destroyed in the 1993 Laguna Fire should re-open by Spring-Summer, 1996). However, a two- to four-mile hike or ride is required to reach the three campgrounds. Nightly camping fees are currently $7.00 to $9.00 per night (depending on the season). The camping fee includes parking. For more information call the park at (714)494-3539. Toilets and water are available at the ranger station-parking area.

CRYSTAL COVE STATE PARK LOOP RIDES
The following are suggested loop rides for riders who may not be familiar with the area. By combining trail segments in various ways, you can make longer or more varied rides.

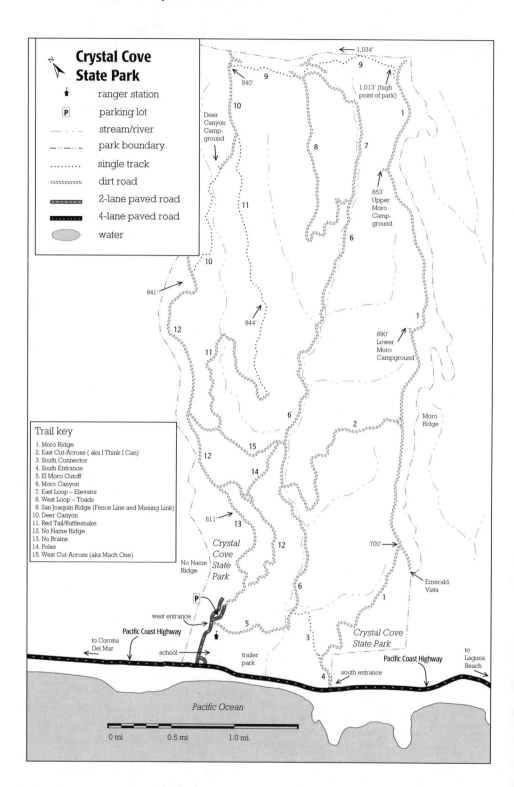

Crystal Cove State Park

N

🧍 ranger station

P parking lot

—·— stream/river

—··— park boundary

········· single track

∿∿∿∿∿ dirt road

▭▭▭▭ 2-lane paved road

▬▬▬▬ 4-lane paved road

⬭ water

Trail key

1. Moro Ridge
2. East Cut-Across (aka I Think I Can)
3. South Connector
4. South Entrance
5. El Moro Cutoff
6. Moro Canyon
7. East Loop – Elevator
8. West Loop – Toads
9. San Joaquin Ridge (Fence Line and Missing Link)
10. Deer Canyon
11. Red Tail/Rattlesnake
12. No Name Ridge
13. No Brains
14. Poles
15. West Cut-Across (aka Mach One)

1,034'

9

940'

9

1,013' (high point of park)

10

Deer Canyon Camp-ground

8

7

1

853' Upper Moro Campground

11

6

10

841'

844'

12

11

890' Lower Moro Campground

1

Moro Ridge

12

6

2

15

12

14

611'

13

700'

12

6

Emerald Vista

Crystal Cove State Park

No Name Ridge

P

west entrance

Pacific Coast Highway

to Corona Del Mar

school

5

trailer park

3

Crystal Cove State Park

1

Pacific Coast Highway

to Laguna Beach

south entrance

4

Pacific Ocean

0 mi   0.5 mi   1.0 mi.

Moro Canyon

CRYSTAL COVE RIDE 1

Distance • 6.0 mile loop

Time Required • 0.75 to 1.5+ hours

Route Rating • 5

Grunt Factor • 3

Technical Rating • 1 to 3 (depending on condition)

Elevation • Start/Finish 160 ft.

Low point 40 ft.

High point 520 ft.

Map • Moro Canyon, below

AFTER HEAVY RAINS IN SPRING 1995, much of the upper part of Moro Canyon Trail was heavily damaged. Until repairs are made, the upper section of this ride is moderately technical with several bike and hike sections around washouts. Under normal conditions, this is a nice and easy ride up this major drainage. Many stands of old oak and sycamore will be found in the upper section of this ride.

THE RIDE

From the main parking area, head back down toward the kiosk (west) until a fireroad is seen on your left (the El Moro Cut-Off). Follow this behind the trailer park down to the bottom of Moro Canyon (0.4 mile). Turn left, and head up Moro Canyon. A few steeper grades will be encountered after 1.3 miles or so (**1.7 mile mark**), but the going is relatively easy. At nearly the **3.0 mile mark**, a fireroad will be seen heading off to the left (West Loop Trail). This marks the turn-around point. Simply retrace your route back to the parking lot.

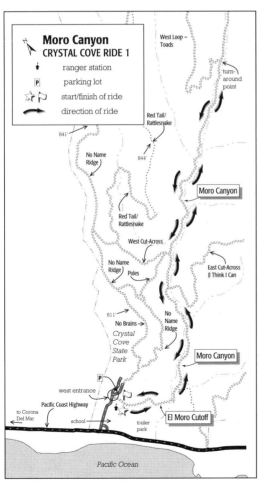

Moro Canyon
CRYSTAL COVE RIDE 1

⚲ ranger station
P parking lot
⚝ start/finish of ride
➤ direction of ride

West Loop – Toads

turn-around point

Red Tail/ Rattlesnake

841'

No Name Ridge   844'

Moro Canyon

Red Tail/ Rattlesnake

West Cut-Across

No Name Ridge   Poles

East Cut-Across (I Think I Can)

611'   No Brains ➤   No Name Ridge

Crystal Cove State Park

P

west entrance

Pacific Coast Highway

Moro Canyon

to Corona Del Mar

school

trailer park

El Moro Cutoff

Pacific Ocean

No Name Ridge- Moro Canyon

CRYSTAL COVE RIDE 2

Distance • 8.1 miles

Time Required • 1.3 hours to 2+ hours.

Route Rating • 5

Grunt Factor • 5

Technical Rating • 2 to 3 (depending on conditions)

Elevation • Start/Finish 160 ft.
Low point 40 ft.
High point 935 ft.

Map • No Name Ridge-Moro Canyon, page 101

THIS RIDE INVOLVES SOME SECTIONS of moderately steep climbing, fun singletrack and a fast glide into the upper portion of El Moro Canyon which is followed downhill to the parking area.

THE RIDE

From the parking area, head up the No Name Ridge Trail, following it for 2.2 miles past several steep uphills, to where a singletrack heads off and down to the right. The main fireroad is fenced a short distance past this point. A steep downhill, a short uphill and then another downhill on the singletrack take you down into Deer Canyon. Continue along next to the stream, then begin an uphill climb on another fireroad (**2.9 mile mark**). At this point Deer Canyon campground will be found on your left. It offers the last shade for a bit.

Continue up the fireroad for 0.5 mile to where it is gated, the San Joaquin Ridge Trail singletrack begins here on your right (**3.4 mile mark**). Follow the singletrack for 0.5 mile to where it joins a fireroad (**3.9 mile mark**). Follow the fireroad a short distance where it splits; take the right-hand fork (more or less straight ahead). This is the West Loop Trail that follows the ridgeline then steeply descends into Moro Canyon. After 1.2 miles, the West Loop Trail joins the Moro Canyon Trail (**5.1 mile mark**).

Follow the Moro Canyon Trail downhill for nearly 2.6 miles. (Note: The upper section of the Moro Canyon Trail may have rain damage that could require some bike carries over washouts.) At the bottom of the Moro Canyon Trail (**7.7 mile mark**), take a fireroad that heads up and right and leads back to the parking area (8.1 total miles).

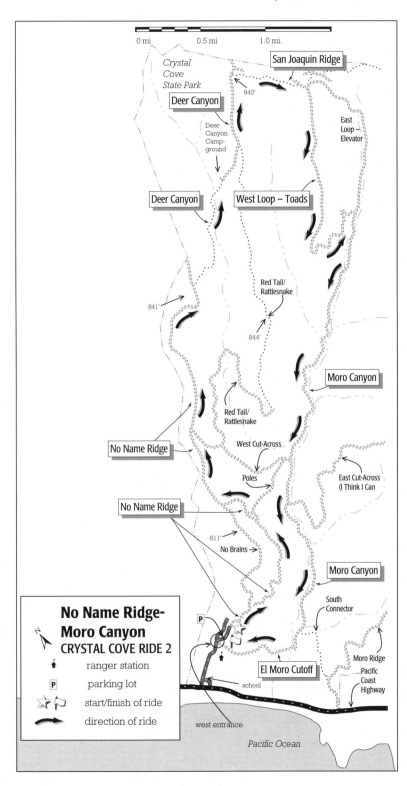

San Joaquin Ridge

Crystal
Cove
State Park

Deer Canyon

940'

East
Loop –
Elevator

Deer
Canyon
Camp-
ground

Deer Canyon

West Loop – Toads

Red Tail/
Rattlesnake

841'

844'

Moro Canyon

Red Tail/
Rattlesnake

No Name Ridge

West Cut-Across

Poles

East Cut-Across
(I Think I Can

No Name Ridge

611'

No Brains

Moro Canyon

South
Connector

**No Name Ridge-
Moro Canyon**

CRYSTAL COVE RIDE 2

Moro Ridge

ranger station

El Moro Cutoff

P   parking lot

Pacific
Coast
Highway

⭐ 🚩 start/finish of ride

school

➤ direction of ride

west entrance

Pacific Ocean

Moro Ridge-No Name Ridge

CRYSTAL COVE RIDE 3

Distance • 8.6 mile loop

Time Required • 1.3 hours to 2+ hours

Route Rating • 6

Grunt Factor • 5+

Technical Rating • 2+

Elevation • Start 160 ft.

Low point 40 ft.

High point 1013 ft.

Map • Moro Ridge-No Name Ridge, page 103

THIS GRAND LOOP COVERS THE ENTIRE perimeter of the park following various ridgelines that provide excellent views of the ocean and the entire San Joaquin Hills. Roughly two miles of the ride involves well-traveled singletrack. This ride can be also ridden as a loop in the reverse direction as described.

THE RIDE

From the parking area, head back down toward the kiosk (west) until a fireroad can be seen on your left (the El Moro Cut-Off). Follow this behind the trailer park down to the bottom of Moro Canyon (0.4 mile). Turn left, and head a very short distance (less than 100 yards) up Moro Canyon. A singletrack will be seen heading off to the right (South Connector Singletrack). Turn right here and head for 0.3+ mile up the South Connector until a partially paved fireroad is reached (the Moro Ridge Trail). Head left (uphill).

The Moro Ridge Trail is quite steep near the bottom, but after a short distance it soon levels. After about 0.8 mile (**1.5 mile mark**), a fork in the road will be encountered. The ride takes the mild left hand turn. The very sharp right-hand turn takes you to the Emerald Point Vista, a short detour with a pleasant ocean view.

Continue along Moro Ridge Trail, passing the East Cut-Across Connector at the **2.2 mile mark**. At the **2.6 mile mark**, atop a short hill, the Lower Moro Ridge Campground will be seen on the left; head right and slightly downhill here. Continue along the ridge for nearly another 1.5 miles, until just past two steep sections a singletrack will be seen heading left (**4.0+ mile mark**). Turn left here and ride a short distance to the top of a small knoll. At 1013 feet, this is the highest point in the park (**4.1 mile mark**).

From here, ride down a singletrack that runs just below the ridgeline until a section of fireroad is encountered (**4.6 mile mark**). Head uphill (right) for a very short distance on this fireroad, then turn left at a gate, along another short section of singletrack, to yet another fireroad (**4.7 mile mark**). Turn right here and head up a short distance to the crest of the hill, turn right again and up to a gate. A singletrack will be seen heading off to the left. Follow this singletrack for about 0.5 mile to where it meets the upper end of the Deer Canyon Trail (5.2 mile mark).

Head left, downhill on the fireroad until you reach the bottom of the hill and the road becomes singletrack (**5.7 mile mark**). The Small Deer Canyon Campground will be passed on your right. Follow the singletrack along the stream, then head up two very steep hills. After 0.7 mile, the singletrack intersects the No Name Ridge Trail fireroad (**6.4 mile mark**). Turn left here and follow the fireroad up and down the ridgeline, then down a long grade for 2.2 miles to return to the parking area (8.6 total mileage).

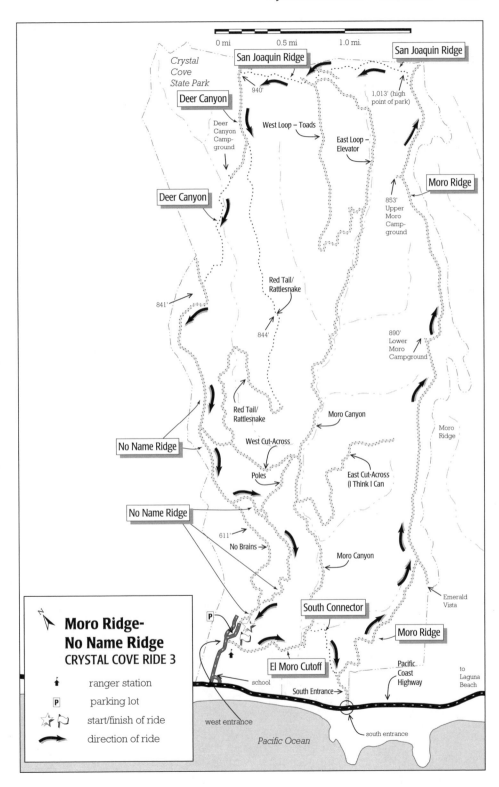

0 mi   0.5 mi   1.0 mi.

San Joaquin Ridge

San Joaquin Ridge

Crystal Cove State Park

Deer Canyon

940'

1,013' (high point of park)

Deer Canyon Campground

West Loop – Toads

East Loop – Elevator

Moro Ridge

Deer Canyon

853' Upper Moro Campground

Red Tail/ Rattlesnake

841'

844'

890' Lower Moro Campground

Red Tail/ Rattlesnake

Moro Canyon

No Name Ridge

West Cut-Across

Moro Ridge

Poles

East Cut-Across (I Think I Can)

No Name Ridge

611'

No Brains

Moro Canyon

South Connector

Emerald Vista

Moro Ridge

**Moro Ridge-
No Name Ridge**
CRYSTAL COVE RIDE 3

El Moro Cutoff

Pacific Coast Highway

to Laguna Beach

school

South Entrance

P   parking lot

start/finish of ride

direction of ride

ranger station

N

west entrance

south entrance

Pacific Ocean

Moro Ridge- Red Tail Ridge

CRYSTAL COVE RIDE 4

Distance • 9.9 miles

Time Required • 1.3 hours to 2+ hours.

Route Rating • 6

Grunt Factor • 5

Technical Rating • 4

Elevation • Start 120 ft.

High point 1013 ft.

Finish 120 ft.

Map • Moro Ridge-Red Tail Ridge, page 105

THIS EXCELLENT LOOP COMBINES THE best of what the park has to offer: fireroads, rolling singletrack and a taste of technical ground. The uphill grades provide a good workout that is following by mostly downhill riding. Well suited for intermediate and better riders as an after-work or early-morning ride.

THE RIDE

From the parking area, head back down toward the kiosk (west) until a fireroad is seen on your left (the El Moro Cutoff). Follow this behind the trailer park to the bottom of Moro Canyon (**0.4 mile mark**) Follow the El Moro Canyon fireroad for nearly a mile (**1.4 mile mark**) and take a right-hand turn onto the East Cut-Across fireroad. (Note: Heavy Spring 1995 rains washed out the road here. Cross the creek on a singletrack just beyond the road turn-off).

Head up the East Cut-Across for about 1.1 miles (gaining 580 feet) to where the road forks; take the left fork and join the Moro Ridge fireroad a short distance farther (**2.5+ mile mark**). Head left on the Moro Ridge road encountering some pavement. Atop a hill, at the 3.0+ mile mark, the Lower Moro Ridge Campground will be seen to the left; head right and slightly downhill here. Continue along the ridge for nearly 1.5 miles. Just past two steep sections, a singletrack will be seen heading left (**4.4+ mile mark**). Turn left here and ride a short distance to the top of a small knoll. At 1013 feet, this is the highest point on your ride and in the park (**4.5 mile mark**).

From this point, you ride down a singletrack that runs just below the ridgeline until a section of fireroad is encountered (**5.0+ mile mark**). Head uphill (right) for a very short distance, and then turn left at a gate along another short section of singletrack to yet another fireroad (**5.1 mile mark**). Turn right here and head a short distance up to the crest of the hill, turn right again toward a gate and where a singletrack will be seen heading off to the left. Follow this singletrack for about 0.5 mile to where it meets the upper end of the Deer Canyon Trail (**5.6 mile mark**).

Head left downhill on the fireroad for 0.3 mile (**5.9 mile mark**) and head off left on a trail (Red Tail Ridge) that splits off the main fireroad. After about a mile of following the ridgeline, the trail heads steeply down a rocky singletrack. This will be the most technical section of the ride. Follow the singletrack until it finally meets a well-graded fireroad (**7.3 mile mark**). Turn right here and follow the fireroad for about 0.7 mile where it joins the West Cut-Across fireroad (**8.0 mile mark**). Turn left and enjoy the 0.5 mile downhill to where the Moro Canyon fireroad is met (**8.5 mile mark**). From here, simply head down canyon (right) and tetrace your ride back to your car.

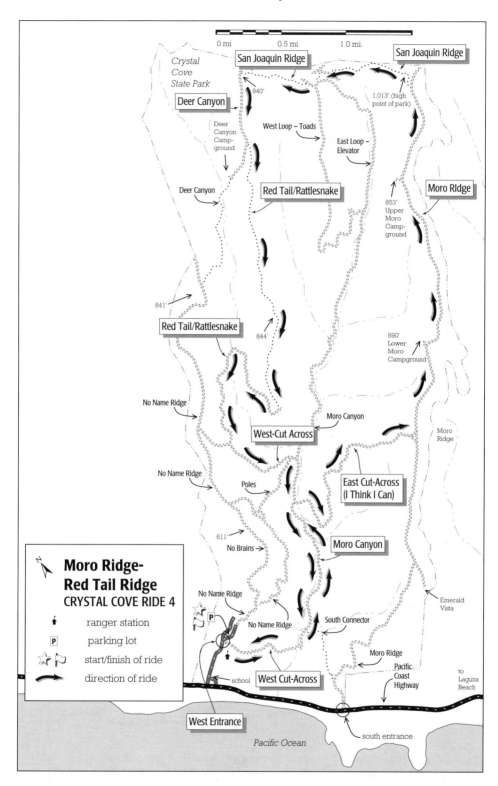

0 mi   0.5 mi   1.0 mi.

Crystal Cove State Park

San Joaquin Ridge

San Joaquin Ridge

Deer Canyon

940'

1,013' (high point of park)

Deer Canyon Campground

West Loop – Toads

East Loop – Elevator

Deer Canyon

Red Tail/Rattlesnake

Moro Ridge

853' Upper Moro Campground

841'

Red Tail/Rattlesnake

844'

890' Lower Moro Campground

No Name Ridge

Moro Canyon

Moro Ridge

West-Cut Across

No Name Ridge

Poles

East Cut-Across (I Think I Can)

611'

No Brains

Moro Canyon

**Moro Ridge-
Red Tail Ridge**

CRYSTAL COVE RIDE 4

Emerald Vista

ranger station

No Name Ridge

parking lot

P

No Name Ridge

South Connector

start/finish of ride

direction of ride

Moro Ridge

school

West Cut-Across

Pacific Coast Highway

to Laguna Beach

West Entrance

south entrance

Pacific Ocean

Trail Segments

The following is a description of all of the various trails in the park. Riders can use this information to devise their own loop rides. Some of the trail designations have been slightly modified from those used in the past. This was done to make trail designations logically consistent and in agreement with standard routes ridden by most riders. The numbers of the segments correspond to the trail numbers on the overview map of the park below.

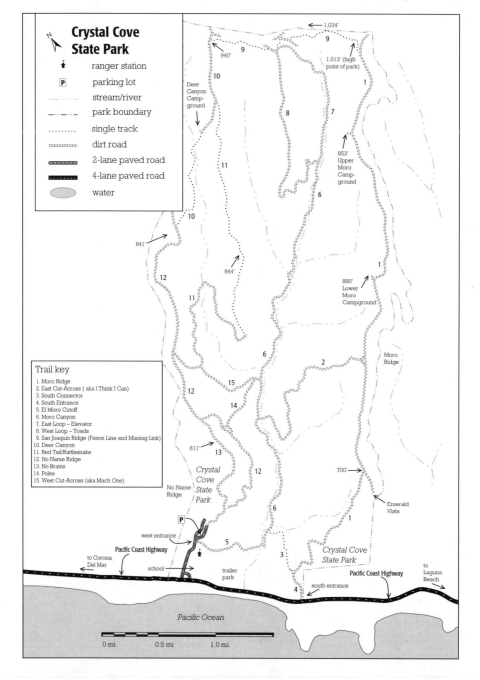

Crystal Cove State Park

♦	ranger station
P	parking lot
—·—·—	stream/river
—··—··—	park boundary
·········	single track
~~	dirt road
━━━━━	2-lane paved road
━━━━━	4-lane paved road
	water

Trail key
1. Moro Ridge
2. East Cut-Across (aka I Think I Can)
3. South Connector
4. South Entrance
5. El Moro Cutoff
6. Moro Canyon
7. East Loop – Elevator
8. West Loop – Toads
9. San Joaquin Ridge (Fence Line and Missing Link)
10. Deer Canyon
11. Red Tail/Rattlesnake
12. No Name Ridge
13. No Brains
14. Poles
15. West Cut-Across (aka Mach One)

Moro Ridge Trail Direct Route

CRYSTAL COVE SEGMENT 1

Distance • 3.4 miles
Route Rating • 3
Grunt Factor • 5+
Technical Rating • 1
Elevation • Low point 190 ft.
High point 1013 ft.

THE DIRECT ROUTE ASCENDS MORO RIDGE directly above the South Entrance. The initial section of this fireroad is steep, with remaining ridge mostly gentle ups and downs. Some short steep sections are found near the end of the trail. Some portions of this fireroad are paved.

East Cut-Across (aka I Think I Can)

CRYSTAL COVE SEGMENT 2

Distance • 1.1+ miles
Route Rating • 3
Grunt Factor • 5
Technical Rating • 1
Elevation • Low point 140 ft.
High point 720 ft.

THE EAST CUT-ACROSS ASCENDS OUT OF Moro Canyon to join the main Moro Ridge fireroad. It is a more moderate grade than the initial section of the Moro Ridge and somewhat more scenic.

South Connector Trail

CRYSTAL COVE SEGMENT 3

Distance • 0.3+ mile
Route Rating • 4
Grunt Factor • 3
Technical Rating • 2+
Elevation • Low point 60 ft.
High point 190 ft.

THIS SINGLETRACK RUNS FROM THE bottom of Moro Canyon to the bottom of the Moro Ridge Trail and South Entrance Connector. It can be a bit soft at times on the uphill direction and novice riders will probably walk the steepest section.

South Entrance

CRYSTAL COVE SEGMENT 4

Distance • 0.1 mile
Technical Rating • 0
Elevation • Low point 120 ft.
High point 200 ft.

THIS IS THE VERY SHORT SPUR ROAD that connects the bottom of the Moro Ridge Trail with the gated entrance along Pacific Coast Highway.

El Moro Cut-Off

CRYSTAL COVE SEGMENT 5

Distance • 0.4 mile
Route Rating • 1
Grunt Factor • 2
Technical Rating • 1+
Elevation • Low point 40 ft.
High point 160 ft.

THIS IS THE SHORT FIREROAD THAT connects the lower end of the main parking lot at the Ranger Station with the bottom of El Moro Canyon.

Moro Canyon Trail

CRYSTAL COVE SEGMENT 6

Distance • 2.6 miles
Route Rating • 5+
Grunt Factor • 2
Technical Rating • 3 (due to rain damage)
Downhill Rating 6
Elevation • 520 ft at top
Low point 40 ft.

ONE OF THE MOST SCENIC RIDES IN THE park, the upper section of this trail passes under old oaks and is one of the few sections of the park that provides a shady respite. The trail begins at the bottom of El Moro Canyon (behind the trailer park) and continues for 2.6 miles until a junction is reached (East and West Loop Trails begin here).

East Loop Trail (aka Elevator)

CRYSTAL COVE SEGMENT 7

Distance • 1.0 mile
Route Rating • 2
Grunt Factor • 5+
Technical Rating • 2
Elevation • 935 ft at top
        520 ft. at bottom

BEGINS AT THE UPPER END OF EL MORO Canyon at the junction with the West Loop Trail. The bottom section is relatively flat, but can be very sandy. The upper section of this fireroad is steep and can be loose. Near the top, stay left to reach the top of the hill.

West Loop Trail (aka Toads)

CRYSTAL COVE SEGMENT 8

Distance • 1.2 miles
Route Rating • 3
Grunt Factor • 4+
Technical Rating • 1
Elevation • Low point 520 ft.
        935 ft. high point

THE EASIEST AND BEST CHOICE FOR connecting the San Joaquin Ridge Trail and El Moro Canyon, no matter what direction you travel.

San Joaquin Ridge Trail (Fence Line and Missing Link)

CRYSTAL COVE SEGMENT 9

Distance • 1.1 miles
Route Rating • 5+
Technical Rating • 3
Elevation • South end 1013 ft.
        North end 935 ft.

THIS IS ACTUALLY THREE SEPARATE sections of singletrack that connect fireroads along the northeastern boundary of the park. These singletracks run from the top of Moro Ridge Trail to the top of East Loop Trail (called Missing Link) and from the top of West Loop Trail to the top of the Deer Canyon Trail (Fence Line).

Deer Canyon Trail

CRYSTAL COVE SEGMENT 10
Distance • 1.2 miles
Route Rating • 5
Technical Rating • 2+
Elevation • High point 935 ft.
Low point 620 ft.

THIS SECTION OF TRAIL BEGINS AS A fireroad at the northern end of the San Joaquin Ridge Singletrack at the park boundary. From here, the trail extends westward and down into Deer Canyon (Red Tail stays on the ridgeline and cuts off to the left). After passing a campground, the trail becomes singletrack which then makes two steep climbs up to meet No Name Ridge at its top.

Red Tail Ridge and Rattlesnake

CRYSTAL COVE SEGMENT 11
Distance • 2.1 miles
Route Rating • 7
Technical Rating • 4
Elevation • Low point 450 ft.
High point 830 ft.

THIS TRAIL FOLLOWS A RIDGELINE AND then the valley below between Deer Canyon Trail and West Cut Across. The top of the trail is located 0.3 mile downhill from the top of Deer Canyon Trail. The bottom intersects West Cut-Across about a quarter of the way down. The section of trail from the high point on the ridgeline down to a fireroad below is the most technical section of singletrack in the park.

No Name Ridge

CRYSTAL COVE SEGMENT 12
Distance • 2.2 miles
Route Rating • 4
Grunt Factor • 5
Technical Rating • 1+
Elevation • Low point 170 ft.
High point 810 ft.

THIS TRAIL RUNS FROM THE MAIN PARK entrance parking area along fireroad to the park boundary on the northwest side of the Park. Deer Canyon Trail meets up here. This trail is a good climb with several up-and-down sections just to make it more strenuous.

No Brains

CRYSTAL COVE SEGMENT 13
Distance • 0.7 mile
Grunt Factor • 4
Technical Rating • 1+
Downhill Rating • 4
Elevation • Low point 250 ft.
High point 611 ft.

A DIRECT ROUTE OVER THE HILLSIDE that No Name Ridge skirts on the right. The trail begins about 0.1 mile up No Name Ridge on the left (north) and rejoins No Name Ridge 0.7 mile later. Much more strenuous than No Name Ridge.

Poles

CRYSTAL COVE SEGMENT 14
Distance • 0.3+ miles
Route Rating • 2
Technical Rating • 2
Downhill Rating • 4
Elevation • Low point 240 ft.
High point 540 ft.

A FAST AND STEEP DOWNHILL OFF THE lower section of No Name Ridge to Moro Canyon.

West Cut-Across (aka Mach One)

CRYSTAL COVE SEGMENT 15
Distance • 0.8 mile
Route Rating • 2
Grunt Factor • 5+
Technical Rating • 1+
Downhill Rating • 4
Elevation • Low point 170 ft.
High point 590 ft.

THIS RIDE CONNECTS NO NAME RIDGE with Moro Canyon.

Laguna Coast Wilderness Park and Irvine Company Open Space Reserve

ABOUT THE PARK

The Laguna Greenbelt is the common name given to some 15,000 acres of contiguous undeveloped coastal hills and valleys surrounding Laguna Beach. Preservation of this unique habitat has been the long-term goal of many committed individuals. Despite the severing of this treasure by the despised San Joaquin Hills Tollroad and threats of development, the creation of the Laguna Greenbelt has been an amazing accomplishment. We strongly urge mountain bikers to contribute to the continuing battle to save what's left. Tax-deductible donations can be made to: The Laguna Canyon Foundation, P.O. Box 4895, Laguna Beach, CA 92652 (714)497-8324.

Currently, Laguna Coast Wilderness Park encompasses only the areas outlined on the accompanying map. The western section of Irvine Co. Open Space Reserve, and the thin sliver connecting it to the northern section of Irvine land, prevents unrestricted access and better management options. However, the County of Orange anticipates acquiring the western section of Irvine land and the aforementioned ridge and adding this land to Laguna Coast. If this goal is achieved, it should be possible to legally ride from Crystal Cove State Park to Aliso-Wood Canyon.

MOUNTAIN BIKING IN THE PARK

From the mountain biker's perspective, matters are still far from ideal. Although trails connect throughout the Laguna Greenbelt from Newport Beach to Laguna Niguel, it remains impossible to legally piece even one ride together. The Laguna Coast Wilderness Park and Irvine Co. Open Space Reserve are open to public use on a very limited basis. Bicycling opportunities are restricted to docent-led tours of selected areas, on specified dates. Advance reservations are required. While the opportunity to legally ride this beautiful landscape is welcome, most serious cyclists may be put off by such group outings.

To obtain information concerning tour availability, dates and reservation requirements, you may call the responsible managing agency directly as follows:

The Irvine Company Open Space Reserve
Managed by The Nature Conservancy
Docent-led tours only, reservations a must.
(714)832-7478

Laguna Coast Wilderness Park
Managed by the County of Orange
Docent-led tours only.
(714)854-7108

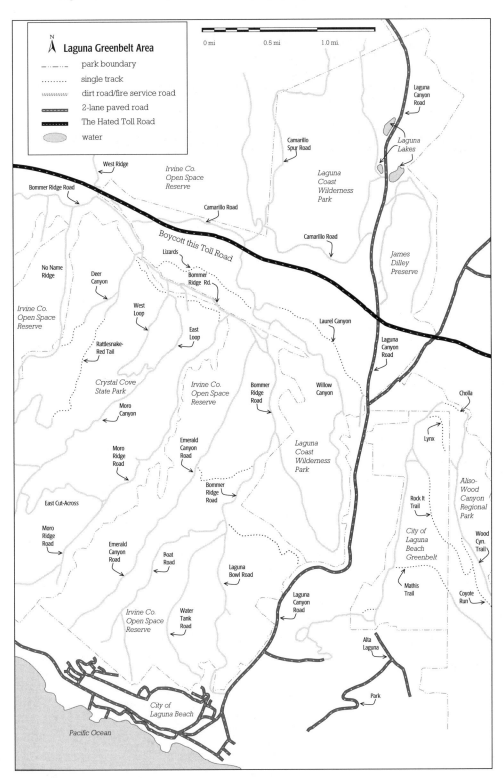

Laguna Greenbelt Area

— · — park boundary
········· single track
∿∿∿∿∿ dirt road/fire service road
▭▭▭▭ 2-lane paved road
▬▬▬▬ The Hated Toll Road
water

N

0 mi   0.5 mi   1.0 mi.

West Ridge

Bommer Ridge Road

Irvine Co. Open Space Reserve

Camarillo Spur Road

Laguna Canyon Road

Laguna Lakes

Laguna Coast Wilderness Park

Camarillo Road

Camarillo Road

Boycott this Toll Road

James Dilley Preserve

No Name Ridge

Deer Canyon

Lizards

Bommer Ridge Rd.

West Loop

East Loop

Laurel Canyon

Laguna Canyon Road

Irvine Co. Open Space Reserve

Rattlesnake-Red Tail

Crystal Cove State Park

Moro Canyon

Irvine Co. Open Space Reserve

Bommer Ridge Road

Willow Canyon

Laguna Coast Wilderness Park

Cholla

Lynx

Moro Ridge Road

Emerald Canyon Road

Bommer Ridge Road

Aliso-Wood Canyon Regional Park

Rock It Trail

East Cut-Across

Moro Ridge Road

Emerald Canyon Road

Roat Road

Laguna Bowl Road

City of Laguna Beach Greenbelt

Wood Cyn. Trail

Mathis Trail

Coyote Run

Irvine Co. Open Space Reserve

Water Tank Road

Laguna Canyon Road

Alta Laguna

City of Laguna Beach

Park

Pacific Ocean

Aliso-Wood Canyon Regional Park and Laguna Beach Greenbelt

Aliso-Wood Canyon Regional Park
28241 La Paz Road
Laguna Niguel, CA 92667
(714)831-2791

PARK HOURS: 7 A.M. to sunset, daily.
Closed for three days after
rain

The Aliso-Wood Canyon Regional Park and the Laguna Beach Greenbelt form a pristine park of over 5,000 acres that is wedged between the cancer-like sprawl of Aliso Viejo and the coastal town of Laguna Beach. The hillsides and valleys give one a taste of old coastal Orange County. The park is undeveloped and fortunately slated to remain so. The aged live oaks, sycamores, meadows, unique sandstone outcrops, coastal sage and variety of wildlife make this park a priceless refuge from the developer's bulldozer.

Notwithstanding what has been saved, development has been allowed to encroach well within the otherwise natural boundaries of the canyons and hillsides. Originally part of the Rancho Niguel land grant, the surrounding area was used for cattle grazing and farming from 1842 until the early 1980s.

MOUNTAIN BIKING IN THE PARK

Aliso-Wood offers the mountain bike rider everything from smooth and level fireroad to the most terrifyingly technical singletrack. There is something for everyone here. The many sandstone rocks found along the steep canyons provide technical challenges unavailable in most areas. As a result, *always use a lot of caution on the these trails*. Accidents (and litigation) of the sort experienced at Whiting Ranch could ruin mountain biking here. Stay off trails that are beyond your experience or technical ability. Remember, if you fall down, it is 100% your fault. Accept responsibility for actions, don't try to blame someone else.

Additionally, due to the large number of hikers, *you should always slow down when visibility is restricted, a controlled stop is impossible, or if other users are present. Always slow down when passing hikers.* A warm greeting wouldn't hurt you (or access) either.

Aliso-Wood Canyon Park is closed for three days after any rain to protect trails from damage. Contact the park headquarters, at (714)831-2791, for further information or to volunteer with trail maintenance projects.

Note About Unlisted Trails: There are a large number of established trails in the Aliso-Wood and Laguna area that have been excluded from this guide. Primarily, these trails have been "closed" either to all traffic or are otherwise restricted. In some instances other access issues may remain uncertain. Please respect closures and ride only on established trail systems. In a few cases, trails that are of interest primarily to local riders or do

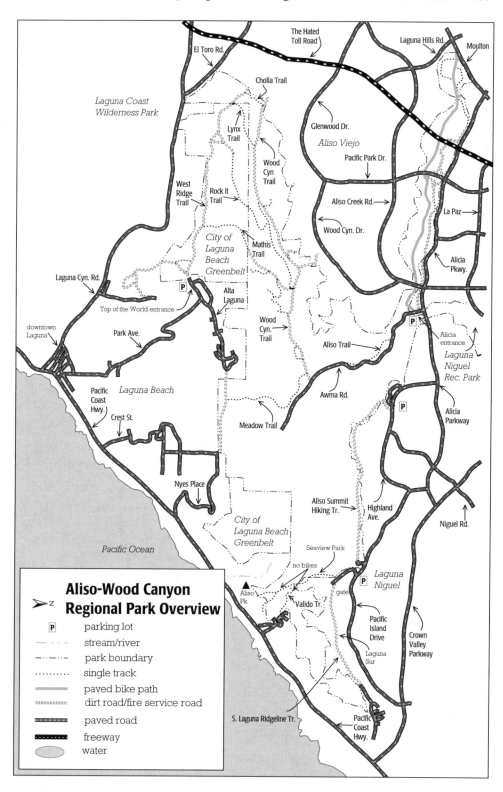

Aliso-Wood Canyon Regional Park Overview

- **P**   parking lot
- — · · ·   stream/river
- — · — · —   park boundary
- · · · · · · · ·   single track
- ▬▬▬   paved bike path
- ▨▨▨▨▨   dirt road/fire service road
- ══════   paved road
- ■■■■■   freeway
- ⬭   water

that are of interest primarily to local riders or do not otherwise connect with park trails have also been excluded.

HOW TO GET THERE

There are three primary ways to access the Aliso-Wood Canyon area. The eastern, Aliso Creek Entrance; the Alta Laguna (Top of the World) Entrance; and the seldom-used Canyon Acres Access. Access is also available from behind Aliso Viejo; this is noted in the relevant Trail Segments descriptions.

Aliso Creek Entrance

This is the entrance that will be used by most people living inland. From the 5 Freeway take Alicia Parkway south for 3.8 miles to where Alicia Parkway crosses Aliso Creek Road. Continue straight on Alicia, crossing Aliso Creek Road, and after 0.25 mile, turn right (west) on a small paved road (a park boundary sign will be seen). After a few hundred feet, you will see a parking area on your left (opposite the Mormon Church). The park entrance is straight ahead. This entrance is favored by cyclists of all kinds, including family groups, because of the mild grade and good roads.

Past the gate entrance, follow the paved road (Awma Road) left and downhill, until signs direct you to stay off the pavement and onto the dirt trail (The Aliso Trail) that parallels the road to its right. Awma Road (owned by Aliso Water Management Agency, AMWA) is private

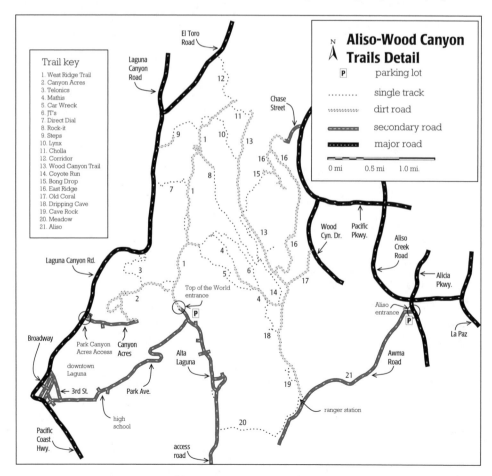

and off-limits to bike use. After 1.5 miles, turn right onto Wood Canyon Trail (a dirt road). A ranger office and information board will be found here. All riding trails described in this section can be accessed from this point.

Top of the World (Alta Laguna) Entrance

This is a far more gratifying way to enter the park, and avoids the rather uninteresting initial 1.5 miles of the Aliso Creek Entrance.

From the south, take Pacific Coast Highway north to downtown Laguna Beach, head inland on Laguna Avenue (across from the historic Hotel Laguna). After a block, Laguna Avenue becomes Park Avenue. Follow Park Avenue uphill to its end where it "T"'s into Alta Laguna Boulevard. Turn left on Alta Laguna and go 0.2 mile to where that street dead ends.

From the north, take Laguna Canyon Road to Forest Ave/Third Street. Take Third up the short, very steep hill. Above, at the stop sign turn left onto Park Avenue. Follow Park uphill to its end where it "T"'s into Alta Laguna Boulevard. Turn left on Alta Laguna and go 0.2 mile to where that street dead-ends.

The park entrance is straight ahead at the end of Alta Laguna. Parking is available in a parking area (Alta Laguna Park) on the right or on the street at the entrance.

The Top of the World Entrance is the highest spot in the park, and the fireroad that heads directly down the ridge ahead is the West Ridge Trail. The West Ridge Trail provides easy access to the top of most of the other trails in the park. Starting your journey at Top of the World means that it is a uphill grind to get back to your car.

Canyon Acres Access

Local riders often use Canyon Acres as a direct access route to Aliso-Wood Canyon. However, most riders are put off by this unrelentingly steep climb. Canyon Acres Road is located off Laguna Canyon Road about 1.0 mile inland from Pacific Coast Highway, and 2.5 miles toward the ocean from El Toro Road. Park in a small dirt parking area on the northeastern corner of Canyon Acres and Laguna Canyon Road. *Do not park on Canyon Acres or Arroyo Drive since parking is very limited and is reserved for local residents.* During the Summer Festivals, parking on Canyon Acres and adjacent streets is by permit only (your car can be ticketed and/or towed).

FEES AND FACILITIES

As of January 1, 1996, there is a charge of $2.00 per vehicle for parking (Aliso Viejo Entrance). No facilities are available.

Aliso-Wood Canyon Loop Rides

The following are a few suggested loop rides for riders who may not be familiar with the area. Obviously, there are many possible combinations of various Trail Segments (see page 116). Many of the trails which are suitable for advanced and expert riders are not included in the suggested loops. Once you have ridden the Aliso Wood Canyon area for a while, you can then incorporate some of these other trails in your rides. Variety is the spice of life.

ALISO ENTRANCE LOOPS

Because of Aliso Entrance's location, the number of loops and segments are more limited than those beginning at the Top of the World.

Aliso Entrance-Cholla Trail

ALISO-WOOD RIDE 1

Distance • 8.8 miles

Time Required • 0.75 to 2 hours

Route Rating • 4

Grunt Factor • 1+

Technical Rating • 1

Elevation • Start 160 ft.

Low point 95 ft.

High point 475 ft.

Map • Aliso Entrance-Cholla Trail, page 119

THIS UP-AND-BACK RIDE INVOLVES maintained trails and well-graded dirt roads on nearly level grade, and is well suited for a family-type outing. The initial section of the ride (Aliso Trail) parallels a paved road and is somewhat uninspiring. However, the ride up the increasingly beautiful Wood Canyon Trail provides wonderful scenery that makes you feel you have stepped back in time to early California days. The final 0.5 mile involves gentle uphill.

THE RIDE

Begin at the Aliso Creek Entrance (see directions page 116). Ride the Aliso Trail for 1.5 miles of slight downhill to the ranger buildings at the start of the Wood Canyon Trail. Be sure to stay off the private paved road.

As you ride the 2.9 miles up Wood Canyon, open meadows give way to sycamore and oak groves. Farther along, a stream crossing (seasonal) then slight uphill riding takes you to open chaparral. The beginning of the Cholla Trail on your left marks your turnaround point. From here, retrace your route back to your car.

VARIATION

For more experienced riders. Take the Coyote Run Trail singletrack (See Trail Segment 14, page 130) on your way back. From the turnaround point, ride 0.8 mile down Wood Canyon Trail, turn right at the sign, cross the stream and follow this singletrack 1.1 miles to its end at the Mathis Trail. At this point, turn left, cross the stream, then turn right to rejoin Wood Canyon Trail.

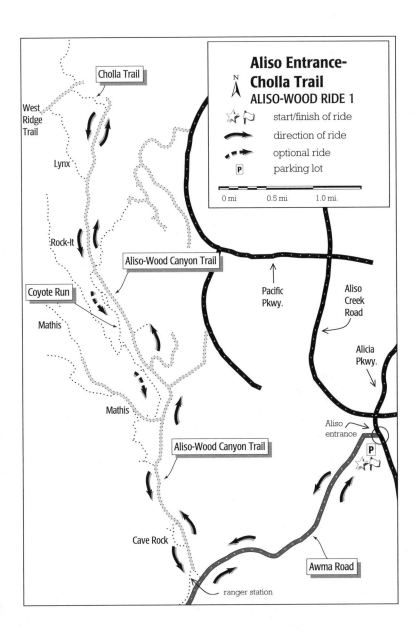

**Aliso Entrance-
Cholla Trail**
ALISO-WOOD RIDE 1

N

⭐ 🚩   start/finish of ride

➡   direction of ride

⇢   optional ride

P   parking lot

0 mi   0.5 mi   1.0 mi.

Cholla Trail

West Ridge Trail

Lynx

Rock-It

Aliso-Wood Canyon Trail

Coyote Run

Mathis

Pacific Pkwy.

Aliso Creek Road

Alicia Pkwy.

Mathis

Aliso-Wood Canyon Trail

Aliso entrance

P

Cave Rock

Awma Road

ranger station

Cholla– Rock-It Loop

ALISO-WOOD RIDE 2

Distance • 10.2 mile loop

Time Required • 1.0 to 2.0 hours

Route Rating • 6

Grunt Factor • 3

Technical Rating • 3/4

Elevation • Start 160 ft.

Low point 95 ft.

High point 780 ft.

Map • Cholla–Rock-It Loop, page 121

THIS CLASSIC LOOP COMBINES EASY fireroad with more technical singletrack riding. An excellent tour for intermediate riders containing some very fun downhill singletrack.

THE RIDE

Begin at the Aliso Creek Entrance (see directions page 116). Ride the Aliso Trail for 1.5 miles of slight downhill to the ranger buildings at the start of the Wood Canyon Trail. Be sure to stay off the private paved road. Ride nearly 2.9 miles up Wood Canyon, a refreshing remnant of old Orange County. After a short uphill, the road widens and the beginning of the Cholla Trail will seen on your left (**4.4 mile mark**). Take this a little more than 0.3 mile to where it joins the lower end of the West Ridge Trail (**4.7+ mile mark**). Turn left here. Continue up the fireroad, pass a gate, then continue up and down the ridge for about 0.8 mile where a road will be seen heading down and left (**5.5 mile mark**). This is the beginning of Rock-It Trail; turn left here.

Photo: Larry Kuechlin

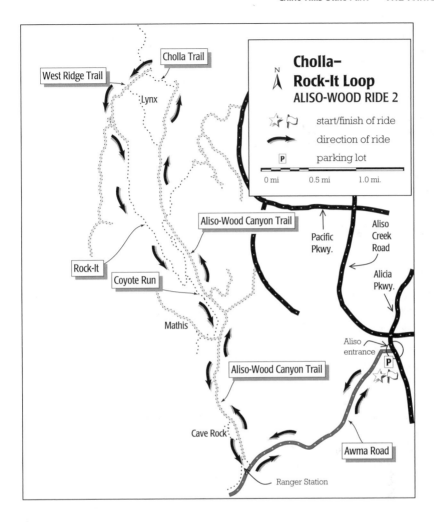

Follow Rock-It down a ridgeline, first on fireroad then singletrack. As you descend you will discover how the trail got its name. Near the bottom, the trail heads down left off the ridge into a grassy area, stay left until you reach the bottom (**6.8 mile mark**). Here Rock-It intersects Coyote Run Trail. Where the trail forks, head right. Follow the Coyote Run Trail until you are dumped off at the bottom of the Mathis Trail (7.6 miles). Turn left, cross the stream, and immediately meet up with the Wood Canyon Trail again. Turn right on Wood Canyon Trail and retrace the first part of your ride back to your car.

TOP OF THE WORLD ENTRANCE LOOP RIDES

Due to the layout of the park and canyons, the Top of the World Entrance provides a much better variety of loop rides than the Aliso Creek Entrance. All the Top of the World rides start at over 1000 feet and immediately proceed downhill. This means that to return to your starting point you must regain that elevation.

Mathis-Cholla Loop

ALISO-WOOD RIDE 3

Distance • 6.2 mile loop

Time Required • 1.0 to 1.5 hours

Route Rating • 6

Grunt Factor • 4

Technical Rating • 3

Elevation • Start 1000 ft.

Low point 195 ft.

Finish 1000 ft.

Map • Mathis-Cholla Loop, page 123

THIS IS A FUN, BUT NOT TOO TECHNICAL loop, with entertaining downhill and beautiful scenery. Although this ride is fairly short, intermediate riders will still find it challenging. A great introduction to the Aliso Wood Canyon area.

THE RIDE

Begin at the Top of the World Entrance (see page 117). Proceed down the West Ridge trail for 0.5+ mile to where the West Ridge Trail is nearly level. Where the West Ridge Trail turns left, take the Mathis Trail pretty much straight ahead. The upper section of Mathis is a combination of deteriorated fireroad and singletrack; several short rocky sections add spice. After passing through the park gate, Mathis becomes a graded road (nevertheless steep in places). At the bottom of the hill, continue on level terrain to the **1.8+ mile mark**, where a quick left turn (just before a major creek crossing) puts you on the Coyote Run Trail singletrack.

After an initial very short, steep section, Coyote Run Trail becomes a classic rolling singletrack that continues for 1.1 miles in an northerly direction, paralleling the upper section of the Wood Canyon Trail. At its end (2.9+ mile mark), Coyote Run crosses Wood Canyon Creek and joins the Wood Canyon Trail fireroad. Turn left onto Wood Canyon Trail. Continue for about 0.7 mile (3.6+ mile mark) where the road widens and the beginning of the Cholla Trail will seen on your left. Take the Cholla Trail a little more than 0.3 mile to where it joins the lower end of the West Ridge Trail. Turn left here. Continue uphill on the West Ridge Trail about 2.2+ miles to your starting point.

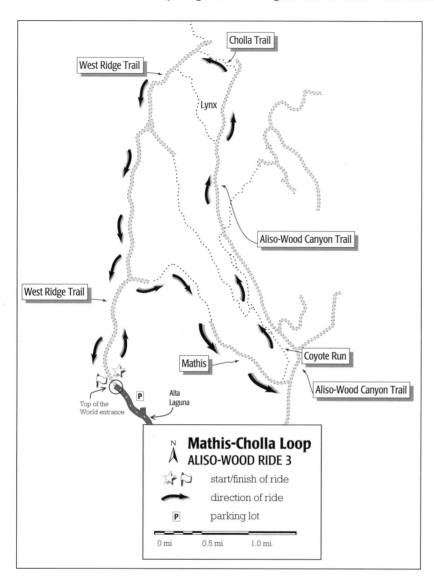

Cholla Trail

West Ridge Trail

Lynx

Aliso-Wood Canyon Trail

West Ridge Trail

Mathis

Coyote Run

Aliso-Wood Canyon Trail

P

Alta
Laguna

Top of the
World entrance

N

Mathis-Cholla Loop
ALISO-WOOD RIDE 3

☆ ⌐   start/finish of ride

━━►   direction of ride

P   parking lot

0 mi   0.5 mi   1.0 mi.

Grand Tour Loop

ALISO-WOOD RIDE 4

Distance • 7.9 mile loop

Time Required • 1+ to 2 hours

Route Rating • 7

Grunt Factor • 5

Technical Rating • 4

Map • Grand Tour Loop, below

THIS RIDE MAXIMIZES THE NUMBER OF trails you get to ride with little repetition. Two downhills and two uphills are involved and you get to ride some of the best and most popular trails in one ride. Great for intermediate riders who want a little more riding fun.

THE RIDE

Begin at the Top of the World Entrance (see page 117). Proceed down the West Ridge trail for approximately 2.0 miles; you will see a park gate on your left. Head more or less straight ahead to the beginning of the Lynx Trail and follow this enjoyable singletrack downhill for 0.6 mile to where it ends at the Wood Canyon Trail (2.6 miles). Turn left here. Head up Wood Canyon Trail for about 0.2 mile and a short uphill. The

road widens, and the beginning of the Cholla Trail will seen on your left (**2.8 mile mark**). Take the Cholla Trail a little more than 0.3 mile to where it joins the lower end of the West Ridge Trail (**3.2 mile mark**). Turn left here. Continue up the fireroad and pass through a gate (the same one you saw near the beginning of Lynx).

A very short distance past the gate, take the singletrack heading up and right. It soon splits. Take the right-hand fork of this short diversion, which after about 0.2 mile dumps you out again on the West Ridge Trail. Continue on the West Ridge Trail for another 0.3 mile where a road will be seen heading down and left (just past a watertank on your right). This is the beginning of Rock-It Trail; turn left here (3.9 miles).

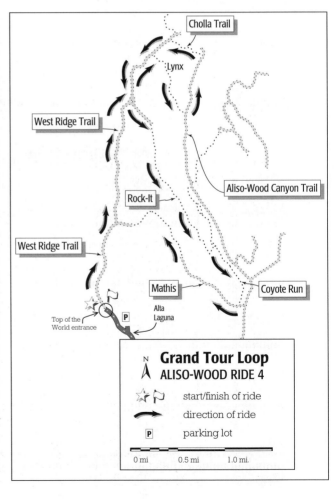

Follow Rock-It down a ridgeline, first on fireroad, then singletrack. As you descend, the trail gets more eroded, and part of the trail descends a sandstone ridge. Near the bottom, the trail heads down left off the ridge into a grassy area, stay left until you reach the bottom (**5.2 mile mark**). Here Rock-It intersects Coyote Run Trail. Where the trail forks, head right along Coyote Run Trail 0.8 mile until you are dumped off at the bottom of the Mathis Trail (6.0 miles).

Turn right and head up Mathis 1.3 miles to the juncture with the West Ridge trail (7.3 miles). Mathis is moderately steep (mostly in the first 0.75 mile) with some moderately technical sections to make it interesting. At the West Ridge trail, turn left and head almost 0.6 mile uphill to your starting point.

Photo: Keith Young

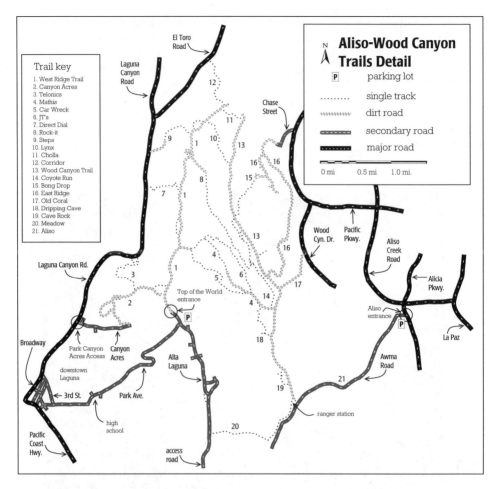

Trail Segments

The following is a description of all of the various trails in the park. Experienced riders can use this information to devise their own loop rides.

Westridge Trail

ALISO-WOOD SEGMENT 1

Distance • 2.2+ miles
Route Rating • 2/3
Grunt Factor • 4 (uphill)
Technical Rating • 1
Downhill Rating • 3
Elevation • High point 1000 feet
              705 ft. at Cholla Trail

THIS FIREROAD RUNS NORTHEAST FROM the Top of the World Entrance to the top of the Cholla Trail. Just past the Cholla Trail is a park gate. Beyond are the upper reaches of Wood Canyon which have been destroyed by development. This fireroad has rolling up and down, with a few parallel single tracks (see map), and is used as a jumping off and/or connecting route for most of the other trails.

Canyon Acres

ALISO-WOOD SEGMENT 2

Distance • 1.2 miles
Route Rating • 3
Grunt Factor • 8
Technical Rating • 2
Downhill Rating • 5
Elevation • Low point 75 ft.
High point 950 ft.

THE QUINTESSENTIAL UPHILL GRUNT IN Orange County. Absolutely guaranteed to get anyone's heart-rate monitor into the triple digits. This fireroad begins at end of Canyon Acres Road and winds its way up to a point just below Top of The World Entrance. Near the top, a nice singletrack off left avoids the final bit of fireroad. See Canyon Acres Entrance information on page 117.

Telonics

ALISO-WOOD SEGMENT 3

Distance • 1.0 mile
Route Rating • 8
Technical Rating • 6
Downhill Rating • 9
Elevation • 810 ft. High Point
130 ft. at Laguna Canyon Road

ARGUABLY THE BEST DOWNHILL JAUNT IN the Canyon; it is technical and rocky in places. Definitely not an uphill ride. Named for Berkeley/Telonic located at the trail's terminus near Big Bend on Laguna Canyon Road. The start is located 0.3+ mile down the Canyon Acres fireroad, just before Canyon Acres' long straight downhill section; hang a right onto this singletrack. Proceed down the ridge, over and down the sandstone rocks, then head down and right on steep terrain.

Mathis

ALISO-WOOD SEGMENT 4

Distance • 1.3 miles
Route Rating • 4
Grunt Factor • 5 (uphill)
Technical Rating • 3+
Downhill Rating • 7
Elevation • Low point 195 ft.
High point 845 ft.

THIS POPULAR FIREROAD WITH SEMI-singletrack on the upper section is commonly ridden in both directions. Mathis Trail connects the upper portion of the West Ridge Trail with Wood Canyon Trail. Only the Cholla Trail provides an easier way up to the West Ridge Trail and Top of the World. From the Top of the World Entrance, ride about 0.5+ mile down the West Ridge Trail. Where the West Ridge Trail turns left, the Mathis Trail heads straight ahead. At the bottom, Mathis becomes a graded road that connects with the Wood Canyon Trail (after the stream crossing) or the Coyote Run Trail (just before the stream crossing). From Wood Canyon Trail, Mathis is the left-hand turn 1.1 miles from the Ranger Station.

Car Wreck (aka Oak Grove Trail)

ALISO-WOOD SEGMENT 5

Distance • 0.8 mile
Route Rating • 8
Technical Rating • 7+
Downhill Rating • 7
Elevation • Low point 220 ft.
High point 800 ft.

THIS SINGLETRACK BEGINS A FEW hundred yards down Mathis and heads down and right. Although the first section is fairly easy, farther down it has some quite technical and steep sections. A little beyond the 0.4 mile point the trail forks. The easier-looking left fork leads to a wrecked car under a tree (you have to walk around the tree to rejoin the trail). The right fork is very technical and after a short distance is joined by the left fork. Below the going is easy and beautiful, but poison oak is very plentiful. Join Mathis at the bottom of the hill.

Direct Dial

ALISO-WOOD SEGMENT 7

Distance • 0.3 mile
Route Rating • 6
Grunt Factor • 5
Technical Rating • 10
Downhill Rating • 6/7
Elevation • Low point 180 ft.
750 ft. high point

A STEEP, DEMANDING SINGLETRACK descent that heads down to Laguna Canyon Road from West Ridge Trail. This very technical trail starts at a point 1.0 mile down the West Ridge Trail from Top of the World Parking area and features several exciting drop-offs. The trail starts as a small footpath perpendicular to the fireroad, then heads right, along the hillside. After some easy switchbacks, things get increasingly interesting as the trail takes a fairly direct route down the rocky ridgeline. The last section can get very rutted, before it terminates at the city "Dog" Park along Laguna Canyon Road.

Rock-It Trail

ALISO-WOOD SEGMENT 8

Distance • 1.3 miles
Route Rating • 7
Grunt Factor • 5
Technical Rating • 4
Downhill Rating • 8
Elevation • Low point 250 ft.
High point 780 ft.

A LONG, SINGLETRACK RIDGELINE THAT gets fairly bumpy, with a short, technical section. Is commonly ridden both directions. The top of this trail is located about 1.5+ miles down the West Ridge Trail from the Top of the World Entrance, just before a watertank. The bottom of the trail is located off of the Coyote Run Trail, 0.8 mile up from Mathis or 0.3 mile down from the Wood Canyon Trail junction.

Stair Steps

ALISO-WOOD SEGMENT 9

Distance • 0.7 mile
Route Rating • 8
Technical Rating • 7
Downhill Rating • 8
Elevation • High point 815 ft.
210 ft. at Laguna Canyon Road

THIS TRAIL BEGINS NEAR THE WATER TANK located above and just west of the West Ridge Trail, about 1.7+ miles from the Top of the World Entrance (about 0.2 mile past the first Rock-It Trail turnoff). The trail begins north of the watertank. Take a trail/road spur west a short distance. The first singletrack on your right is the main ridge route. A second singletrack heads left of the ridge and joins the previous trail about 0.25 mile farther down. The initial section can be quite rutted.

Follow the ridge down increasingly rocky and action-packed riding until it eventually leads to a paved road at another water tank. This road (Phillips Road) leads a short distance down to Laguna Canyon Road.

Lynx Trail

ALISO-WOOD SEGMENT 10

Distance • 0.6 mile
Route Rating • 6
Grunt Factor • 4
Technical Rating • 3
Downhill Rating • 6
Elevation • Low point 360 ft.
High point 735 ft.

THIS NICE SINGLETRACK IS PRONE TO bad ruts after heavy rains. When rutted, it can be particularly challenging if traveled in the uphill direction. This trail is commonly ridden in both directions. The upper terminus of the trail is located down the West Ridge Trail approximately 2.0 miles from the Top of the World Entrance, just before a gate. The trail heads down a ridge on your right. From the Ranger Station, the trail begins on your left some 2.7 miles up the Wood Canyon Trail. This is about 0.5 mile up Wood Canyon Trail past the juncture with the Coyote Run Trail.

Cholla Trail

ALISO-WOOD SEGMENT 11

Distance • 0.35 mile
Route Rating • 5
Grunt Factor • 3-4
Technical Rating • 2
Elevation • Low point 450 ft.
High point 705 ft.

A SHORT, NICELY GROOMED SINGLE-track that provides easy access from the end of Wood Canyon Trail to the bottom of the West Ridge Trail fireroad. The trail is by far the easiest way to get from Wood Canyon to the West Ridge. Avoid using this as a downhill due to the frequent uphill traffic. The trail is found on your left about 2.9 miles up the Wood Canyon Trail from the Ranger Station (0.2 mile past Lynx Trail). The top of the trail is located about 2.2+ miles down the West Ridge from the Top of the World Entrance.

Corridor

ALISO-WOOD SEGMENT 12

Distance • 0.5 mile
Route Rating • 5
Technical Rating • 5+
Downhill Rating • 6+
Elevation • High point 700 ft.
310 ft. at El Toro Road

THIS SINGLETRACK STARTS JUST NORTH of the park gate near the juncture of the West Ridge Trail and Cholla Trail. This trail is subject to closure, so heed any signage to this effect. *Also, this trail stays wet for many days after any rain, let it dry completely before considering using it.* Head out the park gate, turn left (north) staying along the ridge for about 75 yards, then turn left again. Proceed down the narrow winding path that is somewhat technical in the middle section. It eventually drops you off at El Toro Road next to the hated tollroad.

Wood Canyon Trail

ALISO-WOOD SEGMENT 13

Distance • 2.9+ miles
Route Rating • 4+
Grunt Factor • 1+
Technical Rating • 1
Elevation • 95 ft. Low point
475 ft. at top

THIS IS THE DIRT FIREROAD THAT RUNS the length of Wood Canyon. It begins at the ranger station located 1.5 miles from the Aliso Entrance and continues through increasingly scenic terrain to the park gate just past the beginning of the Cholla Trail. An easy, almost flat jaunt, with a few uphills near the end, suitable for any bike. It is used to connect other more technical segments.

Coyote Run Trail

ALISO-WOOD SEGMENT 14

Distance • 1.1 miles
Route Rating • 7
Grunt Factor • 1
Technical Rating • 2
Elevation • 195 ft. at Mathis
290 ft. at Wood Canyon

A CLASSIC ROLLING SINGLETRACK THAT parallels the upper section of the Wood Canyon Trail fireroad. The lower portion is part of a "Nature Loop" that starts off Mathis, just west of the stream crossing. The upper terminus is located about 2.2 miles up Wood Canyon Trail from the ranger station. The Coyote Run Trail can be used to connect Rock-It Trail and other segments, or as a more pleasant variant to the Wood Canyon Trail fireroad. (Note: The upper section of the "Nature Loop" is off-limits to bike traffic).

Bong Drop

ALISO-WOOD SEGMENT 15

Distance • 0.5 mile
Route Rating • 7
Technical Rating • 6 (Final drop-off cannot be ridden.)
Downhill Rating • 7/8
Elevation • Low point 290 ft.
High point 800 ft.

STARTS OFF BELOW MOULTON PEAK—the top of the hill on the east rim of the park—below a water storage tank. This challenging route winds down killer singletrack with occasional technical sections. There is a final large sandstone drop-off that you should not even consider riding. You end your descent on Wood Canyon Trail only a hundred feet or so upcanyon from the Coyote Run junction. To access this trail, turn up Chase Street off Pacific Park and work your way through new development to a dirt road up the hill to the water tank. Old Corral or East Ridge are ways of getting to surface streets from Wood Canyon.

Eastridge Fireroad

ALISO-WOOD SEGMENT 16

Distance • 0.5 mile
Route Rating • 1
Grunt Factor • 3+
Technical Rating • 1/2

THIS TRAIL STARTS 0.1+ MILE UP CANYON from the Old Coral turn-off (about 1.5+ mile up Wood Canyon Trail). The dual-track beginning may be hard to find, it is often obscured by deep grass. Look for tracks that angle slightly off right. After about 0.2 mile you will encounter a park gate on the hill above; this is easily seen from below. Farther on, your on private land with various fireroads that alternatively head up the ridge or head north along the hillsides. Some may be in pretty bad shape. Heading up the ridge will give access to more developmental blight, but may be the easiest legal way to access Bong Drop.

Old Corral Trail

ALISO-WOOD SEGMENT 17

Distance • 0.5 mile
Route Rating • 0
Grunt Factor • 3+
Technical Rating • 1

THIS ROAD IS LOCATED ABOUT 1.4 MILES up Wood Canyon Trail from the ranger station (about 0.3 mile past the Mathis Trail turn-off), and about 1.5 miles down the Wood Canyon Trail from the Cholla Trail junction. It is on the east side of the canyon and proceeds for 0.1 mile through a meadow to the park gate. Beyond the gate, continue straight, then bear left up a steep incline, eventually reaching the paved road of Wood Canyon Drive. Probably only of interest to residents of Aliso Viejo.

Dripping Cave

ALISO-WOOD SEGMENT 18

Distance • 2.0 miles
Route Rating • 5+
Technical Rating • 4

DRIPPING CAVE TRAIL PROVIDES A FUN singletrack link from lower Wood Canyon Trail to lower Mathis Trail. From Wood Canyon Trail, the Dripping Cave Trail proceeds 0.2 mile on dual track, then singletrack to a sandstone overhang/cave believed to have been used by Indians, cowboys and rustlers who corralled livestock here. From near the "cave," the singletrack traverses along the hillside then drops back into the canyon floor to meet Mathis Trail near its bottom.

Cave Rock Trail

ALISO-WOOD SEGMENT 19

Distance • 0.2 mile
Route Rating • 2
Technical Rating • 3/4

THIS SHORT DIVERSION OFF THE WOOD Canyon Trail climbs to, over, down and/or around several slabby sandstone rocks. The lower end of this short trail is located 0.2 mile from the ranger station, the upper end, at about 0.4 mile.

Meadow Trail

ALISO-WOOD SEGMENT 20

Distance • 1.2 miles
Route Rating • 4
Grunt Factor • 10
Technical Rating • 2
Downhill Rating • 7+
Elevation • 95 ft at Ranger Station
High point 810 ft.

THIS TRAIL IS BEST LEFT AS A DOWNHILL run from Top of the World area to Park Headquarters. It is a *very serious* grunt uphill. From Top of the World Entrance, ride south along Alta Laguna for 0.8+ mile to its southerly point. Do not take the gated paved road heading south, rather, about 100+ feet prior to reaching that road, an open lot with short roped-off area along the road frontage, will be seen on your right. Where this ends, at a short wall on the adjacent property, a singletrack takes you about 0.1 mile to the paved fireroad that continues south from here. Ride along the fireroad 0.3+ mile. The Meadow Trail begins on your left and is marked. To head uphill, take the singletrack southwest from the Ranger Station for 0.5 mile paralleling the paved road, then head right and up the relentless hill. The last 0.6 mile will ensure cardiac overload.

Aliso Trail

ALISO-WOOD SEGMENT 21

Distance • 1.4+ miles
Route Rating • 2
Grunt Factor • 0
Technical Rating • 0
Elevation • 160 ft. at Park Entrance
           95 ft. at Ranger Station

THIS IS THE DIRT TRAIL THAT PARALLELS the paved Awma Road running from the Aliso Entrance to the ranger station at the beginning of Wood Canyon Trail. A good outing for the little ones, it is the access route to more challenging rides deeper in the park.

Aliso Creek Trail

ALISO-WOOD SEGMENT 22

Distance • 2.5 to 2.9 miles depending on route taken
Route Rating • 1
Grunt Factor • 0 to 1
Technical Rating • 0 to 1+
Elevation • 250 ft. at Moulton Parkway
           160 ft. at Alicia Entrance

A BIKE PATH (PAVED) AND A DIRT TRAIL run the length on the eastern "arm" of Aliso-Wood Canyon Park between Aliso Entrance and Moulton Parkway. The bike path generally stays on the western side of Aliso Creek and the dirt path on the eastern side. Tollroad construction has blocked part of the dirt trail.

Pectin Loop Trail

ALISO-WOOD SEGMENT 23

Distance • 0.4 mile
Route Rating • 2
Grunt Factor • 0
Technical Rating • 1+

A VERY SHORT SINGLETRACK THAT LOOPS around a hill at the northern apex of the eastern arm of the park, just west of Moulton Parkway. The beginning of the trail is located where the Moulton access to the paved bike path joins. It is signed. It loops around the base of the hill, rejoining the paved bike path farther south. Other informal singletracks wind around the hill and adjacent bluffs.

Aliso Summit Trail

ALISO-WOOD SEGMENT 24

Distance • 2.2 miles
Route Rating • 1
Grunt Factor • 2
Technical Rating • 0+
Elevation • 560 ft. at Ridgeview Park
           850 ft. at Pacific Park

THE TRAIL RUNS ALONG THE EASTERN ridge of the Aliso Creek drainage, on the Laguna Niguel side of the park. It is a broad, even surface that runs behind the many residential developments that line the hillside. Listed for completeness, rather than recommended. A good place for absolute beginners to taste some dirt.

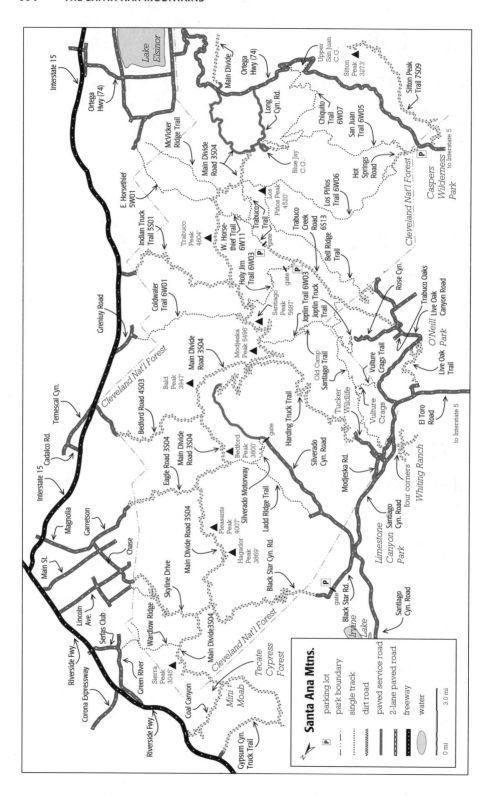

II. THE SANTA ANA MOUNTAINS

The Santa Ana Mountains are an amazingly diverse and wild place. The biological and geological wonders of the Santa Anas are yours to be discovered as you explore the trails that crisscross this mountain range. Orange County residents are privileged to have this resource in our backyard. It is also fortunate that much of this landscape has been preserved for all to visit and enjoy. Most of the "high country" sections of the Santa Ana Mountains are within the confines of the Cleveland National Forest, however, development continues to increase along the edges of this 135,000 acres of federal land, threatening wildlife and open space alike. Some of this land is slated to be set aside in preserves and parks, but the ultimate fate of much of the foothills and canyons remains open.

Mountain bikers should thank the U.S. Forest Service for its policy permitting multiple use of trails and fireroads. This translates into a tremendous variety of mountain biking opportunities throughout the range. By showing respect to the environment and other trail users we can preserve this privilege. The ultimate preservation of the foothills and canyons outside the bounds of the National Forest will not only prevent destruction of wild habitat and incredible scenery, but will open an immense area for potential mountain bike use. The possibilities for extended off-road travel throughout this region are enormous.

In addition to the diversity of natural resources, the Santa Ana Mountains have served as the backdrop for historical events that are part of Orange County's heritage. In the introductory sections of some of the following chapters we have tried to include bits of historically interesting information. Treat these peaks, trails and valleys with respect. Don't leave behind anything but tire tracks and pick up any trash you might encounter.

Black Star Canyon

Black Star Canyon is one of several canyons in the Santa Ana Mountains that was renamed in the 1870s during the few frenzied "mining years." The original Spanish name for this beautiful and remote canyon was Cañon de los Indios – the Canyon of the Indians. The flats near

Hidden Ranch were occupied by native americans for countless years and in 1831 was the site of a bloody confrontation between American trappers and Indian horse thieves.

A group of American trappers came to Los Angeles in 1831 via New Mexico. Americans were not generally welcome in Los Angeles at the time, and in an effort to curry favor with the Spanish, the trappers agreed to help hunt down a group of Indians who were stealing horses. The trappers followed a trail of stolen horses across the Santa Ana river, then east through present day Villa Park, and up Santiago canyon. The trail then headed up Cañon de los Indios.

The trail took the trappers up the steep mountainsides and eventually a small grassy valley was reached. Indians were seen feasting on horseflesh at a campsite in the lower end of what is known today as Hidden Valley. The Indians who were not killed by the rifles of the trappers fled into the brush. The horses were returned to their owners by the trappers. Today the valley is the site of Hidden Ranch and riding off the well-graded Black Star Canyon Road is prohibited. The only signs of Indian habitation remaining are a few grinder holes in some boulders.

In 1879, the Black Star Coal Mining Company began a search for coal deposits in Cañon de los Indios. Miners worked the deposits for several years, but mining activity ceased when the coal was depleted in the early 1880s. Since that time, the canyon has been known as Black Star Canyon. The canyon has also seen placer gold mining activity. One of the Santa Ana Mountains higher waterfalls is to be found in the lower portion of the canyon. However, this 50-foot waterfall is not accessible by bicycle.

Black Star to Main Divide (Beek's Place)

SANTA ANA MTNS. RIDE 1

Distance • 15.7+ miles round trip

(22.2 miles, optional ride to Sierra Peak)

Time Required • 1.5 to 3+ hours

Route Rating • 6

Grunt Factor • 5

Technical Rating • 1+

Elevation • Bottom 970 ft.

Top 2815 ft.

Topos • *Black Star Canyon;* ride map, page 137

ALTHOUGH THIS IS A UP-AND-BACK RIDE, it is worthy of description as a fine ride on its own. This is a wonderful trip in the fall through spring, when temperatures are milder. In the spring the hills are green, wildflowers sprout forth and the views are magnificent. As an option, you can continue north on Main Divide to Sierra Peak, the highest point on the north end of the Santa Ana Mountains.

CAR DIRECTIONS

From North Orange County:
From the 55 Freeway in the city of Orange, take Chapman Avenue east to the intersection with Jamboree. Proceed straight ahead; at this point Chapman becomes Santiago Canyon Road. Drive 6.7 miles on Santiago Canyon Road to the junction with Silverado Canyon Road. Turn left here. Proceed a few hundred yards on Silverado Canyon Road, then make a left turn onto Black Star Canyon Road. Drive to the gate and park off the roadway.

From Irvine Area:

From the 5 Freeway, take Jamboree Blvd east to the intersection of Chapman/Santiago Canyon Road. Turn right here. Proceed another 6.7 miles on Santiago Canyon Road to the junction with Silverado Canyon Road. Turn left here. Proceed a few hundred yards on Silverado Canyon Road, then make a left turn onto Black Star Canyon Road. Drive to the gate and park off the roadway.

From South Orange County:

From the 5 Freeway take El Toro Road eastward for approximately 13.6 miles to the junction with Silverado Canyon Road. Turn right here. Proceed a few hundred yards on Silverado Canyon Road, then make a left turn onto Black Star Canyon Road. Drive to the gate and park off the roadway. Note: El Toro changes its name to Santiago Canyon Road after 7.6 miles.

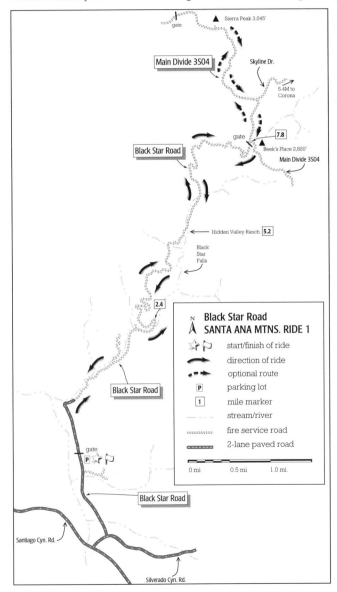

THE RIDE

Park your car outside the metal gate (be sure to park off the road), your ride begins here. Beyond the metal gate proceed on alternatively paved and dirt road of easy uphill in the shaded canyon. At the **2.3 mile point**, take the right fork in the road. Some private residences will be passed, and at about the **2.4+ mile point** the road will begin to quickly gain elevation up a series of steep switchbacks. After gaining elevation to just over 2,000 feet, the road begins to drop slightly down into a valley where the Hidden Valley Ranch is located. Although a sign proclaims "Private Property," use of the road is legal (don't stray off). At this point, rock formations can be seen in the canyon on your right (south). These mark the top of the Black Star Canyon Waterfall, one of the highest in the Santa Anas.

At **5.2 miles** you pass Hidden Ranch in the heart of this high and grassy valley. Cows may be found grazing adjacent to and on the road. Please ride carefully so as not spook these animals. Farther on, the road again steepens and heads up more switchbacks until the junction with Main Divide Road is reached at **7.8+ miles**. The buildings located just to the south are known as Beek's Place. Retrace your ride back to your car.

OPTIONAL RIDE TO SIERRA PEAK: From Beek's Place, turn left (north) on Main Divide (3S04) and continue for about 3.0 miles to Sierra Peak. Retrace your ride to Beek's Place, then down Black Star Road to your starting point.

Black Star Canyon to Silverado Motorway

SANTA ANA MTNS. RIDE 2

Distance • 26.0 miles

19.3 miles with car shuttle

Time Required • 2.5 to 4+ hours

Route Rating • 7

Grunt Factor • 7

Technical Rating • 3

Elevation • Start 970 ft.

High point 3810 ft.

Finish 970 ft.

Topos • *Corona South, Santiago Peak;* ride map, page 139

THIS LOOP RIDE COMBINES GREAT scenery, some stout uphill grinds and a great singletrack downhill finish. This ride is an easier (and more fun) option than riding all the way to Maple Springs Road and down into Silverado (which adds another 1,000 feet in elevation gain and 10 miles to the ride). Like many rides in the Santa Anas, save this one for those cooler days; it can get genuinely hot in the summer. Alternatively, a very early start (e.g. 6:00 A.M.) will keep most of the uphill in the shade and pleasant even on a hot summer day.

CAR DIRECTIONS

Park your car at the gate at Black Star Canyon Road. See previous ride for directions.

THE RIDE

Park your car outside the metal gate (be sure to park off the road), your ride begins here. Beyond the metal gate proceed on alternatively paved and dirt road of easy uphill. After **2.4 miles**, some private residences will be passed, and just past this point the road will begin to quickly gain elevation up a series of steep switchbacks. Above, the road drops slightly down into a valley. Although a sign proclaims "Private Property", use of the road is legal (don't stray off).

At **5.2 miles**, you pass Hidden Ranch. Cows may be found grazing adjacent to and on the road. Please ride carefully so as not spook these animals. Farther on, the road again steepens and heads up more switchbacks until the junction with Main Divide Road is reached at **7.8+ miles**. Turn right here. You are now heading southeast on the North Main Divide.

Now you begin to climb in earnest. Over the next 2.4 miles, you gain nearly 1,000 feet, which is made harder by some elevation drops along the way (**10.4 mile mark**). From here the road drops, then levels a bit, passing on the north side of Pleasants Peak. Stay left

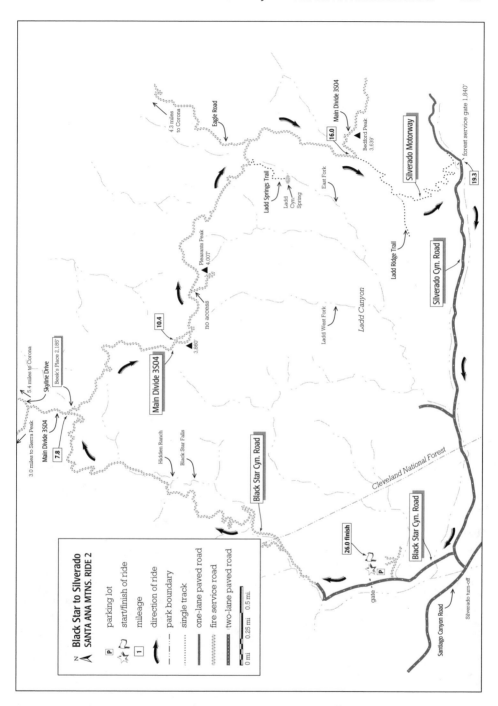

Black Star to Silverado
SANTA ANA MTNS. RIDE 2

- **P**   parking lot
- ⭐   start/finish of ride
- **1**   mileage
- ➤   direction of ride
- — · · —   park boundary
- · · · · ·   single track
- ——   one-lane paved road
- ≈≈≈   fire service road
- ▬▬   two-lane paved road

0 mi   0.25 mi   0.5 mi

3.0 miles to Sierra Peak

5.4 miles to Corona

Skyline Drive

Beek's Place 2,185'

Main Divide 3S04

7.8

Main Divide 3S04

10.4

3,860'

Pleasants Peak 4,007'

no access

Hidden Ranch

Black Star Falls

4.3 miles to Corona

Eagle Road

Ladd Springs Trail

Ladd Cyn. Spring

East Fork

Main Divide 3S04

16.0

Bedford Peak 3,639'

Silverado Motorway

Ladd West Fork

Ladd Canyon

Ladd Ridge Trail

forest service gate 1,840'

19.3

Silverado Cyn. Road

Cleveland National Forest

Black Star Cyn. Road

Black Star Cyn. Road

26.0 finish

gate

Santiago Canyon Road

Silverado turn-off

at the junction with the Pleasant Peak service road. The next five miles are both beautiful and fun rolling fireroad along the ridgeline with incredible scenery. A last uphill leads toward Bedford Peak.

Eventually, at the **16.0 mile mark**, The Main Divide intersects the Silverado Motorway. The Silverado Motorway heads off to the right. There are no signs marking this trail. The trailhead is located were the Main Divide levels a bit and makes a fairly sharp left-hand turn uphill. At the apex of this turn, on your right, a firebreak will be seen. Large, wood barriers block the firebreak. Opposite this point you will note a small sign which states "N. Main 3.S.04."

Take a right turn, heading around the left side of the wood barrier, and proceed slightly uphill along a trail. This excellent trail is 3.2 miles long and quickly becomes singletrack running along the ridgeline. Follow the ridgeline for nearly a mile, until the trail heads down and left (continuing along the ridgeline is the Ladd Canyon singletrack). From here the trail switchbacks to a point 0.1 mile above the Silverado/Maple Springs gate-trailhead. Note: The very bottom of this trail is subject to rain damage.

If you are very lazy, you parked a second car at the Maple Springs gate and your ride is over (19.3 miles). Most riders will save a lot of hassle, gas and time, and just continue down Silverado Canyon Road. The downhill grade makes the return to the car a fun 15 minute excursion. Make sure you mind the 25 mile an hour speed limit! At Black Star Canyon Road, turn right and continue back to your car (26.0 miles).

Photo: Randy Vogel

Skyline Drive Area

Just on the east side of the Orange County border, there is a Santa Ana Mountain riding area unknown to most Orange County riders. The trails of this area center around Skyline Drive, a fireroad that ascends from the city of Corona to Main Divide Road. Skyline Drive also provides easy access to Sierra Peak and the top of Black Star Canyon Road. With some trail maintenance, the opportunities for quality riding could be extensive. Currently however, neglect has allowed several trails to become unpleasant riding prospects. For this reason, we have only described two rides. We have, however, roughly described other routes worthy of further attention.

HOW TO GET THERE

From Orange County, take the Riverside Freeway (91) east. Take the Lincoln Avenue exit and turn right (south). Follow Lincoln about three miles to the intersection of Chase Drive, Lincoln Avenue, and Foothill Parkway. Turn right (west) onto Chase Drive and follow it until you reach Skyline Drive. Skyline Drive is located just after you drive over a concrete water crossing. Turn left (south) onto Skyline and follow it until it dead ends at the gate. *Park along Skyline off the pavement and do not block the gate.*

THE RIDES:

Skyline Drive to Sierra Peak

SANTA ANA MTNS. RIDE 3

Distance • 15.8 miles

Time Required • 1.5 to 2.5+ hours

Route Rating • 5

Grunt Factor • 4/5

Technical Rating • 1

Elevation • Start 1080 ft.

High point 3045 ft.

Finish 1080 ft.

Topos • *Corona South, Black Star Canyon;* ride map, page 142

SKYLINE DRIVE IS ONE OF THE EASIEST ways to get to Main Divide. Beginners who feel intimidated by thoughts of cranking their way up to Saddleback Mountain should set aside a day, especially during the winter, and make their way up Skyline Drive if for no other reason than to sit up on Sierra Peak and soak in the beauty. On a clear, winter day this is the most beautiful place for a picnic lunch in the Orange County area. On the way up you are surrounded by the snow-covered peaks of the San Gabriel, San Bernardino and San Jacinto Mountains. Once you reach the top you'll be treated to a view of the beautiful valley that makes up Hidden Ranch. As you make your way north toward Sierra Peak on North Main Divide you'll see multi-colored sandstone reminiscent of Sedona. Few people have any appreciation of this wonderful scenery because it can not be seen from the 91 Freeway.

THE RIDE

You start the ride by heading through the main gate. Follow the main road as it veers right, skirting the east edge of an orange grove (**0.3 mile mark**). Soon you will leave the relatively flat valley floor and make a 180-degree switchback and begin the real climbing (**1.0 mile mark**). You ascend up easy switchbacks that give you respite from what could be a brutal climb if not for the thoughtful engineers.

The angle of the road steepens from about the **2.5 mile mark** until you reach the **3.6 mile mark**. Again the angle eases and you continue up a moderate grade until Skyline Drive terminates at Main Divide (3S04) at Oak Flat, a grassy area with a few oak trees (**5.1 mile mark**). Turn right on Main Divide and follow it as it roller coasters along the spine of the northern Santa Ana Mountains. Several smaller unmarked roads will be passed heading off Main Divide to one side or the other. Stay on the well-graded Main Divide. After about 2.6 miles, you will come to the turn-off for Sierra Peak (really straight ahead), whereas the Main Divide descends down to the left (**7.8 mile mark**).

Head straight up to the summit (**7.9 mile mark**). Enjoy the view, rest and mostly coast back to your starting point.

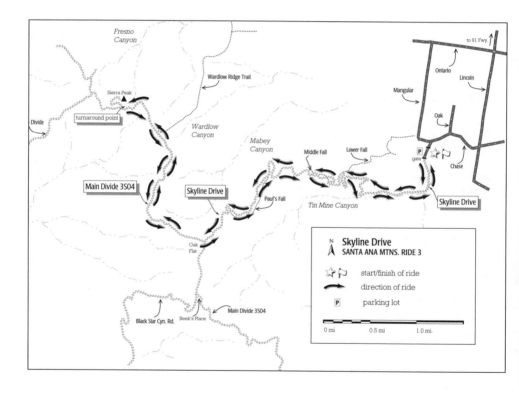

The Fall Zone

SANTA ANA MTNS. RIDE 4

Distance • Variation 1: 9.0 miles

Variation 2: 8.7 miles

Time Required • 1.0 to 2.0 hours

Route Rating • 8

Grunt Factor • 4

Technical Rating • Variation 1: 2/3

Variation 2: 7

Elevation • Start 1080 ft.

High point 2810 ft.

Finish 1080 ft.

Topos • *Corona South, Black Star Canyon;*

ride map, page 144

THIS RIDE GRADUALLY GAINS ALTITUDE UP Skyline Drive, then descends a series of three great singletrack and doubletrack trails adjacent to, across and below Skyline Drive. These three trails are collectively called the Fall Zone. The Fall Zone (Paul Fall, Middle Fall and Lower Fall Zones) are classic downhill rides. The Paul Fall and Middle Fall Zones are suitable for all but beginner riders. The Lower Fall Zone is suitable only for more advanced riders.

THE RIDE

Start your computer at the main gate. Follow the main road as it veers right, skirting an orange grove. Head up the valley floor to a 180-degree switchback, the beginning of the climb up easy switchbacks (**1.0 mile mark**). At the **2.0 mile mark** you'll pass the entrance to the Lower Fall Zone. Remember this spot, because as you come screaming down the hill later, this turn-off will be easy to miss.

Continue uphill on Skyline Drive to the **4.5 mile mark**. You will see the entrance to the Paul Fall Zone on your left (south). Turn left, make a short but steep climb to the top of the ridge. Start down the trail, following the ridge until the trail forks (**4.7 mile mark**). Take the left fork. Continue down the ridgeline to a final technical downhill leg and rejoin Skyline Drive (**5.4 mile mark**).

The next mile of fireroad is very fast, so watch your speed! At the **6.4 mile mark** is a turn-off on your left. This is the Middle Fall Zone, a four-wheel-drive trail that cuts the Skyline Drive switchbacks. It is normally well groomed and well traveled. Use extreme caution on the lower section unless you are prepared to go into orbit. You finally rejoin Skyline again at the **6.7 mile mark**. Continue to your right (downhill).

At the **7.0 mile mark** you will reach that singletrack you noted on the way up (remember?).

VARIATION 1: If you are not a skilled rider, continue past the singletrack, back down the fun last two miles of Skyline Drive to the main gate (**9.0 mile mark**).

VARIATION 2: Lower Fall Zone. Warning: This is where the real technical section of the ride begins. If you lack more advanced riding skills, you have no business being on this leg of the Fall Zone.

Turn left onto this trail. Go uphill a short distance and then begin your descent at a fork in the trail (**7.3 mile mark**). Several choices are presented. At the 7.4 mile mark, veer left and continue to the bottom the hill (**7.8 mile mark**). Make a sharp left turn.

Follow the trail down into a wash and along a flood control channel until you reach the corner of Mangular and Chase (**8.3 mile mark**). Turn right and follow Chase back to Skyline. Turn right onto Skyline and head back to your car (8.7 miles).

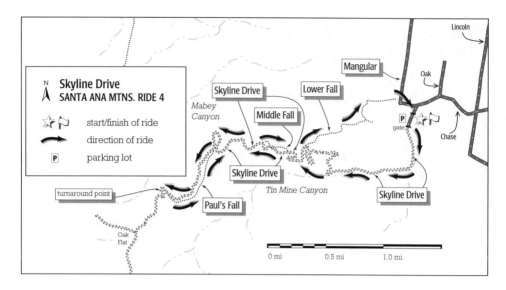

Other Skyline Area Rides:

Wardlow Ridge Trail: This little-known trail is an old firebreak trail that dives off the Main Divide. From the junction of Skyline Drive and Main Divide, turn right and ride about 1.9 miles toward Sierra Peak. Look for this trail on your right (see map, page 142). It descends directly down the ridgeline between Wardlow and Fresno Canyons. Near the bottom, the trail splits, joining various horse trails. These trails lead to the Serfas Club Drive area of western Corona.

This trail has the potential of being one of the best extreme trails in the area. Unfortunately, as of this writing, it is in disrepair and not a very enjoyable ride. Additional traffic and TLC by some dedicated riders could clean this trail up and make it 100% ridable (albeit technically difficult).

Silverado Canyon

The name speaks of mining days long past. But even before American settlers and miners arrived, this canyon was well known to Spanish Californians and their Indian predecessors. The Indian name has been lost to us. The Spanish called it Cañada de la Madera – the Canyon of the Timber. The Spanish built a crude ox-cart trail to the canyon's upper reaches to cut pine timber for construction of adobe buildings. In the early 1860s Sam Shrewsberry and J.E. Pleasants built homesteads in the bits of flat ground in the canyon bottom. Goats and bee keeping were the main activities. Occasionally, grizzly bears visited the canyon, raiding the apiaries for sweet honey.

The quiet was broken one day in the fall of 1877. Two hunters found rocks that looked like silver ore. When the assay report confirmed the find at some $60 of silver per ton, the hunters immediately staked a claim. An article in a Los Angeles paper concerning the discovery of silver in Madera Canyon soon brought some 250-300 men seeking their fortune. Miners changed the canyon's name to Silverado, a name they felt more befitting. Soon the entire Santa Ana mountain range was swarming with miners. The entirety of Silverado Canyon was staked out in short order and a town with three hotels, stores, blacksmith shops and many saloons sprang up.

Coal was quickly discovered near the mouth of the canyon. Southern Pacific railroad surveyed the coal rich lands and soon had ownership. A second town, Carbondale, with its own stores, saloons and post office sprouted. As many as 1,500 people now occupied the canyon. The coal and silver were quickly depleted and by 1883, Silverado and Carbondale were deserted. Little remains of these boom and bust towns, although diligent searches of the canyons reveal telltale mine tailings and occasional mine shafts and rusting equipment.

On the Silverado Motorway   Photo: Ken Larson

Maple Spring Road to Santiago Peak

SANTA ANA MTNS. RIDE 5

Distance • 24.2 miles

15.0+ miles to Main Divide and return

Time Required • 2.5 to 4+ hours

(1.5 to 2.5 hours)

Route Rating • 6

Grunt Factor • 6+

Technical Rating • 1+

Downhill Rating • 6

Elevation • Start 1830 ft.

High point 5687 ft.

Finish 1830 ft.

Topos • *Corona South, Santiago Peak;*

ride map, page 147

THIS RIDE OFFERS THE EASIEST WAY TO mountain bike to the summit of Santiago Peak. This is a moderate up-and-back ride with an option of only riding up Maple Spring Road to the junction with Main Divide Road. As a practical matter, you may turn around at any point to fit the ride to your time-frame or ability. The first 3.2 miles are paved fireroad (don't let this dissuade you) with several stream crossings leading to mostly shaded dirt road. The ride from the junction with the Main Divide to the summit is exposed to the sun and is a bit more strenuous. Once you reach the Main Divide, the views can be wonderful.

CAR DIRECTIONS

From North Orange County

From the 55 Freeway in the city of Orange, take Chapman Avenue east to the intersection with Jamboree. Proceed straight ahead; Chapman becomes Santiago Canyon Road. Drive 6.7 miles on Santiago Canyon Road to Silverado Canyon Road (a left-hand turn). Follow Silverado Canyon Road for 5.4 miles to a parking area and Forest Service gate.

From Irvine Area

From the 5 Freeway, take Jamboree Blvd east to the intersection of Chapman/ Santiago Canyon Road. Turn right here. Follow Santiago Canyon Road 6.7 miles to the Silverado Canyon Road turn-off (a left turn). Follow Silverado Canyon Road for approximately 5.4 miles to a parking area and Forest Service gate.

From South Orange County

From the 5 Freeway take El Toro Road eastward for 13.6 miles to the Silverado Canyon Road turn-off (a right-hand turn). Follow Silverado Canyon Road for approximately 5.4 miles to a parking area and Forest Service gate.

PARKING

Park in the area at the end of Silverado Canyon Road, but *not* in front of the Forest Service gate or where posted "No Parking." If the parking area is full, you may park along Silverado Canyon Road a short distance downstream. *Do not park in or block any private residential driveways.*

THE RIDE

Begin at the Forest Service gate and proceed up the paved Maple Spring Road (5S04) for 3.2 miles making several stream crossings. During winter, these crossings can be quite deep and your shoes will definitely get soaked. Don't let the fact that the first part of this ride is on pavement dissuade you. This part of the ride is still quite nice, and some of the steepest sections are found here.

After the last stream crossing, you turn a sharp corner and the dirt begins. The grade is fairly moderate and as you continue upward, the ride tends to be more in the shade. As you switchback your way up, note the few remnants of pine trees that once were thick in this canyon that the Spanish called Cañada de la Madera (Canyon of the Timber).

After 7.5 miles, you make the last turn and reach a level ridge area at the top of Maple Spring Road. For a shorter ride, admire the view here both east toward the San Gabriel and San Bernardino Mountains and west toward the Pacific Ocean, then turn around and enjoy the glide back to your car. For those continuing to the summit, proceed 0.1+ mile farther—past the Harding Truck Trail (5S08) which descends to your right—turn right (uphill) onto the southbound Main Divide Road (3S04).

The Main Divide Truck Trail gains another 500 feet over the next 1.5 miles to the southwestern ridge of Modjeska Peak (**9.1 mile mark**). Continue slightly downhill for about 1.0 mile, then begin 1.9 miles of climbing to where Main Divide meets the summit access road (**12.0 mile mark**). Turn right on this short road that takes you 0.1+ mile to the radio-tower-encrusted summit of Santiago Peak. The present-day summit is a pretty ugly affair. One can only imagine what a sublime place this was in the last century.

Take the time to ride up and admire the view (which can still be incredible on clear days), ingest liquids and energy bars. Return to the junction with Main Divide, take a left turn, and start your almost entirely downhill journey to your car.

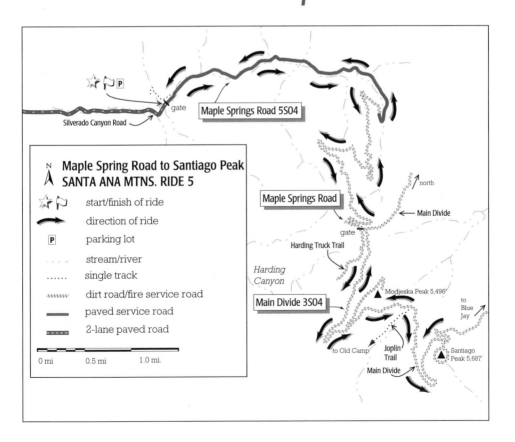

Maple Spring –Silverado Motorway Loop

SANTA ANA MTNS. RIDE 6

Distance • 17.0 mile loop

Time Required • 2 to 4 hours

Route Rating • 8

Grunt Factor • 5

Technical Rating • 3/4

Elevation • Start 1830 ft.

High point 4523ft.

Finish 1830 ft.

Topos • *Santiago Peak, Corona South;*

ride map, page 149

THIS JUSTIFIABLY POPULAR LOOP combines mostly moderate uphill with great vistas, lightning-fast fireroads and an excellent singletrack finish. For slightly more effort than just riding up Maple Springs Road and back, you can complete a loop that finishes right where you began your ride. Note: The Silverado Motorway singletrack is subject to rain damage, but usually by summer, traffic and some TLC fix most of the problems.

CAR DIRECTIONS
See Ride 5 on page 146.

THE RIDE
From the gate you'll proceed up a paved access road—Maple Springs Road (5S04)—for 3.2 miles. During much of the year, you will encounter a number of stream crossings that will soak your pedals.

At the **4.1 mark** the road levels off and gently ascends to the ridge top (**7.5 mile mark**). A short distance farther, at a large flat area, you will see the top of the Harding Truck Trail (5S08) to your right (**7.6 mile mark**). Continue straight for a short distance farther (**7.6+ mile mark**) where Maple Springs ends at the Main Divide Road (3S04). Veer left here. (Going right leads to Santiago Peak.) This is the highest elevation reached on the ride.

From here, the going is largely downhill (with a few short ascents) until you reach the Bedford Road turn-off (4S03) at the **11.3 mark**. Bear left to stay on Main Divide. This is the fastest leg of the journey. Some parts of this fireroad seem so smooth you could just fly, until you find those rutted, loose-rock patches. Be proficient at doing bunnyhops at speed, slow down, or figure on a long stint at the hospital.

Just past the Bedford Road turn-off, you begin your last uphill section. This short (0.7+ mile), but somewhat steep and loose section takes you to the summit of Bedford Peak. As you begin to descend, keep a sharp eye out for the long wooden barrier on the left side of the road (**13.7 mile mark**). This is the longest of several barriers you will have encountered. A North Main Divide numerical marker stands opposite this point.

This is the unmarked, upper terminus of the abandoned Silverado Motorway. It appears to be nothing more than a firebreak at this point. This trail follows the ridgeline on fast singletrack, then heads left, down toward Silverado Canyon. (Note: The Ladd Singletrack continues along the ridge into Ladd Canyon.) At the **16.9 mile mark** you intersect Maple Springs Road just on the uphill side of the first stream crossing. Turn right and continue downhill to you car (**17.0 mile mark**).

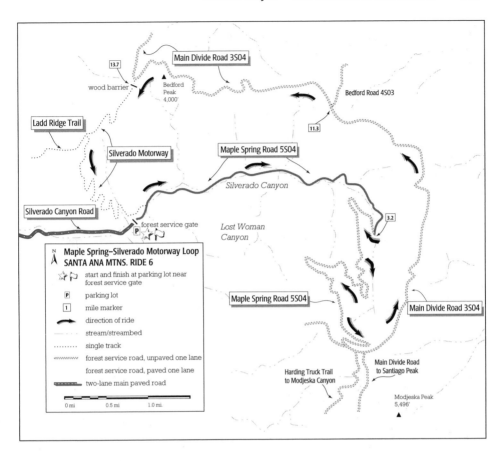

Main Divide Road 3S04

13.7

wood barrier

Bedford
Peak
4,000'

Bedford Road 4S03

Ladd Ridge Trail

11.3

Silverado Motorway

Maple Spring Road 5S04

Silverado Canyon

Silverado Canyon Road

Lost Woman
Canyon

3.2

forest service gate

P

N **Maple Spring–Silverado Motorway Loop**
SANTA ANA MTNS. RIDE 6

start and finish at parking lot near
forest service gate

P   parking lot

1   mile marker

direction of ride

stream/streambed

single track

forest service road, unpaved one lane

forest service road, paved one lane

two-lane main paved road

Maple Spring Road 5S04

Main Divide Road 3S04

Main Divide Road
to Santiago Peak

Harding Truck Trail
to Modjeska Canyon

Modjeska Peak
5,496'

0 mi   0.5 mi   1.0 mi.

Modjeska Canyon

Modjeska Canyon is actually the upper and narrower appendage of Santiago Canyon. Santiago Canyon begins between the two high peaks of Saddleback and extends past Irvine Lake then down through the city of Orange, joining the Santa Ana River. The name Santiago Canyon was bestowed upon this creek in 1769 by early Spanish Settlers, whereas the Santiago's wild upper reaches were named after Madame Helena Modjeska, a world-famous actress who established a summer home in the canyon in 1877. In 1888 she built a permanent residence which was designed by well-known New York architect Stanford White. This residence is still standing and has been restored.

The conglomerate cliffs which lie above the Harding Truck Trail in Modjeska Canyon played a part in the capture of the notorious bandit Juan Flores in 1857. Among other crimes, Flores and his gang looted San Juan Capistrano, killed a storekeeper and murdered Sheriff Barton and his posse. General Andres Pico trapped Flores and his band on the summit of the cliffs, capturing all but Flores and two compatriots. These three managed an escape by spurring their horses down the precipice. Flores was captured a few days later and hung in Los Angeles.

Harding Truck Trail to Santiago Peak

SANTA ANA MTNS. RIDE 7

Distance • 27.9 miles

Time Required • 3 to 5 hours

Route Rating • 7

Grunt Factor • 7

Technical Rating • 1/2

Downhill Rating • 6

Elevation • Start 1380 ft.

High point 5687 ft.

Finish 1380 ft.

Topos • *Santiago Peak;* ride map, page 151

THIS IS AN UP-AND-BACK RIDE TO THE highest point of the Santa Anas, Santiago Peak. If the ride proves a bit much for you the first time on it, you can always turn about at any point and still claim a good ride. Harding Truck Trail is *not* the easiest way to the summit. Maple Spring Road (out of Silverado Canyon) is 1.8 miles shorter and involves less elevation gain.

CAR DIRECTIONS

From North Orange County

From the 55 Freeway in the city of Orange, take Chapman Avenue east to the intersection with Jamboree. Proceed straight ahead; Chapman becomes Santiago Canyon Road. Drive 9.7 miles on Santiago Canyon Road to Modjeska Canyon Road (a left-hand turn). Follow Modjeska Canyon Road for approximately two miles to the Tucker Wildlife Sanctuary.

From Irvine Area:

From the 5 Freeway, take Jamboree Blvd east to the intersection of Chapman/Santiago Canyon Road. Turn right here. Follow Santiago Canyon Road 9.7

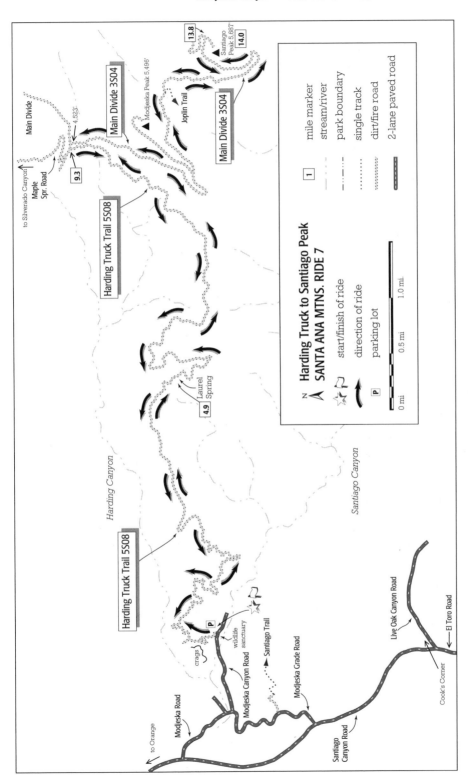

Harding Truck to Santiago Peak
SANTA ANA MTNS. RIDE 7

miles to the Modjeska Canyon Road turn-off (a left turn). Follow Modjeska Canyon Road for approximately two miles to the Tucker Wildlife Sanctuary.

From South Orange County

From the 5 Freeway, take El Toro Road eastward for 10.7 miles to the Modjeska Canyon Road turn-off (a right-hand turn). Follow Modjeska Canyon Road for approximately two miles to the Tucker Wildlife Sanctuary.

PARKING

Park in the small gravel lot next to a small observatory dome, just past the Sanctuary entrance. *Do not park in front of the trailhead or in front of Tucker Wildlife Sanctuary. Parking is limited, and your failure to park in a considerate manner could jeopardize future access.*

Hint: The small store along Modjeska Canyon Road carries a variety of goodies and drinks, including power bars for only 99¢. It is a good place to stock up before or after a ride.

THE RIDE

The Harding Truck Trail (5S08) begins across the road from the Tucker Wildlife Sanctuary parking area. This maintained fireroad is closed to vehicular traffic. Take this dirt road past a metal gate and begin the uphill grind through the chaparral-laden hillsides. As you ascend, you will note a large canyon on your left; this is Harding Canyon. If you look carefully, you can see evidence of mining activity on the opposite slope of the upper reaches of the canyon. In 1878 prospectors found evidence of silver and lead, spawning a short-lived mining boom. Reportedly, the canyon was swarming with prospectors.

After the first 4.0 miles or so the incline eases slightly. At the **4.9 mile point**, a sign for Laurel Spring will be seen on your right (the spring is about 30 yards down). After reaching the 6.6 mile point the road levels then descends for a mile, before a last uphill section to a metal gate.

Just past the gate, at **9.3 miles**, you join Maple Springs Road (coming up from Silverado Canyon). Turn right here. Head uphill for less than 0.1 mile and turn right again onto the southbound (uphill) Main Divide Truck Trail (3S04). The elevation here is 4523 ft.

The Main Divide Truck Trail gains another 500 feet over the next 1.5 miles to the southwestern ridge of Modjeska Peak. Continue slightly downhill for about 1.0 mile (past the juncture with the Joplin Trail) then begin the nearly 2.0 miles of climbing to the junction of the Main Divide (**13.8 mile mark**) and a short road on your right that takes you 0.1+ mile to the radio-tower-encrusted summit of Santiago Peak. The summit is a pretty ugly affair. One can only imagine what a sublime place this was in the last century.

Take the time to ride up and admire the view (which can still be incredible on clear days), ingest liquids and energy bars. Return to the junction with Main Divide and take a left turn to start you on your almost entirely downhill journey to your car.

Harding Truck Trail to Joplin Trail Loop

SANTA ANA MTNS. RIDE 8

Distance • 24.0 mile loop

Time Required • 3.0 to 5.0 hours

Route Rating • 9+

Grunt Factor • 7

Technical Rating • 5/6

Elevation • Start 1380 ft.

High point 5015 ft.

Finish 1380 ft.

Topos • *Santiago Peak,* ride map, page 153

THIS CLASSIC LOOP RIDE HAS IT ALL: A stout uphill grind leading to miles of downhill on scenic, often remote, and technical singletrack. This is one of the best loop rides in the Santa Anas. Like many rides in the Santa Anas, save this one for those cooler winter or spring days; it can get genuinely hot in the summer. Alternatively, strong riders will find a very early start (e.g. 6:00 A.M.) and plenty of fluids can make this and other Santa Ana rides reasonably pleasant on even hot summer days.

CAR DIRECTIONS

Park at Tucker Wildlife Sanctuary in Modjeska Canyon. See Ride 7 (page 150) for directions.

THE RIDE

Take the Harding Truck Trail (5S08) which begins across the road from the Tucker Wildlife Sanctuary parking area past a metal gate and begin your long uphill grind. As you ascend, you will note a large canyon on your left; this is Harding Canyon.

After the first 5.0 miles or so the climb eases a bit and levels at the **6.6 mile point**. The road then descends for a mile, before a last uphill section brings you to Maple Springs Road (9.3 miles). Turn right here. Head uphill for a very short distance and turn right again onto the southbound (uphill) Main Divide Truck Trail (3S04).

Continue up the Main Divide Truck Trail for about 1.5 miles gaining almost 500 more feet on the somewhat rocky surface to a sharp bend around the southwestern ridge of Modjeska Peak. This is the highest point on the ride at 5015 feet. Continue slightly downhill on smoother road for about 0.9 mile (**nearly 11.8 mile mark**) to the juncture with the Joplin Trail (a small sign may mark this spot). This singletrack heads down off the right-hand side of the road.

The Joplin Trail descends rapidly through chaparral and tree-canopied hillside. It varies from smooth dirt to loose and rocky; there a few very tight switchbacks. Rain-ruts and washed-out stream crossings may be encountered, depending on the season. After 2.2 miles of killer and challenging riding, a last stream crossing leads to smooth singletrack for 0.1 mile which takes you to a flat and superb tree-shaded area—Old Camp (**14.0 mile mark**).

The Joplin Trail section of this ride is where all the real technical challenges will be encountered. Care should be taken, and less-experienced riders should dismount and walk some sections. An accident in this remote locale is the last thing you need. Also note: due to often loose soil conditions, the Joplin Trail is an unpleasant uphill riding proposition. Save it as an excellent downhill.

From Old Camp, head up switchbacks along a well-traveled singletrack which then levels and becomes the Santiago Trail. This narrow old road is essentially singletrack for a good portion of the 8.0 miles from Old Camp to the gate at the Old Modjeska Grade Road (**22.0**

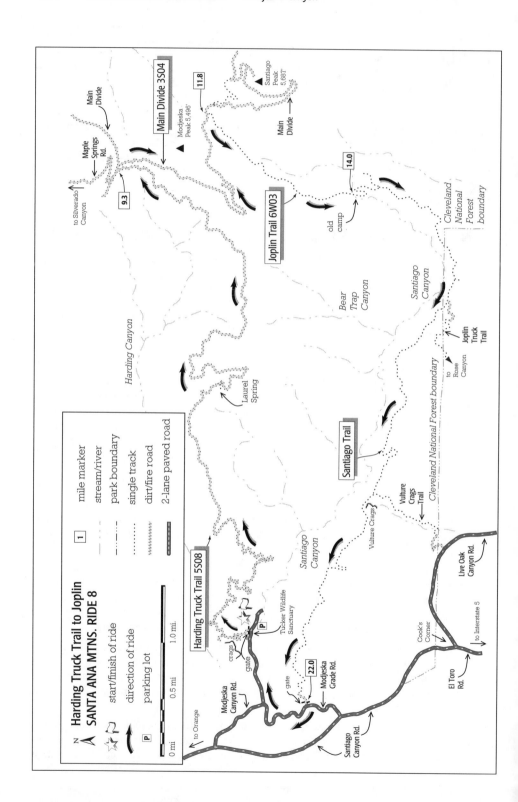

Harding Truck Trail to Joplin
SANTA ANA MTNS. RIDE 8

N

- 1 mile marker
- stream/river
- park boundary
- single track
- dirt/fire road
- 2-lane paved road

- start/finish of ride
- direction of ride
- P parking lot

0 mi   0.5 mi   1.0 mi.

Main Divide 3S04

11.8

Santiago Peak 5,687'

Main Divide

Modjeska Peak 5,496'

9.3

Maple Springs Rd.

Main Divide

to Silverado Canyon

Joplin Trail 6W03

14.0

old camp

Cleveland National Forest boundary

Bear Trap Canyon

Santiago Canyon

Harding Canyon

Laurel Spring

Joplin Truck Trail

to Rose Canyon

Santiago Trail

Cleveland National Forest boundary

Vulture Crags Trail

Vulture Crags

Santiago Canyon

Harding Truck Trail 5S08

Tucker Wildlife Sanctuary

crags gate

P

Modjeska Canyon Rd.

gate

22.0

Modjeska Grade Rd.

to Orange

Santiago Canyon Rd.

Cook's Corner

El Toro Rd.

Live Oak Canyon Rd.

to Interstate 5

mile mark). About 2.1 miles from Old Camp, a road will be seen to your left. This is the Joplin/Rose Canyon Trail. Don't turn, but head straight ahead and uphill. Most of the remaining ride is fun downhill, with one notable uphill.

Note: Be aware that Santiago Truck Trail is extremely popular with mountain bikers and hikers. Watch out for other trail users; **watch** your speed. *Slow down when passing others.*

At the end of the Santiago Truck Trail, pass through a metal gate, turn right on the paved Modjeska Grade Road, and head downhill into Modjeska Canyon. Stay to the right to return to Tucker Wildlife Sanctuary parking area. From the metal gate, it is about 2.0 miles of mostly downhill and flat riding to your car.

Harding to Holy Jim to Santiago Trail (via Santiago Peak)

SANTA ANA MTNS. RIDE 9

Distance • Variation 1 38.4 mile loop
Variation 2 35.9 mile loop

Time Required • 4.5 to 7+ hours

Route Rating • 9

Grunt Factor • 9

Technical Rating • 4+

Elevation • Start 1380 ft.
High point 5687 ft.
Finish 1380 ft.

Topos • *Santiago Peak (El Toro optional);*
ride map, page 156

AN INCREDIBLE LOOP FOR VERY STRONG riders. There is over 6700 feet of elevation gain and plenty of miles of varied terrain. Take lots of fluids and plenty of energy bars for this one. Again, a total classic Santa Ana Mountain ride that has it all. Save this one for those cooler winter or spring days; and leave yourself plenty of time for fluid, food and rest stops. An early start is recommended. Variation 1 maximizes the quality off-road riding experience, Variation 2 offers a somewhat easier (yet still fun) option for finishing the ride.

CAR DIRECTIONS
See Ride No 7 on page 150.

THE RIDE
Take the Harding Truck Trail (5S08), which begins across the road from the Tucker Wildlife Sanctuary parking area, past a metal gate and begin your long uphill grind. As you ascend, you will note a large canyon on your left; this is Harding Canyon.

After the first 5.0 miles or so the climb eases a bit and levels at the **6.6 mile point**. **The road** then descends for a mile, before an easier uphill section brings you to Maple Springs Road (9.3 miles). Turn right here. Head uphill for a very short distance and turn right again onto the southbound (uphill) Main Divide Truck Trail (3S04). The elevation here is 4523 feet.

The Main Divide Truck Trail gains another 500 feet over the next 1.5 miles to the southwestern ridge of Modjeska Peak. Continue slightly downhill for about 1.0 (past the juncture with the Joplin Trail) then begin the nearly 2.0 miles of climbing to the junction of the Main Divide and a short road on your right (**13.8 mile mark**). This access road takes you 0.1+ mile to the radio-tower-encrusted summit of Santiago Peak. Take the time to ride up and admire the view, ingest liquids and energy bars.

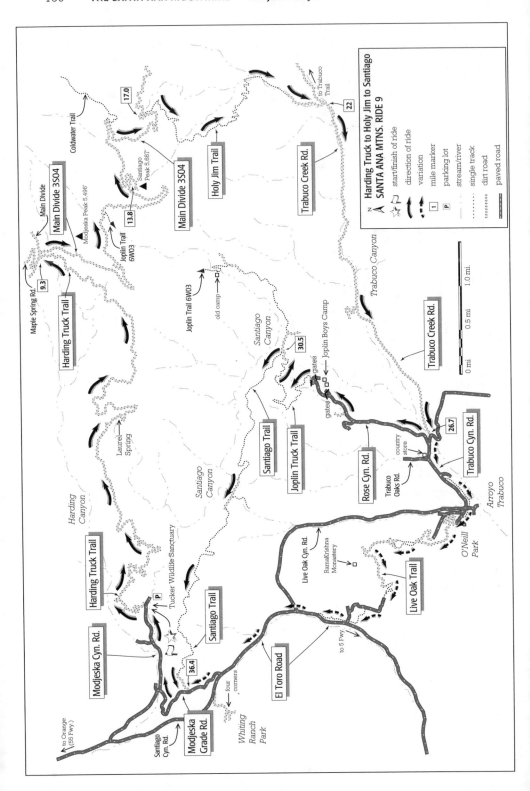

Return down to the junction with the Main Divide (**14.1 mile mark**) and head right. The road surface becomes quite rocky in places (watch your speed) and you lose a fair bit of elevation over the 2.9 miles until the Holy Jim Trailhead (6W03) is seen on your right (**17.0 mile mark**). There are a few initial sections of the Holy Jim Trail that may be washed-out and require short bike-n-hikes. However, as you descend, the trail surface is generally excellent and at a moderate grade.

Note: Holy Jim Trail is extremely popular with hikers. You may encounter dozens of people on their way up and down this trail. Utilize extra caution when riding sections with limited visibility or where you may be required to stop suddenly. Watch your speed! There have been no conflicts between bicycles and hikers on this trail. *It is up to you to keep it that way.*

After 4.5 miles of killer singletrack, dozens of switchbacks and several stream crossings in the canyon bottom, you reach the lower Holy Jim Trailhead (**21.5 mile mark**). Reputedly, Holy Jim Canyon is named after James T. Smith, a canyon resident and beekeeper in the late 1800s famous for his foul language. Smith was nicknamed variously "Cussin' Jim," "Lying' Jim," "Greasy Jim," and "Salvation Jim," but government map-makers bestowed the sanitized "Holy Jim" for the canyon with which he had become closely associated.

From the trailhead, ride 0.5 mile downcanyon on the Holy Jim dirt road (6S14) to the junction with Trabuco Road (6S13) at the **22.0 mile mark**. Turn right and proceed down the wide and well-graded dirt road for 4.7 miles where the paved Trabuco Canyon Road is met (**26.7 mile mark**).

Note: Only 0.2 mile down Trabuco Canyon Road is an old-fashioned general store, replete with cold fluids and a water faucet in front. It is a good place to stop if you feel the need to replenish supplies or yourself.

VARIATION 1: Turn right on the paved Trabuco Canyon Road and proceed about 0.1 mile to Rose Canyon Road. Turn right on Rose Canyon and ride up the paved road (staying right) for 1.4 miles to where the gated entrance of the Joplin Boys Camp (a correctional facility for young offenders) will be seen on your right (**28.2 mile mark**). Stay left here, passing around a gate onto a deteriorating paved road. Follow this for about 0.3 mile where you head left, around another gate onto the dirt Joplin Truck Trail.

The Joplin Truck Trail is an old fireroad that is slowly becoming singletrack. It proceeds for 2.0 miles up a moderate grade to where it terminates at the Santiago Trail (**30.5 mile mark**). Turn left here and proceed on 5.9 miles of excellent downhill (with a small section of uphill) on well groomed singletrack (an old roadbed) until the metal gate at Modjeska Grade Road is reached (**36.4 mile mark**). Turn right on the paved Modjeska Grade Road and proceed about 2.0 miles of mostly downhill back to your car (**38.4 miles**).

VARIATION 2: Turn right on the paved Trabuco Canyon Road, proceed about 0.4+ mile, and cross over to the left side of the road. This is just past the Forest Service Station. Turn left at a gate to O'Neill Park (**27.2 mile mark**). Hang an immediate right onto a singletrack that parallels Trabuco Canyon Road. Follow this for 0.6 mile until you must cross a series of three Park Service roads near the main entrance (**27.8 mile mark**). Continue straight onto a continuation of the singletrack, which heads slightly uphill, then dumps you out onto another paved service road. Proceed up this for a short distance to where the Live Oak Trail dirt road will be seen on your right (**28.1 mile mark**).

Follow the Live Oak Trail uphill for 1.0 mile (stay left at a **28.3 mile** junction) to a four-way intersection (**29.1 mile mark**). Turn left here (through the break in the fence line) and then make an immediate right onto a singletrack. This singletrack is followed 0.3+ mile uphill to where it joins a graded road near a small pond (**29.4 mile mark**). Turn left and proceed straight along the fireroad for 0.3 mile (some gravel) as it descends. At a three-way intersection, make a very sharp left turn and continue down fast fireroad to its end. Turn left and go over a small bridge (**30.5 mile mark**).

A fun, short section of singletrack goes up and then switchbacks down a small ridge. Proceed on the trail next to a nursery and behind residences until a paved road (Meadow Ridge Drive) is reached (**30.9 mile mark**). The Live Oak Trail runs on the left side of Meadow Ridge Drive for 0.3 mile, then turns left, up and over a hillside, then down to El Toro Road (**31.5 mile mark**).

Turn right and stay on the Live Oak Trail. Live Oak Trail remains dirt and runs along the right side of El Toro Road until it joins a paved bicycle path at a tunnel under El Toro Road. From here, proceed along El Toro Road, past Cook's Corner to the **33.3 mile mark**, where Modjeska Grade Road turns off to the right. Grunt up this then glide down the other side. Stay to the right and you eventually end back at your car (35.9 miles)

Harding to Silverado to Joplin Loop

SANTA ANA MTNS. RIDE 10

Distance • 40.9 mile loop

Time Required • 5 to 8 hours

Route Rating • 10

Grunt Factor • 9

Technical Rating • 5/6

Elevation • Start 1380 ft.
High point 5015ft.
Finish 1380 ft.

Topos • *Santiago Peak, Corona South (El Toro optional);* ride map, page 159

HERE IS A GREAT RIDE FOR RIDERS WHO want to get some mileage, a killer workout, and explore some of the best terrain in the Santa Ana Mountains. This "loop" is actually a figure eight, which essentially combines Ride 6 and Ride 8. You get a maximum of mileage, without repeating any of your route. This is not a ride for those in poor condition. The ride is 33% singletrack, 55% fireroad, 7% paved service road (no cars) and 5% paved road. This is an incredibly beautiful ride that takes you through some remote areas.

CAR DIRECTIONS
See Ride 7 on page 150.

THE RIDE
The Harding Truck Trail (5S08) begins across the road from the Tucker Wildlife Sanctuary parking area. Take this dirt road past a metal gate and begin the uphill grind through the chaparral-laden hillsides. The large canyon on your left is Harding Canyon. After reaching the **6.6 mile point** the road levels then descends for a mile, before a last uphill section to a metal gate. Just past the gate, at

9.3 miles, you join Maple Springs Road coming up from Silverado Canyon. [Note: You will ascend up Maple Springs to this point later in the ride as you cross the center of your figure eight.] Turn right here. Head uphill for less than 0.1 mile and turn left (north) onto the Main Divide Truck Trail (3S04).

From here, the going is largely downhill and fast (with a few short ascents) until you reach the Bedford Road turn-off (4S03) at the **13.0 mile mark**. Keep your eye out for the occasional rutted and loose sections. Plenty of riders have dumped their bikes along this stretch at high speed. At the Bedford Road junction, bear left, staying on Main Divide.

Just past the Bedford Road turn-off, Main Divide makes a short but somewhat steep and loose climb to the summit of Bedford Peak. As you begin to descend, keep a sharp eye out for a long wooden barrier on the left side of the road (**15.7 mile mark**). This is the longest of several barriers you will encounter. A North Main Divide numerical marker stands opposite this point.

This is the unmarked, upper terminus of the Silverado Motorway singletrack. It appears to be nothing more than a firebreak at this point. This trail follows the ridgeline on fast singletrack, then heads left, down toward Silverado Canyon. At the **18.9+ mile mark** you intersect the lower paved section of Maple Springs Road just uphill from the Forest Service gate. Turn left and start climbing again. After 3.0+ miles and several stream crossings, the angle of ascent lessens and the pavement ends (**22.0 mile mark**).

Follow good fireroad to the ridge top, past the Harding Truck Trail junction on your right (**26.2 mile mark**), to the Main Divide Road again. This time, turn right and head uphill on Main Divide Truck Trail for about 1.5 miles on a somewhat rocky surface to a sharp bend around the southwestern ridge of Modjeska Peak. This is the highest point on the ride at 5015 feet. Continue slightly downhill on smoother road for about 0.9 mile (**nearly 28.7 mile**

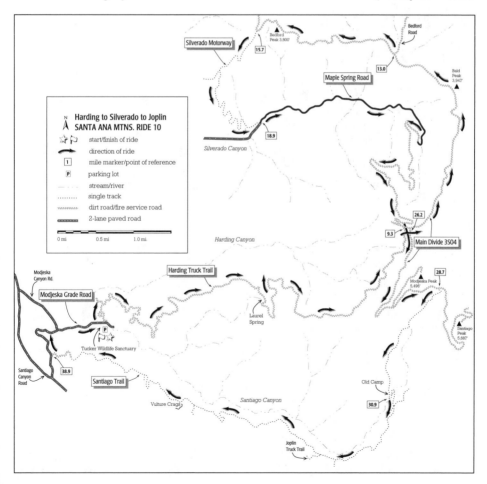

mark) to the juncture with the Joplin Trail (a small sign may mark this spot). The Joplin Trail singletrack heads down off the right-hand side of the road.

Joplin Trail descends rapidly through chaparral and tree-canopied hillside. It varies from smooth dirt to loose, rocky and technical; there a few very tight switchbacks. This is a remote locale. An accident is the last thing you need. After 2.2 miles of some of the best singletrack in the Santa Anas you reach a flat tree-shaded area – Old Camp (**mile 30.9**).

From Old Camp, head up switchbacks along a well-traveled singletrack which then levels and becomes the Santiago Trail. This narrow old road is very popular with hikers, runners and other cyclists and is essentially singletrack, so watch your speed. Stay right at any junctions you encounter. Most of the remaining ride is downhill, with one notable uphill. It is 8.0 miles from Old Camp to the gate at the Old Modjeska Grade Road (**38.9 mile mark**).

At the end of the Santiago Trail, pass through a metal gate, turn right on the paved Modjeska Grade Road, and head downhill into Modjeska Canyon. Stay to the right to return to Tucker Wildlife Sanctuary parking area. From the metal gate, it is about 2.0 miles of mostly downhill and flat riding to your car (**40.9 total miles**).

The Vulture Crags Singletrack   Photo: Ken Larson

Santiago Trail

Santiago Trail-Vulture Crags Singletrack Loop

SANTA ANA MTNS. RIDE 11

Distance • 7.1 mile loop

Time Required • 0.75 to 1.5+ hours

Route Rating • 6

Grunt Factor • 3/4

Technical Rating • 3+

Elevation • Start 1650 ft.

High point 2340 ft.

Finish 1400 ft.

Topos • *Santiago Peak (El Toro optional);* ride map, page 161

THIS IS A SHORT, FUN LOOP RIDE. It is perfect when time is short and you want to get in a nice ride. This and the following ride are two of the most popular mountain biking routes in the Santa Anas. The Santiago Trail is a former fireroad that is being encouraged to revert to a nice singletrack. The Santiago Trail leads 8.0 miles to Old Camp (see next ride). However, you only ride the first 3.3 miles until heading down the moderately technical Vulture Crags singletrack. The last portion of this ride follows Live Oak Canyon Road downhill to Cook's Corner then back to your car.

Access Note: Until August of 1995, it was legal to park along Modjeska Grade Road near the entry gate. It is now signed "No Parking." Inconsiderate mountain bikers who blocked car traffic and residents' driveways ruined this parking option for everyone. Your behavior affects everyone.

CAR DIRECTIONS

From North Orange County:
From the 55 Freeway in the city of Orange, take Chapman Avenue east to the intersection with Jamboree. Proceed straight ahead; at this point Chapman becomes Santiago Canyon Road. Drive 11.5 miles on Santiago Canyon Road to the junction with the Modjeska Grade Road (a left-hand turn).

From Irvine Area:
From the 5 Freeway, take Jamboree Blvd. east to the intersection of Chapman/Santiago Canyon Road. Turn right here. Proceed another 11.5 miles on Santiago Canyon Road to the junction with the Modjeska Grade Road (a sharp left-hand turn).

From South Orange County:
From the 5 Freeway, take El Toro Road eastward for approximately 8.9 miles to the Modjeska Grade Road turn-off (a right-hand turn about 1.3 miles past Live Oak Canyon Road turn-off [aka Cook's Corner]). El Toro becomes Santiago Canyon Road past Cook's Corner.

PARKING

Park on the east side of Santiago Canyon Road, well off the pavement, either north or south of the junction with Modjeska Grade Road. There is also some limited parking near the bottom of Modjeska Grade Road toward the junction with Santiago Canyon Road. If you park along the lower part of Modjeska Grade Road, park well off the road surface and do not impede traffic. See "About This Ride: Access Note" above.

THE RIDE

Ride up the steep Modjeska Grade Road to a point just below its crest. A steel gate and the trailhead will be seen on your right. Reset your computer here. Please respect any fire or other closure signs. The initial section of trail is on So Cal Edison property; they have been very favorable to allowing access—don't mess this up!

Proceed up the fairly moderate grade, with some ups and downs. Stay left at the **2.2 mile mark**. A final short, but somewhat steep, downhill leads to a level area. Looking up to your right, you will see some cliffs composed of conglomerate rock (river stones welded together with compressed silica). These are Vulture Crags. Prior to the 20th century, this was a roosting area for the now endangered California Condor. Like the mighty grizzly bear (also a former resident of the Santa Anas), the soaring condor was laid low by rifle bullets and poison.

At **3.3+ miles**, a small spur road on your right heads through a notch, then downhill. It quickly becomes a singletrack. From here the trail winds its way down the side of the shady upper Live Oak Canyon. This trail has been in use continuously for more than one hundred

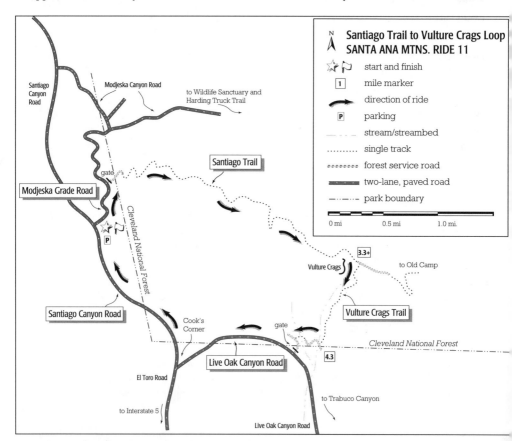

years (by miners, hikers and now cyclists) as an excellent route from Live Oak Canyon to Upper Santiago Canyon. It is not maintained and can suffer at the hands of winter rains.

After 1.0 mile of fun, the singletrack terminates at a dirt service road (**4.3 mile mark**). Turn right and downhill here (straight ahead is private property), cross the creek and then up a short, but steep, switchback on the other side. A short descent leads around, then across, a streambed. Turn left to join another dirt road. This road turns paved and, at the **4.8 mile mark**, ends at a gate. Proceed around the gate and you will find yourself at the top of the hill on Live Oak Canyon Road, above Cook's Corner. Turn right here and glide down to Cook's Corner (**5.8 mile mark**).

From Cook's Corner, turn right on Santiago Canyon Road and head 1.3 miles of slight uphill to your car (**7.1 miles**). Actual total mileage is closer to 7.5 miles when your initial ride up to the gate is included.

Santiago Trail to Old Camp

SANTA ANA MTNS. RIDE 12

Distance • 16.0 miles

Time Required • 1.5 to 3+ hours

Route Rating • 7

Grunt Factor • 5+

Technical Rating • 2+

Elevation • Start 1650 ft.
High point 3190 ft.
Finish 1650 ft.

Topos • *Santiago Peak, El Toro;* ride map, page 164

THIS IS A CLASSIC IN-AND-OUT RIDE along an old fireroad that is now largely singletrack. The relatively mild grade, ease of access and ability to turn around at any point, make this one of the most popular rides in the entire Santa Ana Mountain range. The Santiago Trail follows a ridge above the upper Santiago Canyon, until it drops into the canyon. The ride ends at Old Camp, in the high reaches of Santiago Canyon below Santiago and Modjeska Peaks. Old Camp is reputedly an old Indian camp and was used by early hunters. Its shady stream-side location makes it a fine place for a rest and lunch.

Note: Some inconsiderate slobs regularly leave litter at Old Camp. If you can't pick up your energy bar wrappers, why don't you take up road riding?

CAR DIRECTIONS
See Ride 11 on page 161.

PARKING
Park on the east side of Santiago Canyon Road, near Modjeska Grade Road, well off the pavement. Some parking is also available on Modjeska Grade Road, near Santiago Canyon Road. The upper section of Modjeska Grade Road is marked "No Parking." Please read the parking Access Note for previous ride (Ride 11).

THE RIDE
The ride starts at the crest of the Modjeska Grade Road. The unmarked Santiago Trail starts on the east side of the road at a large metal gate. Start your mileage computer at the gate.

As with the prior ride, the initial section follows the Santiago Trail fireroad (which is slowly reverting to singletrack) up a mostly moderate grade with a few steeper sections and some

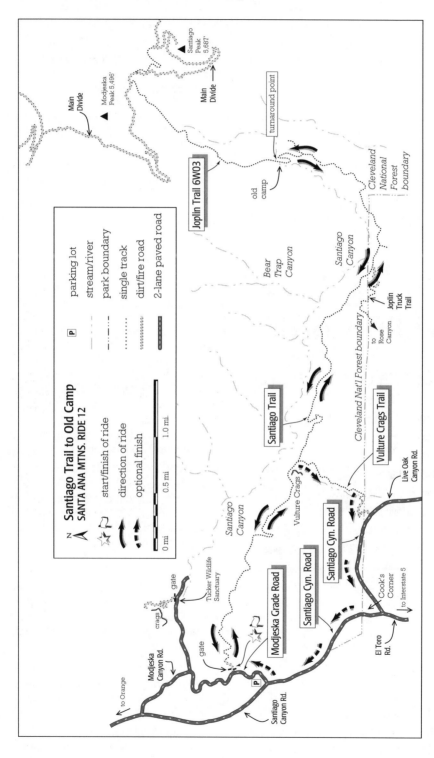

Santiago Trail to Old Camp
SANTA ANA MTNS. RIDE 12

N

start/finish of ride
direction of ride
optional finish

0 mi   0.5 mi   1.0 mi

P   parking lot
stream/river
park boundary
single track
dirt/fire road
2-lane paved road

Main Divide

Modjeska Peak 5,496'

Santiago Peak 5,687'

Main Divide

Joplin Trail 6W03

turnaround point

old camp

Cleveland National Forest boundary

Bear Trap Canyon

Santiago Canyon

Joplin Truck Trail

to Rose Canyon

Santiago Trail

Cleveland Nat'l Forest boundary

Vulture Crags Trail

Live Oak Canyon Rd.

Santiago Canyon

Vulture Crags

Santiago Cyn. Road

Santiago Cyn. Road

Cook's Corner

to Interstate 5

El Toro Rd.

Modjeska Grade Road

Tucker Wildlife Sanctuary

gate

crags

gate

Modjeska Canyon Rd.

to Orange

P

Santiago Canyon Rd.

downhill. After a rocky descent, at the **3.3+ mile mark**, you pass the turn-off for the Vulture Crags Singletrack on your right. Continue straight. Past this point, the trail climbs for a bit, then proceeds at a nearly level grade. At the **5.9 mile point**, a fireroad will be seen descending to your right. This is the Joplin Truck Trail. Continue straight.

Continue along the Santiago Trail, for another 1.7+ miles to a three- or four-way junction (**7.6 mile mark**). At this junction, go straight ahead and downhill into Santiago Canyon to a grassy area under ancient oaks and sycamore next to a creek (**8.0 mile mark**). This is Old Camp. Rest here and enjoy the scenery. Leave the place cleaner than when you arrived, then retrace your ride back to your car. (16.0 miles) Watch your speed as the Santiago Trail is heavily used by hikers, runners and other cyclists.

OPTIONAL FINISH: On your way back down the Santiago Trail, 4.7 miles from Old Camp (**12.7 mile mark**), turn left onto the Vulture Crags singletrack. Follow this downhill for 1.0 mile, then turn right, cross a streambed and climb steeply up the other side. More singletrack and another creek crossing bring you to a dirt road. Turn left. The road becomes paved and ends at a gate at Live Oak Canyon Road (**14.2 mile mark**). Go right, down Live Oak Canyon Road 1.0 mile to Cook's Corner, turn right onto Santiago Canyon Road, and ride the remaining 1.3 miles back to your car (16.5 miles total).

Photo: Larry Kuechlin

Trabuco Canyon

Holy Jim Trail to Santiago Peak

SANTA ANA MTNS. RIDE 13

Distance • 16.1 miles

Time Required • 3 to 4.5+ hours

Route Rating • 7

Grunt Factor • 7+

Technical Rating • 4+

Elevation • Start 1740 ft.

High point 5687 ft.

Finish 1740 ft.

Topos • *Santiago Peak;* ride map, page 167

A VERY FUN UP-AND-BACK RIDE TO THE summit of Santiago Peak. This is the shortest (but not the easiest) way to the highest point in the Santa Ana Mountains. There is lots of elevation gain over fairly short distances. This ride is not suitable for inexperienced or poorly conditioned riders. Much of the ride is along excellent singletrack, however, the Main Divide fireroad is quite rocky and steep and is far from a fun uphill ride. This route is heavily traveled by hikers. Courtesy is paramount at all times. If you can't properly share the trail, stay off! Don't ruin access for others.

CAR DIRECTIONS

From North Orange County:
From the 55 Freeway, in the city of Orange, take Chapman Avenue east to the intersection with Jamboree where it becomes Santiago Canyon Road. Proceed another 12.8 miles on Santiago Canyon Road to the Live Oak Canyon Road (aka Cook's Corner) turn-off (a left turn). Turn left and follow Live Oak Canyon Road for approximately 4.4 miles to where the road crosses the Trabuco Creek (just past Rose Canyon Road). Turn left onto the Trabuco Creek dirt road (6S13) heading up the wide canyon bed. Follow the dirt road for 4.7 miles where the Holy Jim Canyon Road (6S14) turn-off is met. Park in the large flat area just before the intersection of Trabuco Creek Road and Holy Jim Canyon Road.

From South Orange County:
From the 5 Freeway, take El Toro Road eastward for 7.6 miles to the Live Oak Canyon Road turn-off [aka Cook's Corner]. Turn right. Follow Live Oak Canyon Road for approximately 4.4 miles to where the road crosses the Trabuco Creek (just past Rose Canyon Road). Turn left onto the Trabuco Creek dirt road (6S13) heading up the wide canyon bed. Follow the dirt road for 4.7 miles where the Holy Jim Canyon Road (6S14) turn-off is met. Park in the large flat area just before the intersection of Trabuco Creek Road and Holy Jim Canyon Road.

Parking Note: Do not drive up Holy Jim Canyon Road. Traffic is restricted to local residents and there is no legal parking available.

THE RIDE

From the parking area, turn left and ride 0.5 mile up Holy Jim Canyon Road (6S14) to the Holy Jim Trailhead. The Holy Jim Trail (6W03) is one of the heaviest used hiking trails in the Santa Ana Mountains. The initial section along the canyon floor has several stream crossings that may require you to bike-and-hike.

After the last stream crossing, the trail switchbacks up the western slope of Holy Jim Canyon, steadily gaining altitude. The trail then continues upward, following the contour of the mountainside, until it crosses eastward, around a ridge, eventually terminating at the Main Divide Truck Trail (3S04) at the **5.0 mile mark**. Several short sections of the Holy Jim Trail (particularly higher up) have seen rain damage and may not be rideable.

Now the work begins. You have gained over 2,000 feet in the last 4 miles and have another 1,700+ feet to go over the next 2.9 miles. Turn left of the Main Divide and proceed up a fairly unrelenting grade. The Main Divide has more than several sections that are very loose and

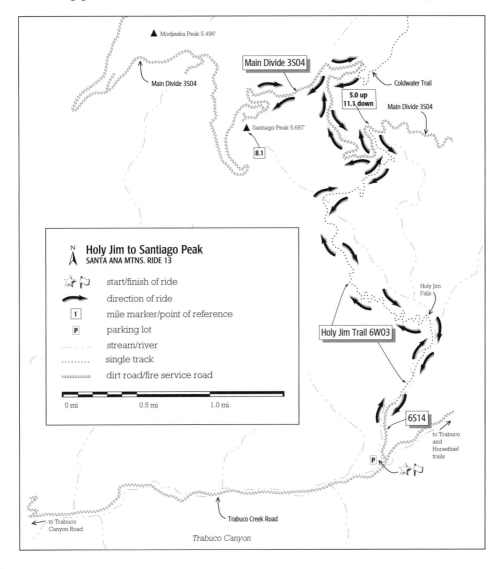

rocky. At the **7.9 mile mark**, you finally reach a service road that proceeds 0.1+ mile to the radio-tower-infested summit of Santiago Peak (**8.0+ mile mark**).

The view can be inspiring, despite the desecration of the summit, particularly on those special and rare crystal-clear days. After fluids, food and rest, turn around and reverse your course. Enjoy the downhill ride that you earned on the way up.

Now is the time to be extra careful of your speed, particularly on the narrow Holy Jim Trail singletrack. If you can't see ahead, slow down so a sudden stop is possible. There are almost always hikers on this trail. Slow when passing, and always give a friendly greeting (even if it is not reciprocated). At the **16.1 mile mark**, you are back at your car.

Trabuco Canyon- West Horsethief Loop

SANTA ANA MTNS. RIDE 14

Distance • 10.4 mile loop

Time Required • 2 to 4 hours

Route Rating • 8

Grunt Factor • 6

Technical Rating • 4

Downhill Rating • 6

Elevation • Start 1970 ft.
High point 4194ft.
Finish 1970 ft.

Topos • *Alberhill, Santiago Peak;*
ride map, page 169

A FANTASTIC LOOP RIDE THAT IS 75% singletrack. The Trabuco Trail takes you through some particularly beautiful and remote terrain that is mostly far away from the traditional biking crowds. Although only 10.4 miles, it feels farther and the more technical uphill nature keeps the duffer and thrash-and-crash downhillers away. All the better.

CAR DIRECTIONS

From North Orange County:
From the 55 Freeway in the city of Orange, take Chapman Avenue east to the intersection with Jamboree where it becomes Santiago Canyon Road. Proceed another 12.8 miles on Santiago Canyon Road to the Live Oak Canyon Road (aka Cook's Corner) turn-off (a left turn). Turn left and follow Live Oak Canyon Road for approximately 4.4 miles to where the road crosses the Trabuco Creek (just past Rose Canyon Road). Turn left onto the dirt road heading up the wide canyon bed. Follow the dirt road for 5.7 miles (passing at 4.7 miles the Holy Jim turn-off) to its end. Park here. The Trabuco trail begins directly at the end of the road.

From South Orange County:
From the 5 Freeway take El Toro Road eastward for 7.6 miles to the Live Oak Canyon Road turn-off (aka Cook's Corner). Turn right. Follow Live Oak Canyon Road for approximately 4.4 miles to where the road crosses Trabuco Creek (just past Rose Canyon Road). Turn left onto the dirt road heading up the wide canyon bed. Follow the dirt road for 5.7 miles (passing at 4.7 miles the Holy Jim turn-off) to its end. Park here. The Trabuco trail begins directly at the end of the road.

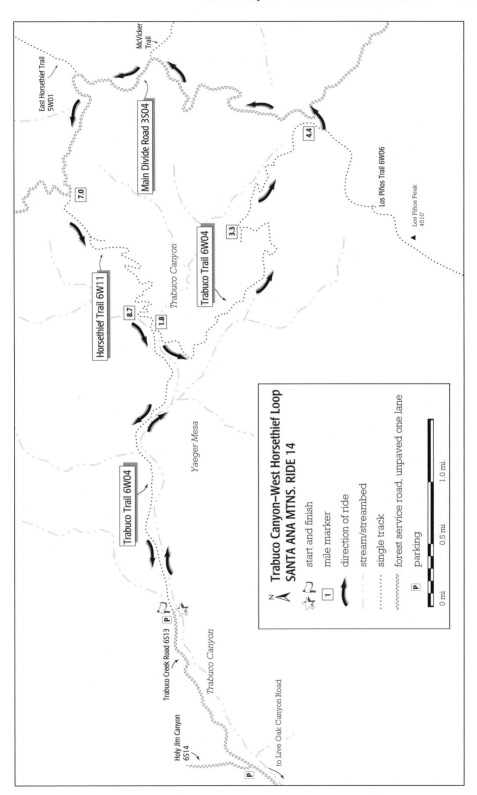

East Horsethief Trail 5W01

McVicker Trail

Main Divide Road 3S04

7.0

Horsethief Trail 6W11

8.7

1.8

Trabuco Canyon

4.4

Trabuco Trail 6W04

3.3

Los Piños Trail 6W06

Los Piños Peak 4510'

Yaeger Mesa

Trabuco Trail 6W04

N

Trabuco Canyon–West Horsethief Loop
SANTA ANA MTNS. RIDE 14

start and finish

1 mile marker

direction of ride

stream/streambed

single track

forest service road, unpaved one lane

P parking

| 0 mi | 0.5 mi | 1.0 mi. |

Trabuco Creek Road 6S13

P

Holy Jim Canyon 6S14

Trabuco Canyon

to Live Oak Canyon Road

P

PARKING

If the small parking area at the trailhead is full, do not bock access to the several private residences nearby. Rather, park farther downhill, off the roadway. The parking area at the Holy Jim Canyon turn-off is large and recommended. Use the extra distance for a warm-up.

THE RIDE

After leaving the parking area, the Trabuco Trail singletrack gradually gains elevation, and crosses the creek bed several times (bike carries probably necessary). Farther, the trail stays on the left side of the creek to the **1.7+ mile mark**. At this point, the Trabuco Trail splits off to the right (across the creek) and the Horsethief Trail heads up on the left. A sign marks this juncture.

Take the Trabuco Trail across the creek bed (head right), as the loose sharply switchbacked Horsethief Trail would be an very unpleasant uphill ride (this is the downhill return). The next mile or so of the Trabuco Trail has some rocky and loose, gravely sections that make uphill progress more work than it should be, but persevere. Soon the trail becomes leaf covered, under a canopy of trees and brush that is a pleasure to pedal and for the eye.

At the **3.3 mile mark**, you will see a trail heading up a ridge on your left. Do not take this. Rather turn right and continue up for another 1.1 miles to a sudden intersection with the Main Divide Truck Trail (**4.4 mile mark**). Just as you pop out onto Main Divide, on your right you will see a trail marked 6W06. This is the infamous Los Piños Trail. (See Ride 15.)

Head left (north) on the Main Divide fireroad for 2.6 miles of ups and downs, with great views both east and west, to the West Horsethief Trail, 6W11 (**7.0 mile mark**). A small sign and a small wooden barrier on your left may mark the trailhead. (Note: After 1.8 miles on Main Divide—the **6.2 mile mark**—you will pass the trailhead for the East Horsethief Trail that heads down toward Lake Elsinor.)

Take the West Horsethief Trail down the ridgeline for short ways, then where the trail splits, stay right and descend down below and around the ridgeline. Now the trail steepens and becomes full of small loose stones that require you to watch your speed and the control of your bike. The trail has a number of very sharp switchbacks, so be extra careful and prepare to stop. This trail is popular with hikers and runners, so watch your speed. After 1.7 miles of great downhill singletrack, you reach the canyon floor and the junction with Trabuco Trail (**8.7 mile mark**).

Now simply retrace your ride 1.7 miles back to the car (**10.4 mile mark**). You will be amazed how much easier and faster this first section seems on the downhill run!

Ortega Corridor

The southern section of the Santa Ana Mountains has seen less development and intrusion by man, but is split by the heavily traveled Ortega Highway. This two-lane highway runs from San Juan Capistrano to Lake Elsinor and commemorates Sergeant Jose Francisco Ortega, a scout for Portola, whose party passed though the Santa Ana Mountain foothills in 1769. The road was completed in 1933 and generally followed an old wagon track, which had its origins in the Juaneno Indian Trail.

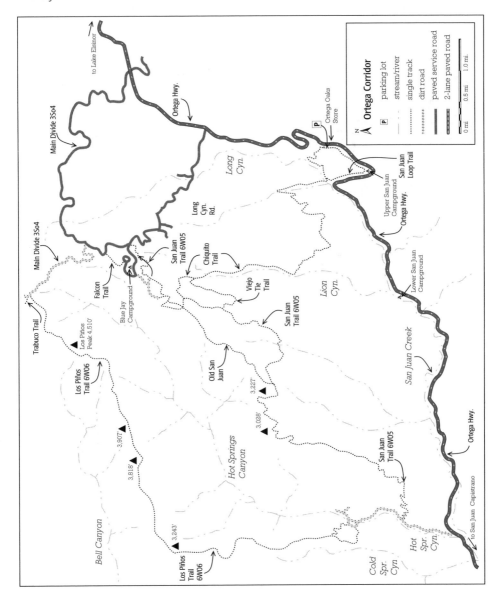

Few roads are found in the mountains between Ortega Highway and Trabuco Canyon, but many excellent and remote singletrack trails and even more primitive pathways can be found throughout this area. We have included only the well-recognized trails on the western slope of the range in this edition. Future editions will expand upon this information and include other trails and rides. Much of the mountain range's sweep to the south of Ortega Highway is designated wilderness area and off-limits to bicycle traffic ,and hiking trails located within that region are accordingly excluded from this guide.

Of the several trails in this region, the most well-known is the San Juan Trail. This 11.9 mile singletrack is well maintained and considered by many to be the best single trail in Orange County. The more remote and poorly maintained Los Piños Trail sees few visitors, but features spectacular vistas and wild downhills. Riders should exercise caution, ride responsibly and always leave the area cleaner than you found it.

The Los Piños Trail

SANTA ANA MTNS. RIDE 15

Distance • 11.0 miles

Time Required • 2.5 to 4+ hours

Route Rating • 7

Grunt Factor • 6

Technical Rating • 5+

Elevation • Start 3600 ft.

High point 4520ft.

Finish 805 ft.

Topos • *Alberhill, Santiago Peak, Cañada Gobernadora;* ride map, page 173

THIS RIDE REQUIRES A CAR SHUTTLE TO descend one of the most remote and wildest trails in the Santa Ana Mountains. The Los Piños Trail is, for much of its length, a singletrack remnant of an old firebreak that proceeds directly along a high ridgeline. Steep ascents and descents are involved. It is not uncommon for sections of the trail to be overgrown. Protective clothing and eyewear are strongly recommended. As of early 1996, one section of the trail (running west from Peak 3818) is severely overgrown and unridable. Some pruning shears need to be applied. This ride is suggested for strong riders with good technical skills. In addition to fluids, we also suggest bringing a good tool kit, including spare tubes. It could be a long walk if you have a mechanical problem.

CAR DIRECTIONS

From the 5 Freeway, take the Ortega Highway exit and head east for 12.5 miles to Hot Springs Canyon Road. It is currently marked with a sign for the Lazy W Ranch (just before the San Juan Fire Station). Turn left. Follow this paved and dirt road 0.9 mile to where you will reach a large parking area in a shaded clearing—the "Lower Parking Area." Park your second car here as this is where you will finish your ride.

Take your other car and drive up Ortega Highway 21.9 miles (9.4 miles past the Hot Springs Canyon turn off) to Long Canyon Road (6S05), on your left. Turn left and follow this paved road for 3.5 miles, passing the entrance to Bluejay Campground, to where you join Main Divide Road. Make a sharp left and drive 0.5 mile up Main Divide to a metal gate. Park off to the right, taking care not to block the gate or the road.

THE RIDE

From the gate, ride up Main Divide, gaining some 600 feet to the Los Piños Saddle (**1.1+ mile mark**). At this point, the Los Piños Trail (6W06) and the Trabuco Trail (6W04) join Main Divide on your left. You actually start the Los Piños trail where the Trabuco Trail hits Main Divide, but head up the trail on the left.

Proceed up the steep trail/firebreak that constitutes the Los Piños Trail, along the ridge. After 1.1 miles, you reach the summit of Los Piños Peak at 4,520 feet (**2.2 mile mark**). On clear days, the view is spectacular both east and west. From the summit, the route is obvious. Simply follow the sharp ridge between Hot Springs Canyon (on your left) and Bell Canyon (on your right). The long somewhat loose descent from Los Piños Peak is an exciting adventure.

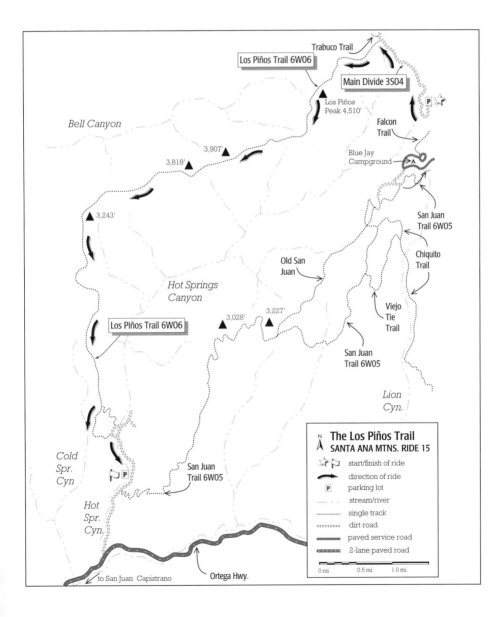

The Los Piños Trail
SANTA ANA MTNS. RIDE 15

start/finish of ride
direction of ride
parking lot
stream/river
single track
dirt road
paved service road
2-lane paved road

0 mi   0.5 mi   1.0 mi.

After nearly 2.0 miles of isolated up-and-down riding, you reach the top of Peak 3818 (**4.1+ mile mark**). The next mile of the trail literally disappears into the thick underbrush. Though the trail surface is fine, the chaparral has grown so thick that unless you are about 24 inches high, prepare to do battle. A small workcrew with clippers, axe and what not could clear this section and much of the remaining trail in a few afternoons effort. Eventually, the trail emerges, but you are glad for the extra clothing as the trail is still overgrown in places. (We lost our mileage count in the last section as we had to carry the bikes through a lot of brush).

When you reach the top of Peak 3243, you are now heading straight south on a ridge between Cold Springs Canyon (on the right) and Hot Springs Canyon (on the left). Eventually, the trail winds right, then heads left down the ridge, onto some switchbacks. From here the route is obvious and the underbrush less of a bother. Stay on the ridge, avoiding any turn-offs until some rocky switchbacks lead to where the trail descends into Hot Springs Canyon. At the bottom of the trail, you reach a fireroad. Head right and ride 0.8 mile back to your car.

The San Juan-Los Piños Loop

SANTA ANA MTNS. RIDE 16

Distance • 26.0 mile loop*

Time Required • 5 to 8+ hours

Route Rating • 9

Grunt Factor • 8+

Technical Rating • 5+

Elevation • Start 805 ft.
High point 4510 ft.
Finish 805 ft.

Topos • *Alberhill, Santiago Peak, Sitton Peak, Cañada Gobernadora;* ride map, page 175

THIS RIDE COMBINES TWO OF THE longest and most remote singletrack trails in the Santa Ana Mountains to create a loop ride of tremendous variety and challenge. The loop ride begins with an ascent of the San Juan Trail, then finishes down the wild and rugged Los Piños Trail. This ride is suggested for strong riders with good technical skills. Be sure to bring adequate fluids and food and protective clothing (lots of brush). Allow sufficient time for completion of the ride. We also suggest bringing a good tool kit, including spare tubes. It could be a long walk if you have a mechanical problem. 85% singletrack, 9% fireroad, 6% paved road.

CAR DIRECTIONS

From the 5 Freeway, take the Ortega Highway exit and head east for 12.5 miles to Hot Springs Canyon Road. It is marked currently with a sign for the Lazy W Ranch (just before the San Juan Fire Station). Turn left. Follow this paved and dirt road 0.9 mile to where you will reach a large parking area in a shaded clearing—the "Lower Parking Area." You will see signs that denote various trail heads, including the San Juan Trail (6W05). You begin and finish your ride here.

THE RIDE

Start up the seemingly endless switchbacks of the San Juan Trail, steadily gaining elevation for the first few miles. Higher up, the terrain becomes more moderate up-and-down type of riding. Stay right at the 6.5+ mile mark (junction with the Old San Juan Trail), and then lose some elevation to the 7.7 mile point where you cross a stream under tree cover. From here, head uphill and rolling up-and-down, making sure to stay left at any turn-offs (**9.1 and 9.7 mile marks**).

At the 9.8+ mile point and again at the **10.4 mile mark**, go straight across a junction with the Old San Juan Trail. At the **10.5 mile point**, stay right, reaching the end of the San Juan Trail at 11.9 miles. Turn left and take the paved Long Canyon Road 1.5 miles to the junction with Main Divide (**13.4 mile mark**). Make a sharp left onto Main Divide (which becomes dirt) and follow it 0.5 mile to a gate. Past the gate, another 1.1 miles of fireroad bring you to the Los Piños Saddle (**15.0 mile mark**). At this point, the Los Piños Trail (6W06) and the Trabuco Trail (6W04) join Main Divide on your left.

Take the left-hand Los Piños Trail which switchbacks up to the ridge, and becomes a firebreak type trail along the ridge. After 1.1 miles, you reach the summit of Los Piños Peak at 4520 feet (**16.1 mile mark**). On clear days, the view is spectacular. From the summit, the route is obvious. Simply follow the sharp ridge down steep and somewhat loose singletrack trail. After nearly 2.0 miles, you reach the summit of Peak 3818. Break out the long pants and

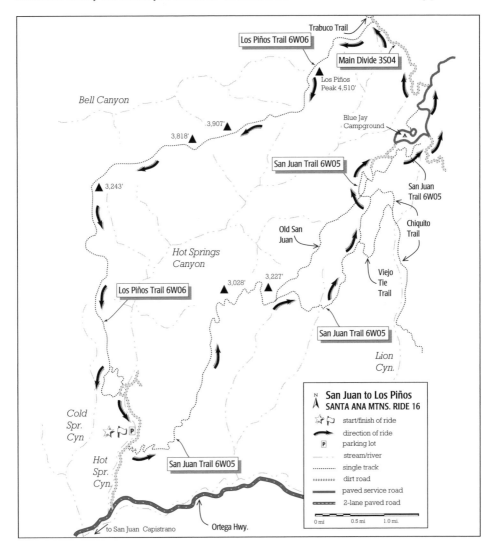

shirt. The next mile of the trail is, as of January, 1996, severely overgrown. We found it unrideable and nearly impassable. Persevere, the trail opens up again and despite overgrown brush, the rest of the trail is rideable. Eventually, the trail improves and finally descends into Hot Springs Canyon. When you reach the fireroad at the trail end, turn right and proceed 0.8 mile back to your car and your starting point. 26.0 miles

The San Juan Trail

SANTA ANA MTNS. RIDES 17a AND 17b

Distance • Ride 17a (downhill with car shuttle) 11.9 miles

Ride 17b (up and back) 23.8 miles

Time Required • Ride 17a 1.2 to 2.5+ hours

Ride 17b 2.7 to 6+ hours

Route Rating • 10

Grunt Factor • Ride 17a 3

Ride 17b 6+

Technical Rating • 4 (with some slightly more difficult spots)

Downhill Rating • 6

Elevation • Bottom 805 ft.

Top 3387 ft.

Topos • *Alberhill, Sitton Peak, Cañada Gobernadora; ride map, page 178*

THE SAN JUAN TRAIL, OR THE BLUE JAY Trail as it is also known, is an outstanding ride whether you are an intermediate or an expert rider. Although often ridden downhill with a car shuttle, this trail is not particularly strenuous as an up-and-back ride. The San Juan is a little more technical than it has been in the past because of substantial damage from the infamous winter of '95.

The San Juan Trail is too difficult for beginner riders, but for all others it can be done as long as you are careful to walk areas that have the smell of death lingering over them. This trail has seen several major accidents from riders who have failed to exercise caution. Ride within your limits and don't assume that everything is clear around that next blind corner. Always slow down when the way ahead can't be seen or you are not in control of your bike. There are no sponsors waiting at the bottom with a stop watch. Have fun.

CAR DIRECTIONS

From the 5 Freeway, take the Ortega Highway exit and head east for 12.5 miles to Hot Springs Canyon Road. It is marked currently with a sign for the Lazy W Ranch (just before the San Juan Fire Station). Turn left. Follow this paved and dirt road until you will reach a large parking area in a shaded clearing—the "Lower Parking Area." You will see signs that denote various trailheads, including the San Juan Trail (6W05). For an up-and-back ride, you begin and finish here.

To ride the downhill as a car shuttle, leave a second car at the Lower Parking Area, and drive up Ortega Highway 21.9 miles (9.4 miles past the Hot Springs Canyon turn off) to Long Canyon Road (6S05), on your left. A sign for Bluejay Campground will also be seen. Turn left on Long Canyon Road and follow this winding paved road for 2.5 miles. Just before you finally reach the campground, is a small parking area (holds about 10 cars). If this lot is full, there is additional parking along the side of the road, past the campground. The main parking area is located directly in front of the trailhead. Always park off the road surface and do not block the road or other cars.

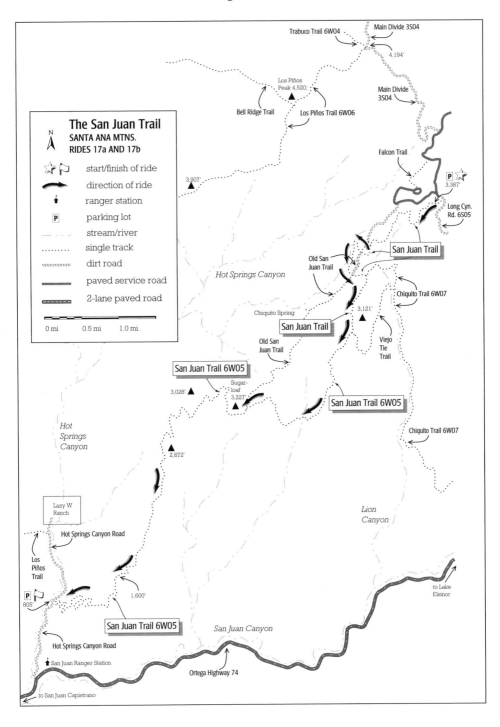

The San Juan Trail
SANTA ANA MTNS.
RIDES 17a AND 17b

★ ⚑   start/finish of ride
➤   direction of ride
✝   ranger station
P   parking lot
----   stream/river
....   single track
~~~~~~   dirt road
▬▬▬   paved service road
▬▬▬▬   2-lane paved road

0 mi   0.5 mi   1.0 mi.

Trabuco Trail 6W04
Main Divide 3S04
4,194'

Los Piños Peak 4,520;
Main Divide 3S04

Bell Ridge Trail   Los Piños Trail 6W06

Falcon Trail

P ★
3,387'

Long Cyn.
Rd. 6S05

3,907' ▲

Old San
Juan Trail

San Juan Trail

Chiquito Trail 6W07

Hot Springs Canyon

Chiquito Spring   3,121' ▲

San Juan Trail

Old San
Juan Trail

Viejo
Tie
Trail

San Juan Trail 6W05

3,028' ▲   Sugar-
loaf
3,227'
▲

San Juan Trail 6W05

Chiquito Trail 6W07

2,672' ▲

Hot
Springs
Canyon

Lion
Canyon

Lazy W
Ranch

Hot Springs Canyon Road

Los
Piños
Trail

to Lake
Elsinor

P ⚑
805'

1,600'

San Juan Trail 6W05

San Juan Canyon

Hot Springs Canyon Road

✝ San Juan Ranger Station

Ortega Highway 74

to San Juan Capistrano

THE RIDES

Ride 17a (Downhill with a Car Shuttle)

The San Juan Trail has been rebuilt in recent years, adding additional trail sections and more switchbacks. The newer sections cross the Old Trail several times. The Old Trail is a steeper, more direct, firebreak affair beginning at the bottom of the Bluejay Campground. The general lack of good signage makes the intersections between Old and New Trails confusing. This ride description attempts to follow the New San Juan Trail. Connections with the Old Trail are noted for those wanting to ride it for variety.

The trailhead, marked only with a "Trail" sign, is located on the left side of the parking area. The San Juan Trail dives off the top of the ridge and makes its way in and out of small canyons and slowly descends the side of the ridgeline. At the **1.4 mile mark**, a small trail joins from the right. This is not particularly confusing because it heads back uphill to the Old San Juan Trail and the campground.

At the **1.5 mile mark**, you reach a four-way intersection. This is the first crossing of Old and New Trails. A small metal sign marks this junction. Continue straight on the singletrack. At the **2.0 mile mark**, you reach another four-way intersection (crossing of Old Trail). Continue straight. (see map page 177) Note: The Old Trail eventually rejoins the New Trail at the **5.3+ mile mark** and shortens your ride, but is a bit more technical.

At the **2.2 mile mark**, you will come to the junction with the Chiquito Trail (a sign may be present). Stay right here, and continue through dense chaparral to the **2.8 mile mark**, staying right past the junction with the Viejo Tie Trail. At the **4.1+ mile mark** you descend into a small ravine with a seasonal stream, poison oak and nice shade (the last of any of these until you reach your car).

The trail climbs a bit from here until the **5.3+ mile mark**, where the Old Trail rejoins from your right. From this point on, there are no confusing turn-offs. As of this writing, farther down the trail some portage activity is required due to gaps in the trail (watch out!). These are being slowly repaired, mostly through the efforts of a single individual (who we think should be made a saint). The areas he has repaired are better that new, and make the trail much better to ride.

Many of the switchbacks, especially the long series just before the end of the trail, may require some riders to tripod or even dismount their bike. Less skilled riders should be aware that in some places they will be required to ride the outside (cliff side) of the trail on the top of rounded berms to avoid ruts. These can be loose and scary if you are not conversant in singletrack. There are also frequent narrow spots on inside corners. This is not the trail to experience singletrack riding for the first time.

You arrive, despite any injuries you received along the way, back at the Lower Parking area at the **11.9 mile mark**. Once you do this ride, you will be back for more.

Ride 17b (Up-and-Back)

Although the San Juan Trail may seem an intimidating prospect to ride up and back, the relatively moderate grade makes this longer ride a reasonable proposition for many riders, given enough time. For those of you who feel that car shuttles are often more hassle than they are worth, no further enticement is needed. You start your ride at the Lower Parking area off Hot Springs Canyon Road.

A long, but reasonable, uphill featuring many switchbacks levels after the first several miles, leading to mostly moderate up-and-down type of riding for the bulk of the uphill leg of your journey. Stay right at the **6.5+ mile mark** (junction with Old Trail) and then lose some elevation to the **7.7 mile point** where you cross a stream under tree cover (the only real shady spot). From here, head uphill and rolling up-and-down, making sure to stay left of both the Viejo Tie Trail at the **9.1 mile mark** and the Chiquito Trail at the **9.7 mile mark**.

At the **9.8+ mile point**, go straight across a junction with the Old San Juan Trail, and again at the **10.4 mile point**. Stay right at a junction at the **10.5 mile point**, reaching the Upper Parking area at **11.9 mile**s. Simply retrace your ride back to your car, or for some variety at the junction with the Old San Juan Trail, turn and follow it until you rejoin your route about 2.5 miles later. Take extra care on the lower sections of the trail where it steepens and you are more tired. 🏁

The Chiquito Trail

SANTA ANA MOUNTAINS RIDES 18a AND 18b

Distance • Ride 18a 11.5 miles (downhill with car shuttle)

Ride 18b 18.0 miles (up and back)

Time Required • Ride 18a 2 to 3 hours

Ride 18b 3.5 to 5 hours

Route Rating • 6

Grunt Factor • Ride 18a 4 (shuttle)

Ride 18b 7+ for being tedious (up-and-back

Technical Rating • 6

Topos • *Alberhill, Sitton Peak;* ride map, page 180

THE CHIQUITO TRAIL RUNS FROM ORTEGA Highway, near Upper San Juan Campground to the San Juan Trail, at a point 2.2 miles below the San Juan Trail's upper trailhead. This ride can be ridden either as a downhill ride with a car shuttle, or as an up-and-back ride. Due to trail conditions, the car shuttle is recommended. Parts of the Chiquito Trail are eroded and boulder strewn. As a result, some bike-and-hike is necessary (particularly on the "uphill" loop ride). Nevertheless, the Chiquito Trail is a good mountain biking adventure.

CAR DIRECTIONS

From the 5 Freeway, take the Ortega Highway exit and head east for about 19.5 miles to the Ortega Country Cottage General Store. Park at the trailhead, on the left side of Ortega Highway, across the street from the store. For an up-and-back ride, your ride begins here. For a car shuttle, leave your second car here and drive to the beginning of the San Juan Trail. See directions for Ride 17a on page 176.

THE RIDES

⭐ **Ride 18a (Downhill with a car shuttle)**

The San Juan trailhead, marked only with a "Trail" sign, is located behind the parking area. Follow the San Juan Trail as it makes its way in and out of small canyons and slowly descends. At the **1.5 mile mark**, you reach a four-way intersection. Continue straight on the singletrack. At the **2.0 mile mark**, you reach another four-way intersection, continue straight. At the **2.2 mile mark**, you will come to the junction with the Chiquito Trail (a sign may be present). Turn left here onto the Chiquito Trail.

The Chiquito Trail drops into Lion Canyon and runs next to the Lion Canyon creek for several miles. Soon you begin to climb out of Lion Canyon, and the trail becomes more technical and rocky. At the **7.1 mile mark**, you reach the crest of the ridgeline. From here the trail drops down a series of switchbacks. This section of the trail is eroded in places and chock-full of granite boulders. The trail alternates between a smooth surface and challenging technical ground over the next 2.0 miles. Some bike-and-hike may be necessary. After this rocky descent, you reach the bottom of another canyon and a creek bed (**9.3 mile mark**). Follow the trail as it runs next to and crosses the creek bed for about 0.8+ mile to where you join the San Juan Loop Trail, 5W08 (**10.1 mile mark**). Turn right, and ride the last 1.0 mile to your second car. 11.1 miles total. 🏁

18b (Up-and-Back Ride)

This is a challenge for advanced riders with very good technical climbing skills. Start your ride on the San Juan Loop Trail (5W08) which begins in a parking area across from the Ortega Country Cottage General Store. Head out the right side (north) of the parking area, and make a fairly technical descent into a canyon until the trail levels and you reach an intersection with the Chiquito Trail (**1.2 mile mark**).

Turn right onto the Chiquito Trail (6W07) and ride up a creek drainage for 0.8+ mile, make a last stream crossing (**2.0+ mile mark**), then begin a tiresome grind up switchbacks on the steep hillside. This next section varies from smooth pleasant riding to an eroded and boulder-filled trail. Plan on technical climbing and some bike and hike. After nearly 2.0 miles of this unpleasantness you reach the crest of the ridgeline (**4.0 mile mark**). Now you begin a somewhat rocky and occasionally technical descent into Lion Canyon.

Proceed up along Lion Canyon for several miles until the trail crosses the creek and begins to head up the ridge on the other side. Stay right at the junction with the Viejo Tie Trail. At the **9.1 mile mark** you reach the junction with the San Juan Trail (6W05). The Chiquito Trail ends here. Simply turn your bike around and follow your route back to the junction with the San Juan Loop Trail (5W08). Turn right onto the San Juan Loop Trail (it is technically easier in this direction and you complete that loop). Ride 1.0 mile back to your car (18.0 miles total). 🏁

The San Juan Loop Trail

SANTA ANA MTNS. RIDE 19

Distance • 2.2 miles

Time Required • 0.25 to 0.75 hour

Route Rating • 6

Grunt Factor • 2

Technical Rating • 5

Topos • *Alberhill, Sitton Peak;* ride map below

THE SAN JUAN LOOP TRAIL (5W08), A short, though somewhat technically challenging loop along Ortega Highway, is not to be confused with the San Juan Trail (6W05), the long remote singletrack. This singletrack loop ride is never far from civilization and begins and ends near the Ortega Country Cottage General Store. A great short ride, but it is a fairly long drive to get there.

CAR DIRECTIONS

From the 5 Freeway, take the Ortega Highway exit and head east for 19.5 miles to the Ortega Country Cottage General Store. Park off the left side of Ortega Highway, in a parking area across the street from the store. The trail begins here.

THE RIDE

Start your ride on the right (north) side of the parking area across from the Ortega Country Cottage General Store. Head right on this loop trail, making a somewhat technical (rocky) descent down some switchbacks into a canyon. The trail starts in open chaparral and as it levels proceeds under a canopy of old oaks. At the **1.2 mile mark**, you pass the junction with the Chiquito Trail. Stay to the left and continue on pleasant, shady trail to Upper San Juan Campground. Stay left as the trail heads behind the campground. Now you proceed on a wide section of trail that climbs back into more open terrain and eventually arrives at the parking area (**2.2 mile mark**).

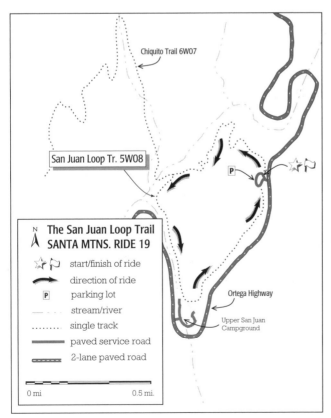

Chiquito Trail 6W07

San Juan Loop Tr. 5W08

P

N

The San Juan Loop Trail
SANTA MTNS. RIDE 19

⭐ 🚩 start/finish of ride

➤ direction of ride

P parking lot

— · · · · stream/river

· · · · · · · single track

——— paved service road

═════ 2-lane paved road

Ortega Highway

Upper San Juan
Campground

0 mi   0.5 mi.

Santa Ana Traverse Rides

Black Star to Ortega Highway (aka The Grand Traverse)

SANTA ANA MTNS. RIDE 20

Distance • 59.5 miles

Time Required • 8 to 12+ hours

Route Rating • 10

Grunt Factor • 10

Technical Rating • 5

Elevation • Lots and lots of up and down

Topos • *Black Star Canyon, Corona South, Santiago Peak, Alberhill, Sitton Peak, Cañada Gobernadora;* ride map, page 183

CAR SHUTTLE OR DROP-OFF/PICK-UP IS required. This is a long ride that takes you from nearly one end of the Santa Ana Mountains to the other. Continued closures of routes from Gypsum and Coal Canyons to the North Main Divide deny riders the best trans-Santa Ana rides possible, but this ride is an excellent substitute. While the ride described may not be the easiest trans-Santa Ana ride possible (see page 186 for other routes), it may be the best. Prepare for a tremendous, though strenuous ride. Don't attempt this ride alone, if you are not in great shape, or without adequate water, food and tools. You can bail-out at either Silverado or Trabuco Canyons if needed.

CAR DIRECTIONS

Drive up Ortega Highway 12.5 miles to Hot Springs Canyon Road (Lazy W Ranch sign here). Turn left. Drive up the paved, then dirt Hot Springs Canyon Road to the parking area at the bottom of the San Juan Trail. Your ride finishes here. Leave the first car here.

Proceed on Santiago Canyon Road to the junction with Silverado Canyon Road. Turn left here. Proceed a few hundred yards on Silverado Canyon Road, then make a left turn onto Black Star Canyon Road. Drive to the gate and park off the roadway. (See Santa Ana Mountains Ride 1 (page 136) for more detailed driving instructions). Leave the second car here.

Our Recommendation: Avoid a car shuttle by having someone drop you off and pick you up. Save gas and lots of time (which you will need for the ride). Although this may try the patience of the good Samaritan who volunteers to drive you (due to the difficulty in predicting how long the ride will take), it works extremely well.

THE RIDE

Start your computer at the Black Star Canyon gate. Proceed on alternatively paved and dirt road in the shaded canyon. At about the **2.4+ mile point** the road will

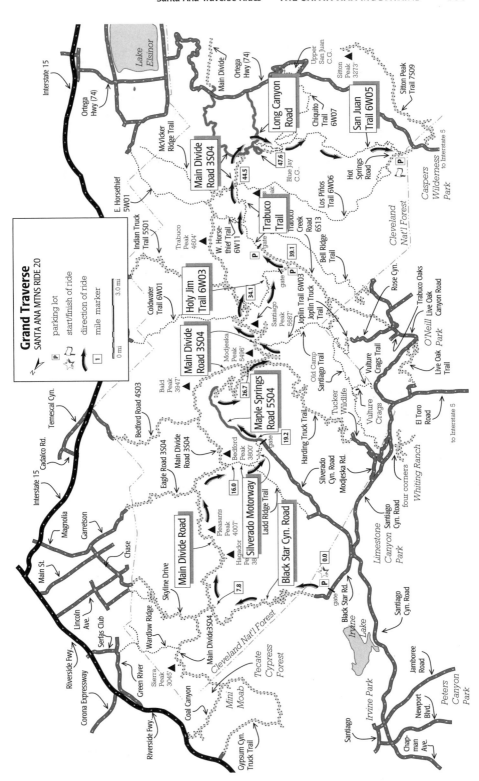

Grand Traverse
SANTA ANA MTNS RIDE 20

P parking lot
☆ start/finish of ride
→ direction of ride
1 mile marker

0 mi   3.0 mi

begin to quickly gain elevation up a series of steep switchbacks. Eventually, the road begins to drop slightly down into a valley where the Hidden Valley Ranch is located. Although a sign proclaims Private Property, use of the road is legal (don't stray off). At **5.2 miles**, you pass Hidden Ranch.

The road again steepens and heads up more switchbacks until the junction with Main Divide Road is reached (**7.8 mile mark**). Turn right on Main Divide Road.

Over the next 2.5+ miles, you gain nearly 1,000 feet, which is made harder by some elevation drops along the way (**10.4 mile mark**). From here the road drops, then levels a bit, passing on the north side of Pleasants Peak. Stay left at the junction with the Pleasant Peak service road. The next five miles are both beautiful and fun rolling fireroad along the ridgeline with incredible scenery. The last uphill leads toward Bedford Peak.

Eventually, at the **16.0 mile mark**, the Main Divide intersects the Silverado Motorway singletrack. There are no signs marking this trail. The trailhead is located were the Main Divide levels a bit and makes a fairly sharp left-hand turn up hill. At the apex of this turn, on your right, a firebreak will be seen. Large, wood barriers block the firebreak. Opposite this point you will note a small sign which states "N. Main 3.S.04."

Take a right turn onto the Silverado Motorway. This excellent trail is 3.2 miles long and quickly becomes singletrack running along the ridgeline. Follow the ridgeline for a nearly a mile, until the trail heads down and left as it descends into Silverado Canyon. Do not continue along the ridgeline. At the **19.2 mile mark**, you reach Maple Springs Road (a paved service road) in the bottom of Silverado Canyon.

Turn left and head up Maple Springs Road. After several stream crossings, the road steepens, makes a last stream crossing and becomes dirt. Soon the grade eases. After riding about 7.5 miles up Maple Springs Road, you will pass a right-hand turn-off for Harding Canyon then a hundred yards farther you reach Main Divide Road again (**26.7 mile mark**). Make a right-hand turn, heading uphill, on Main Divide. You are on the northwestern slope of Modjeska Peak.

The next 1.5 miles of somewhat rocky fireroad bring you to a sharp left turn in the road where you descend along for about a mile to a point just below the saddle between Modjeska and Santiago Peaks (29.2 miles). From here, Main Divide climbs for another 2.0 miles along the slopes of Santiago Peak. At the **31.2 mile mark**, a spur road on your right takes you 0.1+ mile to the actual summit. It is worth the short jaunt to the summit to enjoy the view and take a chance to drink fluids and eat a few energy bars.

Continue downhill on Main Divide (or if you went to the summit, return down to the junction with the Main Divide and head right). The road surface becomes quite rocky in places and you loose a fair bit of elevation over the 2.9 miles until the Holy Jim Trailhead (6W03) is seen on your right (**34.1 mile mark**). Turn right. A few sections of the Holy Jim Trail may be washed-out, however, the trail surface is generally excellent and at a moderate grade.

Note: The Holy Jim Trail is extremely popular with hikers. You may well encounter dozens of people on their way up and down this trail. Utilize extra caution when riding this trail.

After 4.5 miles of excellent singletrack, you reach the lower Holy Jim Trailhead (**38.6 mile mark**). From the trailhead, ride 0.5 mile downhill on the Holy Jim dirt road (6S14) to the junction with Trabuco Road (6S13) at the **39.1 mile mark**. Turn left and proceed up the dirt road for 1.0 mile where it ends at a small parking area. The Trabuco Trail singletrack begins here (**40.1 mile mark**).

After leaving the parking area, this singletrack trail gradually gains elevation and crosses the creek bed several times (bike carries probably necessary). After 1.7+ miles, the

Trabuco Trail splits off to the right (across the creek). The Horsethief Trail heads up on the left. A sign marks this juncture.

Take the Trabuco Trail across the creek bed (head right). The next mile or so of the Trabuco Trail has some loose sections that make uphill progress work. Soon the trail becomes leaf covered, under a canopy of trees and brush. At the **44.5 mile mark** you suddenly reach the Main Divide Truck Trail yet again. Turn right onto Main Divide.

Follow Main Divide downhill for 1.1 miles to a gate. Continue downhill to where Main Divide becomes paved at a road junction (**46.1 mile mark**). Make a sharp right at the road junction and head downhill toward Blue Jay Campground, on paved road, for 1.5 miles to the San Juan Trail trailhead (just past the Blue Jay Campground entrance). Turn right and follow the San Juan Trail. After 1.5 miles, you reach a four-way intersection (**49.1 mile mark**). Continue straight on the singletrack which makes a long switchback and after 0.5 mile you reach another four-way intersection (**49.6 mile mark**). Continue straight. 0.2 mile farther, you will come to the junction with the Chiquito Trail (a sign may be present). Stay right here and again at the junction with the Viejo Tie Trail (**50.4 mile mark**). At the **51.7+ mile mark** you descend into a small ravine with a seasonal stream.

The trail climbs a bit from here until the **52.9 mile mark** where the Old Trail rejoins from your right. Farther down the trail some portage activity may be required due to gaps in the trail (watch out!). The last several miles feature many switchbacks, including an especially long series just before the end of the trail. You are probably tired at this point and should take extra care not to dump your bike.

After 59.5 miles, this ride finally ends at the Hot Springs Canyon parking area. Now who said there were no challenging rides in Orange County?

20a SKYLINE DRIVE VARIATION

This is the same ride as above, except that you start up Skyline Drive (see Santa Ana Mountains Ride 3 on page 141) instead of Black Star Canyon. This saves some climbing and 2.2 miles. Skyline Drive hits Main Divide at the 5.1 mile mark, turn left (south) and after 0.5 mile you reach the Black Star-Main Divide junction. From here the ride is the same. Merely subtract 2.2 miles from all the mile marks along your route. Total distance: 57.3 miles.

Other Santa Ana Traverse Rides

The preceding rides are certainly not the easiest possible way across the Santa Ana Mountain Range, neither are they the hardest. They do combine a variety of excellent trails and scenery. Nevertheless, many possibilities exist for putting other rides trans-Santa Ana together. Here are some other suggestions:

Skyline to Main Divide Traverse

SANTA ANA MTNS. RIDE 20b
Distance • 35.8 miles
Route Rating • 7+
Grunt Factor • 8
Technical Rating • 2/3

THIS IS THE EASIEST TRANS-SANTA ANA ride and follows fireroad the entire distance. Ride 5.1 miles up Skyline Drive to Main Divide Road (see Ride 3), turn left and follow Main Divide south to just below the summit of Santiago Peak (**24.7 mile mark**). From here it is another 11.1 miles to the metal gate which lies 0.5 mile north of the Main Divide-Long Canyon Road junction (**35.8 mile mark**). This is where the ride ends and where you should park your second car.

Black Star to Main Divide Traverse

SANTA ANA MTNS. RIDE 20c
Distance • 38 miles

RATINGS ARE COMPARABLE TO THE previous ride (Ride 20b). Ride 7.8+ miles up Black Star Canyon Road (see Ride 1, page 183), turn right onto Main Divide and follow the above ride to its end.

The Death March

SANTA ANA MTNS. RIDE 20d
Distance • 92.1 miles
Route Rating • 10
Grunt Factor • 12
Technical Rating • 6+

TRAINING FOR THAT SPECIAL OFF-ROAD nightmare? This ride will prepare you for most anything, and then some. This route hits most every Santa Ana Mountain trail and combines them into a true death march. Follow The Grand Traverse (Ride 20, page 182) to the Harding Truck Trail. Now turn right and descend 9.3 miles to Modjeska Canyon. Ride Modjeska Canyon Road to the Modjeska Grade Road, which you follow uphill to the Santiago Trail trailhead (2.0 miles). Ride up Santiago Trail to Old Camp (8.0 miles), then up the Joplin Trail (2.2 miles) to Main Divide. Head up to Santiago Peak (2.1 miles), then down to the Holy Jim Trail (2.9 miles). Take the Holy Jim Trail to Trabuco Canyon (5.0 miles), turn left onto the Trabuco Trail (1.0 mile). Head up the Trabuco Trail to the Main Divide (4.4 miles) and just as you meet Main Divide, turn right onto the Los Piños Trail. Break out the long pants and shirt about 3.0 miles into the Los Piños trail, which ends in Hot Springs Canyon (9.9 miles). Take that last bit of energy and ride up the San Juan Trail to the Chiquito Trail (9.7 miles). Finally, follow the Chiquito Trail to the parking area along Ortega Highway (8.9 miles). You could have people re-supply you at Silverado Canyon, Modjeska Canyon, Trabuco Canyon and Hot Springs Canyon.